For Dorothy and Edward Thompson.
Friends and teachers for thirty years.

CONTENTS

CONTENTS

FOREWORD

Women in Movement is one of several studies growing from the Women's Programme of the World Institute for Development Economics Research (WIDER), which is part of the United Nations University. Recognizing that to add gender onto existing economic theory is to miss important issues raised by feminist critiques of economic development, WIDER has encouraged research that explores the scope of existing definitions of economics. Consequently the WIDER Women's Programme has drawn on sociology, anthropology, philosophy, cultural studies, history, and political science, as well as economics.

Women in Movement provides students with an historical account of concepts that have played a crucial role in economic theory: "progress," "development," "modernization," "tradition," "equality," "entitlements," "rights," and "needs" are situated in social contexts. Sheila Rowbotham shows how debates about the aims of economic and social development have a long history. In many different countries women have sought to enlarge definitions of "economy" to include, for example, domestic labor, the reorganization of family life, consumption, community, and daily life. They have done this not only through debate, but by taking action around production and consumption.

This introductory text will enable students to follow a wide range of economic, social, and political movements all over the world, through which women have sought access to resources and more democratic control over their lives.

The author, one of the research advisers in WIDER's Women's Programme, combines historical knowledge with awareness of significant issues in contemporary social and economic policy and has been active in the women's movement since the late 1960s.

Lal Jayawardena
Director of WIDER

SERIES EDITOR'S PREFACE

This book, like its companions in the *Revolutionary Thought/Radical Movements* series, challenges contemporary society and civilization.

Perhaps the heart of this challenge is a deeply felt anguish and outrage over the sheer magnitude of human suffering—along with the terrible frustration of knowing that much of this suffering could be avoided. Radicals refuse to blame homelessness and starvation, the rape of women and abuse of children, the theft of labor and land, hope and self-respect on divine Providence or unchangeable human nature. Rather, they believe that much of it comes from injustice, exploitation, violence, and organized cruelty that can be eradicated. If we drastically alter our social arrangements in the direction of equality, justice, and human fulfillment, the brutal realities of the present can give way to vastly increased material security, social harmony, and self-realization.

Philanthropists and political reformers share radicals' concern for human suffering. But unlike reformers and philanthropists, radicals and revolutionaries address whole *systems* of injustice. In these systems, particular groups are humiliated, denied rights, and subject to unjust control. The few become rich while the many suffer from poverty or economic insecurity. The select get privileges while millions learn submission or humiliation. We are conditioned to false needs for endless consumption while nature is poisoned. The powers that be profit from these systems, "common sense" enshrines them as necessary, and ideological mystification obscures their origin and nature by blaming the victims. Responses to people's pain, if they are to be truly and lastingly effective, must be aimed *at the system:* at capitalism, sexism, racism, imperialism, homophobia, the bureaucratic state, and the domination of nature.

Governments and economies, families and culture, science and individual psychology—all are shaped by these systems of domination and exclusion. That is why the radical ideal goes beyond piecemeal improvements to a Utopian vision, and tries to realize that vision in everyday struggles for a fair distribution of power, human dignity, and a livable environment. Revolutionaries have argued that a modern economy can be democratically controlled and oriented to human needs rather than profit, can do without vast differences of wealth and power, and can preserve rather than destroy the earth. Radicals claim that in a true "democracy" ordinary men and women would help shape the basic conditions that affect their lives: not just by an occasional trip to the ballot box, but by active involvement in decisions about political and economic life.

How will these sweeping changes take place? Revolutionaries have offered many answers—from large political parties to angry uprisings, from decentralized groups based in consciousness-raising to international organizations. In any case, however, the conception of radicalism that informs the series stipulates that authentic revolutionary change requires the self-action of sizable groups of people, not the self-promotion of a self-proclaimed revolutionary "elite." The only way to prevent the betrayal of the revolution by a privileged bureaucracy is to base radical politics on free discussion, mutual respect, and collective empowerment *from the beginning.* This is one of the clearest and most painful lessons from the history of communism.

Of course much of this sounds good on paper. Yet it may be—as many have claimed—that radical visions are really unrealistic fantasies. However, if we abandon these visions we also abandon human life to its current misery, with little to hope for but token reforms. Radicals reject this essentially cynical "realism," opting for a continuing faith in the human capacity for a fundamentally different and profoundly liberating form of life.

In fact, people have always dreamed of a better world. Yet it is only since the late eighteenth century that organized groups developed a systematic theoretical critique of social life, and tried to embody that critique in mass political movements designed to overthrow the existing order of economic ownership and political control. American revolutionaries claimed that "All men are endowed with certain inalienable rights." The French revolution demanded "liberty, equality, fraternity."

Since then Marxist, socialist, feminist, national liberation, civil rights, gay and lesbian liberation, and ecology movements have been born. Each movement utilized some of the accomplishments of its predecessors, criticized the past for its limitations, and broke new ground. *Revolutionary Thought/Radical Movements* will focus on the theory and practice, successes and failures, of these movements.

While the series' authors are part of the radical tradition, we are painfully aware that this tradition has committed grave errors and at times failed completely. The communism of the Eastern bloc, while maintaining certain valuable social welfare programs, combined economic inefficiency, brutal tyranny, and ecological devastation. Many of us who took to the streets in the 1960s joined arrogance with idealism and self-indulgence with utopian hopes. Much of contemporary radical or socialist feminism fails to reach beyond a circle of the already converted.

These and other failures of radicalism are certainly apparent today. Daily headlines trumpet the collapse of the Eastern bloc, the victory of the United States in the Cold War, the eternal superiority of capitalism and free markets, and the transformation of yesterday's radicals into today's yuppies. Governments of countries that had called themselves "socialist" or "communist" (however much they were distorting the meaning of these terms) trip over each other rushing west for foreign corporate investment and economic advice.

But there are also *successes,* ways in which radicals have changed social life for the better. Though these achievements have been partial reforms rather than sweeping revolutions, many of the basic freedoms, rights, and material advantages of modern life were fought for by people called radicals, dangerous revolutionaries, or anti-American:

- restrictions on the exploitation of workers, from the eight-hour day to the right to unionize;
- resistance to cultural imperialism and racial discrimination;
- a host of government programs, from unemployment insurance to social security, from the Environmental Protection Agency to fair housing laws;
- restrictions on opportunistic and destructive American foreign policy in Vietnam, El Salvador, Nicaragua, and other nations.

Although radicals have not been alone in seeking these goals, they have often led the fight. Perhaps more important, they have offered a theoretical analysis that shows the *connections* among problems that may appear to be separate. They have argued that the sexist treatment of women and ecological devastation may have the same root. They have shown the links between the private control of wealth and an expansionist foreign policy. They have analyzed the family, the factory, the army, and the government as parts of the same system of domination.

Along with both the concrete successes and the global vision, radicals have—sadly—too often reproduced the ideas and relationships they sought to destroy. Marxists demanded an end to unjust society— yet formed authoritarian organizations where dissent was repressed. Radical feminists proclaimed "sisterhood is powerful," but often ignored black women or poor women. At times ecologists, in trying to save nature, have been disrespectful of human beings.

Some of the worst failures came not from being radical, but from *not being radical enough:* not inclusive enough, not honest enough, not willing to examine how radical political programs and group behavior reproduced an oppressive, unjust society. Awareness of these failures reminds us that revolutionary thought cannot limit itself to critique of the larger society, but also requires self-criticism. Although this process can degenerate into petty sectarian hostilities, it also shows that authentic radicalism is not a dead graven image, but a living quest to learn from the past and change the future. In the attempt to create solidarity and community among the oppressed, for instance, radicals have recently spent much effort trying to address and appreciate fundamental differences in social experience—between black and white workers, men and women, temporarily able-bodied and disabled, gay/lesbian and straight. In this effort, radicals have wrestled with the paradox that persons may simultaneously be victims of one system of domination and agents of another one.

The books in this series are part of this radical quest for revolutionary change and continued self-examination. In an era of the sudden fall of totalitarian communism and the frightening rise in the federal deficit, of the possibility of a peace dividend and the specter of the death of nature—these discussions of revolutionary thought and radical movements are needed more than ever before.

Roger S. Gottlieb

*Thanks for editorial suggestions to Bland Addison, Mario Moussa, Miriam Greenspan, Tom Shannon, and John Trimbur.

ACKNOWLEDGMENTS

This book originated in courses at Paris VIII, Kent University, and City Polytechnic. Some of the material was also used in seminars and classes at York University, Ontario, the Islington Sixth Form Centre, Kingsway College of Further Education, Northern College, The Institute of Contemporary Arts, and the Open University.

I am grateful to WIDER UNU Women's Programme for financial assistance while *Women in Movement* was being researched and written and for the stimulation and opportunity to learn about social and economic issues facing women in Third World countries through WIDER seminars.

For material, references, information, discussion, and ideas about women internationally I am indebted to Nahla Abdo, Hugh and Pat Armstrong, Vinay Bahl, Himani Bannerji, Rosalyn Fraad Baxandall, Eileen Boris, Claire Crocker, Charlene Gannagé, Linda Gordon, Hermione Harris, Judith Adler Hellman, Jane S. Jacquette, Temma Kaplan, Delia Jarrett-Macauley, Kumari Jayawardena, Renana Jhabvala, Govind Kelkar, Deniz Kandiyoti, Radha Kumar, Sara Leiserson, Meg Luxton, Fatima Mernissi, Partha Mitter, Swasti Mitter, Valentine Moghadam, Maxine Molyneux, Kumudhini Rosa, Jennifer Schirmer, Marja-Liisa Swantz, Aili Mari Tripp, Stephanie Urdang, Eléni Varikas, Virginia Vargas, Amrit Wilson, and Nira Yuval-Davis.

Any errors in interpretation are my own.

For advice based on their extensive teaching experience thanks to Alison Kirton, Jean McCrindle, and Janet Rée. I am grateful to the series editor Roger S. Gottlieb and to my student readers Shelley Mclennan from Islington Sixth Form Centre and my class at Richmond College. For great patience as I groaned and moaned on the telephone because the writing was much harder than I had thought— particular thanks to Sean Hutton, Delia Jarrett-Macauley, Partha and Swasti Mitter, Lynne Segal, and Hilary Wainwright. And big thanks to The Typing Pool and to Margaret Hanbury for their labor and kindness.

INTRODUCTION

THEMES FOR DISCUSSION

* What is feminism?
* The meanings and uses of the term "gender."
* Do you think people could be feminists before the word was invented?
* Why have women needed democracy?
* The advantages and disadvantages of linking women's emancipation with the transformation of the whole society.

GENERAL INTRODUCTION

Women in Movement is an historical introduction to the ideas, organizations, and activities that have influenced a wide range of emancipatory
movements among women from the late eighteenth century to the
present. It traces the origins of feminism in relation to political thought
and action in many countries. It also describes other economic, social,
and political movements in which women have participated, not only
in Europe and North America, but also in the Third World.

Themes that run through the historical accounts include equality,
women's difference, the personal and the political individualism, collectivity, the scope of rights, and the definition of needs.

Relevant to women's studies, gender studies, women's history and politics courses, it could also be used as background in sociology, politics, history, and economic development.

Each section gives students a starting point from which they can take off in several directions, either historically or by studying texts theoretically, depending on their own interests. Themes for discussion are drawn out before each section. These are not intended as exclusive statements of the questions raised, but as guidelines for students new to the historical material.

The short general bibliographies suggest first steps and indicate texts that are comprehensible without much background knowledge. These could be followed up by reading other works quoted in the footnotes after each chapter, which in turn would provide more references.

Women in Movement can be read in the customary manner from beginning to end, but it is designed to be read in sections, so it could cover several courses. Conceivably it could even be read backward by those who prefer to approach the past from the present!

1

WHAT DO WOMEN WANT?

Women receive less than one-tenth of the world income, but do two-thirds of the world's work. Although earning less than men, they work longer hours—2 to 5 hours more in developed countries, 5 to 6 hours more in Latin America and the Caribbean, and as much as 12 to 13 hours more in Africa and Asia. When housework and child care are taken into account, women on average have a 60 to 70 hour week.

Facts such as these suggest a common sense answer to the question what do women want? They also suggest why, throughout the world today, there are women's movements and organizations that are struggling for better conditions. However, human beings wants and needs are never that simple and women are as capable as men of having contradictory and different desires. Consequently there are many kinds of women's movements, some aiming to conserve, rather than change women's position. Moreover, within the movements for change there are many conflicting emphases and perspectives.

From the late 1960s there has been a resurgence of feminism in many countries, making this the movement that most people associate with the effort to change women's lives. But even if we narrow our question to what is feminism, the replies will vary considerably. "Feminism" itself is a word that has been given a range of shifting meanings, even in the modern women's movement. There is nothing unique in this of course; every set of political concepts possesses contrary interpretations, and as soon as these are applied to reality they acquire yet more nuances. By looking at ideas historically, it is possible to reveal implicit assumptions that accumulate around a political term, but then become overlaid and forgotten in every day usage.

When women's groups formed in the late 1960's, feminism was sometimes regarded with suspicion: the term "women's liberation" was used. It was thought that feminism was too limited because it had been only about women's civil and political rights. One early anthology, for example, had the title *From Feminism to Liberation*.[1] In contrast, when Amanda Sebestyen edited a book in 1988 on the history of the recent movement in Britain, she called it *From Women's Liberation to Feminism,* saying that,

> Liberation was once something for which a thousand different schools of thought contended. Women's liberation saw itself as one of those schools.[2]

The use of the term "feminism" served to highlight women's specific oppression in relation to men, preventing this from being submerged, amid all the other unequal relationships existing in society. Thus feminism is sometimes confined to women's struggles against oppressive gender relationships. In practice, however, women's actions, both now and in the past, often have been against interconnecting relations of inequality and have involved many aspects of resistance around daily life and culture that are not simply about gender.

Some feminists have stretched the meaning of the word and given it a wide span. Judith Astellara, writing on the modern Spanish movement, presented this definition of feminism in 1984:

Feminism is a proposal for social transformation as well as a movement that strives to end the oppression of women. In this double aspect, feminism has always existed as part of the historical societies in which it has developed: it has been influenced by the specific social, economic and political traits of its society. As a movement, feminism has a long history of rebellion, more or less organised but always expressing opposition to the social institutions that made possible the inferiority of women. This opposition has not been isolated from other forms of social struggle and this relationship has influenced both the ideology and the organisation of the movement.[3]

Not all women would accept this view. Sometimes feminism is seen as quite separate from any kind of politics in which men are involved. Also it is often regarded as a movement for limited reforms not for social transformation. It has also been characterized as being restricted to a particular group, for example, as expressing the interests of middle class and white women in Western capitalism.

It is not then self-evident what people mean when they speak of "feminism" and within feminist politics there are several differing political perspectives. Very broadly, "radical feminists" emphasize the primacy of women's subordination to men, which they regard as the key to changing society as a whole. "Liberal feminists" argue that women should have equal opportunities within society to jobs and education and oppose discrimination against women. "Socialist feminists" think women are oppressed not only by men, but by other forms of subordination, such as class and race inequality. None of these divisions is absolute and within each category it would be possible to find rather different emphases. Moreover, these are by no means the only lines of demarcation. Not only have many disputes occurred in the modern movement about what women's problems are and how they should be changed, but the idea of "women" as a unified group has been brought into question in a series of challenges to perspectives that ignored and denied the experience of groups such as lesbians, black women, working class women, aboriginal women, Jewish women, older women, disabled women, and many others.

Conflict over who has the power to speak for women as a group and disagreement about the meaning of feminism are not peculiar to the contemporary movement. So an historical awareness can enable us to take a wider view of present day disputes. Feminism is not an abstract category but a word that human beings have used over time in various ways. At the height of the women's suffrage movement in Britain in 1913, a sharp, young feminist journalist called Rebecca West observed,

> I myself have never been able to find out precisely what feminism is, I only know that people call me a feminist whenever I express sentiments that differentiate me from a doormat or a prostitute.[4]

The word "feminist" was invented by a French socialist, Charles Fourier, in the early nineteenth century. He imagined a "new woman" who would both transform and be herself transformed by a society based on association and mutuality, rather than on competition and profits. His views influenced many women and combined self-emancipation and social emancipation. Changing oneself was part of changing the world.

"Feminist" appeared for the first time in English to describe women campaigning for the vote in the 1890s. By this time organizations had developed in many places that sought to extend liberal ideas of individual rights to women. These sought a reform within existing societies. However, the demand for the suffrage also involved a more fundamental challenge to the denial of autonomy to women as citizens. Feminists argued that if liberalism meant every individual standing alone endowed with equal rights that were universally comparable, women could not be included within the male franchise. Democracy involved women's franchise.

In nineteenth-century radical and revolutionary movements the assertion not only of individual equal rights but of popular sovereignty was made. If the people are seen to have the right to shape society then, women argued, this must include them, as half of the people.

Another claim to citizenship was made in terms of women's service as mothers and workers to society as a whole. The citizen-mother had a right to a democratic political voice and a social right to resources because her reproductive capacity and her labor contributed to material existence.

Some women also believed that women had a moral duty to improve society by gaining power through the franchise. Women's mission was to bring their specific values into the public arena of politics and make a better society. Definitions of this womanly alternative varied: banning alcohol, redesigning housing, challenging militarism, and improving sanitation.

Redemption had a conservative side; white women or rich women have determined the moral sphere as upholding Anglo-Saxon "civilization." Women's mission also had its socialist wing; women were to bring about social well-being and welfare for the working class. The family could be the basis for a better community and the household the model for a benign, homely state.

The meanings of feminism extended beyond the campaign for the vote. In the early twentieth century "feminism" was being used in the United States and Europe to describe a particular strand in the women's movement that stressed the uniqueness and difference of women rather than seeking equality. Indeed difference was sometimes taken to imply women's superiority to men. Thus to remake the world in women's image would be to improve society.

However, there was no unanimity on what these alternative womanly values actually were. Womanliness was at once the conserving of the personal care and responsibility of hearth and home and the adventurous process of a discovery of a potential new womanhood.

Mari Jo Buhle, in her history of *Women and American Socialism 1870–1920,* quotes a journalist in the early 1900s:

> We have grown accustomed in these years to something or other known as the Woman Movement. That has an old sound—it is old. Therefore no need to cry it down. But Feminism![5]

Feminism in this context was used to describe the cultural assertion of the "new woman." Personal self-realization was a vital element. It could be linked to the project of social emancipation or it could focus on the unfolding of personality as an end in itself. Drawing on the philosophers of will, Nietzsche and Bergson, this interpretation of feminism maintained that the true subject of enquiry was the human being rather than the attempt to change external social institutions. Opposing reason and progress, this strand of feminism broke with the liberal values and assumptions that had predominated in the nineteenth-century middle-class "Woman Movement." Instead of the Christian ethic of moral reform that had mingled with the idea of universal rights, the new women were inclined to defy social conventions and were ready to risk unrespectability.

However, it was not difference or bohemianism that upset Arabella Kenealy in 1920. She argued in *Feminism and Sex-Extinction* (an early "postfeminist" tract) that

> Feminism, the extremist—and of late years the predominant cult of the Woman's Movement, is Masculinism.[6]

She believed feminism *denied* women's uniqueness by demanding equality with men. Feminists were endangering the reproduction of healthy children and holding back the evolution of society.

One of her main targets was the South African writer Olive Schreiner whose book, *Woman and Labour,* in 1911, had stressed the significance of women's role in production as a source of power in society. Olive Schreiner argued it was not enough to wave the "poor little 'women's rights' flag on the edge of the platform."[7] Women were not simply victims of the wrongs done by men. To alter women's lives a change wider than simply an equal political status with men was necessary. She opened up an approach to women's material and social existence as a whole that was to influence particularly socialist women who felt equal rights did not tackle the actual economic and social dependence of many working class and lower middle-class women.

They did not, however, have a common strategy. Was improved pay and working conditions the answer or more welfare benefits? Should women have special protection at work because of biological differences and their work in the home?

Feminism came to be an all inclusive term by the 1920s and 1930s, being used to describe not only political campaigns for the vote but also economic and social rights ranging from equal pay to birth control. From around the World War I some young women, convinced that feminism alone was not enough, called themselves "socialist feminists." Other socialist women opposed feminism, which they saw as exclusively expressing the interests of middle-class professional women.

Before "feminism" came into common usage in English phrases such as "Womanism," "the Women's Movement," or "the Woman Question" had been current. Marxists continued to refer to "The Woman Question," presenting an approach that viewed women's position historically and within specific social relations. They looked at women's lives as a whole, rather than seeing emancipation simply as gaining the right to vote. However, inequality between men and women in society was regarded as a problem that would end with class equality.

The emergence of the modern women's liberation movement in the late 1960s put the stress once more or women struggling to free themselves in an autonomous movement, restoring self-emancipation as a factor. Many ideas have appeared in the modern movements among women that can be found in the past, for example, women's claim to control their own bodies, or the protest against inequality at home, because women tend to do more housework and child-care even if they go out to work. It is possible to find similar disputes as well; should women demand equality with men or seek reforms from within a different situation? How should biological differences be approached? Are they best minimized or celebrated as a basis for specific needs? These frequently involve a strategic dilemma about whether to enter a male-defined sphere of politics and ideas or to try and reshape the public terrain that has been established in men's image.

Although looking at women's movements historically can enable us to situate contemporary preoccupations, it is always important to be sensitive to the contexts in which concepts and opinions have been expressed, rather than simply interpreting them arrogantly in terms of what we might believe. There have been women's movements, for example, that did not think they were feminist, but in whose ideas and work modern feminist historians have detected feminist aspects. There is a thin dividing line between recognizing elements in past movements that were outside the terms of reference of contemporary definitions and rather condescendingly deciding other people were not capable of making up their own minds and that we know better.

It would be pedantic to deny that awareness of injustice had to await the arrival of the term feminist. On the other hand, there is a danger in approaching the past as colonizers, bearing the superior wisdom of our present day women's studies departments, as we arbitrarily label all and sundry as feminist. For this reason I have been wary of extending the term, and mainly kept to words people used themselves, stating explicitly when definitions have been created posthumously by historians.

An historical perspective of the differing forms of women's struggle for emancipation is just as vital in understanding women's wants as finding a wider tradition of feminist action in the past. Indeed, other forms of inequality besides gender, such as race and class, can be of as much consequence as being born a woman.

Thus there are reasons for women making alliances with men who are affected by social inequality as well. Our needs are not determined by our gender alone. Moreover, feminism has focused on interests between men and women that are dissimilar, but there have been, and continue to be, movements that stress what particular groups of men and women have in common, for instance, trade unions or tenants struggles. Women have played a part in such movements and they have had an important impact upon their lives. Consequently it is necessary to balance the awareness of women's subordination in relations with men with the mutuality and shared interests that have also been elements of movements for emancipation in which women participated.

The concept of gender was developed by feminists in the 1970s as a means of recognizing that women do not relate to men in the same way in every culture and that the position of women in society has varied over time. The idea of gender thus posits a social rather than a biological situation of women and of men. Sometimes the phrase "sex–gender relations" is used; this reminds us that there is a link between biological differences between men and women and the social assumptions about masculinity and femininity.

Gender has come to be applied in several ways; it has described women's relationship to men in particular societies as well as the experiences of women and men in movements for political or social emancipation. Thus nationalist or antiimperialist struggles or trades unionism can be given a gender dimension, because they have implicitly held images of how men and women could be and attempted to recast new ways of being men and women. Gender issues are to be observed in apparently objective economic policies, for these can have consequences that affect women's lives by making access to natural and social resources more difficult.

By looking at gender in connection with other grievances and concerns that have led women to protest it is possible to understand a wider range of women's movements and action in the present and in the past. For instance, Louise Tilly describes women expressing their needs through crowd action, long before any organized movement for women's rights.

> women were participants in group politics whether or not they had formal political rights. The forms of collective action in which women have taken part have been shaped by interest and organisational bases rooted in the economic and social structures in which they lived.[8]

Assertion of demands by the unprivileged predated political representation. This direct action against oppression has involved the poor of both sexes. However, by asking how these have been affected by the relations of gender in specific societies, we can observe both the wants women have shared with men and the differing emphases that are sometimes apparent in their actions.

Under slavery women and men suffered a common bondage. Lucille Mathurin traced a long history of rebellion among Caribbean women slaves throughout the seventeenth and eighteenth centuries. The Caribbean "rebel woman"[9] participated and even led resistance in which they fought and died for freedom just as did men. However, she also notes oppositions to the daily life of slavery that are specific to women, for example, delaying weaning as a means of refusing work to the slave owner. Awareness of gender provides a way of looking at the forms rebellion has taken. This avoids the mistake of imposing a feminist aim of altering gender relations upon all women's struggles in an ahistorical manner.

In distinguishing among differing kinds of oppressive relationship historically it becomes apparent that women do not always feel that their gender is the main source of their trouble in life, and that they have not necessarily regarded other women as allies.

In the modern movement, the word "identity" has been used as a means of ensuring that particular groups of women's needs and views are not overruled by others in positions of greater privilege. Identity has been a means of staking out a distinct territory, opening up space for many diverse experiences, instead of presenting a limited interpretation of what women might want, based on a narrow elite. However, the problem with the concept of identity is that it tends to become rigid, fixing individuals artificially into a single aspect of their lived experience. It does not convey the dynamic process of an individual becoming aware, within a network of interconnecting relationships. Becoming conscious of oneself and one's place in the world occurs in relation to others; it is an exceedingly complex process never determined completely by external factors.

One of the most fascinating puzzles of history is the attempt to understand how people came to identify with groups and causes in particular times and places. For example, at the first women's rights convention held at Seneca Falls, New York in 1848, Charlotte Woodward spoke not in terms of abstract rights, but of a consciousness of herself that had developed from her life as a homeworker. She was only nineteen but she went to the heart of a complex problem. Does a consciousness exist before it has expression philosophically, politically, organizationally?

> We women work secretly in the seclusion of our bed chambers because all society was built on the theory that men, not women, earned money and that men alone supported the family. . . . But I do not believe that there was any community in which the souls of some women were not beating their wings in rebellion. In my own obscure self I can say that every fibre of my being rebelled although silently, all the hours that I sat and sewed gloves for a miserable pittance which as it was earned would

never be mine. I wanted to work, but I wanted to collect my wages. That was my form of rebellion against the life into which I was born.[10]

Charlotte Woodward's rebellion against the life into which she was born, partly as a woman, partly because of her social position, happened to coincide with an event that is sometimes taken to be the beginning of an organized movement for women's rights. But women had been sewing gloves for hundreds of years before 1848. What were they thinking? Charlotte Woodward believed that her position as a *woman* in the economy was the crucial reason for her low wages. But in the same period many women in the British Chartist movement campaigning for the male franchise believed they were oppressed, not because they were women, but because they were poor. They interpreted similar circumstances in a different political language of class.

The relation between circumstances and concepts is never simple.

An historical awareness of how concepts are used and understood reveals their complexity. Categories are helpful in sorting out strands of thought and differentiating forms of action and organization in social and political movements. But it is only by looking at how these are shaped by people in history that we are able to see how things *move*. The processes of experience and the shifts in the meanings of ideas are dynamic; theoretical definitions are static. The real challenge is holding these differing ways of seeing and understanding human social action together.

Finding a word to illuminate what people might want can be a powerful means of summing up what is otherwise a confusing welter of demands and aspirations. Still it is important to be conscious of how the terms we use have arisen and recognize that they need to be constantly overhauled and redefined. To return to what people themselves say and do is a necessary corrective to becoming enclosed within our own immediate assumptions. It may well be that our assessment of the experience of others will always be approximate—truth being a slippery customer. This need not leave us though with an absolute relativity; the aim is to arrive at the closest possible approximation.

2

WOMEN, POWER, AND
POLITICS.

The idea that women and politics should not mix is extremely ancient. Consequently political organization among women, especially poor and uneducated women, has frequently been regarded as a trespass on the public domain of power. Commenting on present day mobilization of poor Third World women claiming access to resources, Maxine Molyneux notes that they are confronting, "entrenched ideas . . . with a provenance that goes back in political theory to Aristotle and beyond."[1]

The argument that women possess distinct natures because of their biological difference from men has frequently accompanied views of women's separate sphere. This has reinforced divisions in hierarchical societies, which excluded all but the rich and powerful from political power, and continued to form a barrier, even when democratic movements have sought to extend the base of participation.

Opinion and facts are not, however, quite the same. In practice royal and aristocratic women have exerted political power, leading armies into battle, devising laws, and engaging in statecraft. And in situations of extreme oppression and conflict, in wars and during foreign occupation or colonization, even humble women have been swept into public prominence, leaving a record in many cultures. For example the dream of a young Vietnamese peasant woman, who, more than a thousand years ago, imagined a different way of being a woman, has survived the centuries. In 248, Trieu Thi Trinh, told her brother,

> My wish is to ride the tempest, tame the waves, kill the sharks. I want to drive the enemy away to save our people. I will not resign myself to the usual lot of women who bow their heads and become concubines.[2]

True to her word, she led an uprising with her brother against the Chinese overlords, which drove them from the land. When they returned with reinforcements, she took her own life rather than submit to serfdom.

The public realm of politics is not, of course, the only kind of power that exists. In peasant societies, for example, women have possessed economic power because they have contributed an essential part to the productive process. Similarly, many rituals and beliefs have grown up around women as bearers of children. Women's reproductive capacity has been invested with magical and mysterious forms of power, though the actual circumstances of childbirth were hazardous.

Poetry and songs by women survive in many differing cultures from early times with themes frequently about personal relations between men and women, preserving a memory of sensual as well as spiritual yearnings. Language, music, and art are means of giving expression to one's feelings and thoughts; thus creativity can be seen as a kind of power.

The interaction between production and the reproduction of life in society, the role of culture, and the type of religious faith are all relevant for an understanding of women's position and gender relations. How society as well as politics are organized have important consequences on women's lives, one element being how public and personal aspects of life are actually divided. So, in examining how and why movements emerge and develop among women, knowledge of both the structures and relationships within a given society is vital.

Ideas of what is male and what is female have varied greatly in different cultures and periods. Similarly concepts of nature, personal life, the individual society, and politics are not fixed categories but are formed by people in response to diverse circumstances. The boundaries between personal life and what is seen as the public sphere have been shifted and reconstituted thus as people have disputed and recast prevailing values.

Long before any political movement for women's rights came into being, women challenged definitions of their natures imposed by men through secular and religious culture. This involved contesting what constituted culture and could lead to questions about how the boundaries determining personal and public affairs were set. In 1404, for instance, Christine de Pisan, a French writer, produced a book called *The City of Women* in which she confronted men's power to decide the scope and content of learning and scholarship. *The City of Women* was to be a "cloister of defence."[3] Imaginatively she sought to create a citadel fortified by argument whereby women of all stations might withstand male critics. She took over the separate space that existed in the cloister as an image and gave it a new meaning. Metaphorically she created a place that could provide women with the means of refuting male interpretations of culture. Culturally she was reworking the boundaries of male and female experience to counter the power that surrounds the shaping and codifying of knowledge.

Women's assertion of power has taken not only the secular form that we associate with modern politics, but has also involved protesting the roles ascribed to them by religious leaders. Sometimes these have led women to reject or to try and redefine the whole framework of religious beliefs in the process, with important implications not only for cultural hierarchy but for social and political authority.

For example, Fatima Mernissi describes the rejoicing of women after the death of the Prophet, who were called "the harlots of Hadramant"[4] in 632 when a movement of apostasy swept the Arabian peninsula. There was also Aicha, the Prophet's third wife, who went into battle against a Khalife in 656 and herself made religious laws. In India, from the eighth century, the bhakti movement, a popular rebellion against Vedic Hinduism, involved women saints and poets who broke with their families and wrote in regional languages. They had to struggle with the men to be accepted as spiritual equals. In the thirteenth and fourteenth centuries in Europe, women called the "beguines" were part of a movement of lay spirituality that sought to live the apostolic life. Ursula King in a study of *Women and Spirituality* says they were among the people accused of the heresy of the Free Spirit.

> It taught that man and woman could attain perfection on earth through a direct personal relationship between God and the soul which made the mediation of the church unnecessary. Many beguines are also reported to have had visions of an impending third age in which the Holy Ghost would be incarnate in a woman.[5]

Belief in a woman redeemer, or the conviction that women as a group were to rescue a morally corrupt male-dominated society, was to resonate in women's movements, influenced by Christianity, many years later. Equally the notion that an individual might gain a direct, personal relationship to God was to exert an influence on subsequent radical movements.

In the seventeenth century puritan women sought to redefine women's sphere of activity by drawing on the legitimation of religious doctrine in standing up to the authority of fathers, husbands, priests, and political leaders. The Puritan revolution created a ferment in which all forms of hierarchy were rejected by members of the radical sects in Britain and the impact was felt among those who settled in America. The Puritans disagreed among themselves about the degree of democracy that the rights of individual conscience actually required. For many of the men it stopped short at women and servants.

Nonetheless women in Britain and the American colonies claimed inspiration and personal judgment of conscience moving fleetingly into the public discourse that had been set by religious dissent. In Britain women petitioned parliament and in both countries women began to interpret the scriptures and to preach. The men, in response, marked the boundaries more firmly. "You have stepped out of your place,"[6] the Calvinist Church fathers told Anne Hutchinson, a preacher in the Massachusetts Bay Colony, and another Calvinist John Bunyan in Britain grumbled about women in his church who wanted to form a separate group, even after the defeat of Cromwell's Commonwealth.

Ideas of individual rights and the concept that all souls were equal proved difficult to contain or to suppress completely. In European countries such as Britain and France, women of the "middling" strata were in this period losing the capacity to participate in society and the economy. They began to demand the "right" to education and access to the "male" sphere of political and civil society.

By the eighteenth century enlightenment thinkers were presenting a self-conscious critique of women's position based on a secular concept of the reasonable reconstitution of society and politics. Their theories thus were to open up a new approach to the public arena of politics, a potential space based on every individual as the possessor of inalienable rights, which enabled women to make claims for admission to education in order to cultivate the reason necessary for wielding power according to the enlightenment ideal.

The enlightenment is a confusing body of thought in which there are many strands. Nature as well as reason was asserted. In Germany enlightenment philosophers stressed self-realization through the unfolding of the potential of human personality, a theme that was to be revived by the romantics and influence liberalism, socialism, and feminism. Although Rousseau believed women's passions were so powerful they would overwhelm men's capacity for reason, most enlightenment writers, in France, England, and Scotland urged that women's education and unjust laws should be changed so that women could themselves develop reason. It was the ordering of society that was to blame for the 'peculiar foibles and vices'[7] of women declared the radical Catherine Macauley in 1790.

In contrast to earlier theories presenting hierarchy and inequality as necessary and inevitable, by the late eighteenth century a set of philosophic assumptions existed that took for granted the desirability of amending and improving society by the application of principles founded on reason rather than on custom. Some thinkers were prepared to include women as well as men, the poor as well as the rich. It is hardly surprising that the philosophic visions of the enlightenment should be influential in shaping the course of the demands for women's emancipation.

There were, however, certain snags in the project of the enlightenment. These were to have long-term implications, intellectually and politically. Karl Marx was to point out one problem forcibly in the mid-nineteenth century: abstract notions of equal rights and the force of reason failed to consider the actual economic and social inequalities among individuals, which greatly affected how rights could be exercised. Principles might be very fine, but the poor had to live in the meantime. Some advocates of women's emancipation from the 1820s noted another difficulty; to say all individuals could acquire reason ignored that reason itself was culturally formed. They began to argue that men had the power to set the terms of culture and to make reason thus in their own image. Women's emancipation consequently required the transformation of culture, not just gaining access to existing culture.

Within the enlightenment there was a knot of ambiguity about whether women had distinct natures, which was Rousseau's position, or whether women would have the same natures as men if allowed the benefit of education. Should humanity be measured by differing or by universal standards?

From women's points of view both perspectives were to have radical and conservative implications. The argument for distinct natures could provide a source for a cultural opposition to prevailing values defined by men. By characterizing women as more virtuous, more spiritual, or more passionate than men, it was possible to say that they possessed crucial qualities on which a greater degree of social and political power should be established. On the other hand the same stance could lead, as it did in the case of Rousseau, to the insistence that women should be kept apart from the public world of power

politics. The argument that women, being potentially reasonable crea-
tures, should gain equal rights to education, employment, politics and
wealth on the same terms as men recognized that human beings were
commensurate, yet tended to dismiss women's specific needs and experiences, without acknowledging male cultural and social power. These
issues are still with us and recur in modern feminist debates.

Moreover, the enlightenment left a problematic legacy not only for
class and gender, but also for race and ethnicity. Some enlightenment
writers idealized non-European cultures as natural, whereas others saw
them as inferior. As women in the East began to demand rights around
the late nineteenth century they were to face a dilemma; western
assumptions about emancipation were frequently imposed in a rigid
and abstract manner with little regard for customs that had protected
and sustained poor women in particular. On the other hand the idealization of oriental customs could restrict women's aspirations for
emancipation. Never simply intellectual matters these views were to
become increasingly political as movements against colonialism developed and were to leave a very deep mark.

The cultural biases in what came to be called feminism were thus
present from its early years. In the modern women's movement they
have been exhaustively debated, as more and more Third World
women have come to grapple with the recasting of the terms of liberation.

However a critical historical approach to the enlightenment and
awareness that reason was not confined to the West need not lead to a
dismissal of all aspects of the philosophic traditions which influenced
the early claims for women's rights.

Enlightenment concepts of reason and nature have had an extremely important influence on arguments for the emancipation of
women not only in the West but in the East. They presented a means
by which complaint and resistance could find a self-conscious expression in relation to a wider project of social transformation. As a result,
for better or worse, these eighteenth-century debates and the extraordinary event of the French Revolution are crucial in shaping the overall
terms in which particular experiences of oppression were to be defined

and expressed as part of a vision of a new social order and a new individuality.

Inspired by the principles of enlightenment thinkers, Mary Wollstonecraft, a teacher and writer in London radical circles, published *A Vindication of the Rights of Woman* in 1792. She believed individuals had natural rights to self-determination, opposed arbitrary and hereditary rule, and asserted "natural," simple values against aristocratic pomp and cynicism. She optimistically assumed human beings—including women—were capable of perfecting society themselves and that equality would be the basis for new relations among people.

The *Vindication* and her other writings are fired by her own experiences as a woman who was economically and sexually vulnerable. She had to struggle to make her own living. She had a child during the French Revolution with an American, Gilbert Imlay, to whom she was not married. When he deserted her, she attempted suicide. Though she found happiness with the radical philosopher William Godwin, who she married, she died from childbirth in 1797, just as reaction against the French Revolution was consolidating.

In the *Vindication* Mary Wollstonecraft argued for reason as the basis for women's equal part in society and politics. How could men deny women the opportunity to reason and then use this as an excuse to bar them from a useful active life? Though she used some of Rousseau's views about nature, she rejected the idea that one's gender should restrict human rights.

In her letters and novels there is also a self-conscious presentation of herself, a search for self-knowledge, and an attempt to acknowledge contrary passions that reaches towards romanticism. She asked in her novel *Mary,*

> Are desires implanted in me only to make me miserable? Will they never be gratified? Shall I never be happy? My feelings do not accord with the notion of solitary happiness. In a state of bliss it will be the society of beings who can love . . . that will constitute a great part of our happiness.[8]

This was to be one of the most problematic aspects of the quest that was to be called feminism. How were women to express passion without being overwhelmed and abandoning an autonomous sense of self. "I cannot live without loving but love leads to madness."[9]

Mary Wollstonecraft is a thinker who faces two ways. She draws on the arguments of educated enlightenment women and men and looks forward to the socialism and feminism of the early nineteenth century. In one sense she is the lonely individual voice, the Promethean spirit of whom her son-in-law Shelley was to write, releasing women to dare to be and do the inconceivable. But she also intimates a collective project, a concept of "women" as an identifiable group.

"She considered herself as standing forth in defense of one-half of the human species"[10] wrote William Godwin when she died.

It was not so simple of course. Mary Wollstonecraft expressed mainly the grievances of the middling strata. Like other radicals of her day she considers principles that come from a particular social predicament as universal, which, as Marx later pointed out, was the catch in demanding equal rights in theory while ignoring actual social inequalities. She was, moreover, inclined to be complacent about the inherent progress and superiority of Western civilization—other enlightenment thinkers were more self-critical.

Nonetheless, her *Vindication,* written in six weeks and brimming with revolutionary enthusiasm, was read by early nineteenth-century rebels who were not afraid of her posthumous lack of respectability and is still a source of fascination for modern feminists.

I

RIGHTS, SOVEREIGNTY, AND EMANCIPATION

THEMES FOR DISCUSSION

* The pros and cons of arguments for women's emancipation based on universal rights.
* The significance of a consciousness of social and economic entitlements in women's collective action.
* The connection between self-emancipation and social emancipation in women's movements.
* The division between public and personal spheres in society in relation to gender.
* The strategic consequences of demanding equality with men within the existing framework of society.

3

THE TOCSIN OF REASON: WOMEN IN THE FRENCH REVOLUTION

In 1789 the outbreak of the French Revolution meant that individual rights, reason, citizenship, and the sovereignty of the people were no longer simply ideas, but part of an assault on hereditary power. Their abstract quality was shed as they became part of politics. They gained historical legitimacy and lost their innocence, all in a few short years.

It is hard for us to imagine the impact of such an extraordinary event. Power, which had seemed absolute, was overturned. The new dawn of reason and liberty brought a fervor of hope and terrible disappointment.

A butcher's daughter turned playwright, Olympe de Gouges,

exploded in The Declaration of the Rights of Woman and the Citizen-
ess in 1791:

> Woman, wake up, the tocsin of reason is being heard throughout the
> whole universe; discover your rights. The powerful empire of nature is
> no longer surrounded by prejudice, fanaticism, superstition and lies . . .
>
> Oh women, women when will you cease to be blind? What advantage
> have you received from the Revolution?[1]

Olympe de Gouges' call to women to rally to the tocsin of reason
was to have a rough ride in the years of revolution. Most of the
men who supported the revolution, regardless of their own political
differences, did not believe that liberty, equality, and fraternity applied
to women. "The People" not the King were declared to be sovereign.
But sovereignty was restricted in the constitution of 1791—"Active
citizens" were allowed to make laws and "passive" citizens were simply
protected by them. Women and the poorer working men did not have
the vote and were not allowed to join the National Guard. Despite the
efforts of the philosopher Condorcet, who argued for women's rights,
and despite the militant participation of women in the revolution,
subsequent versions never endorsed the demand for women to be
active citizens.

Though without formal rights, women did exert their influence
within the revolutionary situation. They were, however, divided economically, socially, and politically.

The French Revolution paradoxically made possible the *idea* of
there being a common predicament of women that the transformation
of state and society should affect. But the reality was that women
were in very differing circumstances and wanted as many conflicting
changes as the men.

In January 1789, women of the "Third Estate," from the families
of the "middling" and professional classes petitioned for "enlightenment and jobs."[2] Education, legal rights, and employment were their
main concerns. They also protested against what they regarded as
affronts to their modesty—prostitution and men entering midwifery.

In October 1789 the Parisian market women marched to Versailles followed by the National Guard. Bread was not reaching the city and they returned escorting the King and Queen, who they jokingly called the baker and the baker's wife, with a familiarity toward absolute power that divested the monarchy of some of its authority.

Poor women had taken crowd action as a means of exerting some control over prices and consumption long before the revolution. But the targets had been usually the bakers. Now they were holding the king, or head of state, responsible for supplying bread.

The King was to be executed and "the People," through the National Convention, became sovereign. France became embroiled in a war, for other European regimes were alarmed by the example of revolution. Slaves also rebelled in the French colonies. Amid turmoil and dislocation prices rose and in February 1793 poor women went to the Convention to protest. They were told it was about to adjourn for two days and would not hear their case. The women angrily criticized the unresponsive people's state that prevaricated over their families needs.

When our children ask us for milk we don't adjourn them until the day after tomorrow.[3]

These women of the people mobilized not around their individual rights as women but in relation to their kin. Their social responsibilities as mothers legitimated their questioning of state and economy. In the context of revolution the exercise of their direct power to curb market forces assumed a new political meaning. In Lyon in 1792 they actually seized control of the city government and raided shops for bread and meat, which they sold at prices they regarded as just. Such actions indicate assumptions about sovereignty involving a state responsive to the needs of the poor and a moral vision of an economy in which basic commodities should be distributed at prices regarded as fair and just.

Certain limited civil rights were granted. In September 1792 marriage was made a civil contract and divorce was possible. It was agreed that when parents separated the girls went with the mother and the boys with the father. Under the old regime the mother had no rights of custody. In 1793 wives got the right to share family property and girls got equal inheritance rights. However for poor urban women the most crucial measure was the decree of 1793 which fixed a maximum on grain and flour.

The demand of poor women for a just price and for regulation of consumption was bound up with a power struggle about what forces decided the course of the revolution and the future shape of French society. The left in 1793 was pressing for price control. Women active in the radical society of Revolutionary Republican Women were part of this agitation. They expressed the interests of the urban poor, "the sans-culottes" literally "those without breeches." But the predicament of the women of the sans-culottes differed not only from the women of rich merchant and professional families, but also from peasant women, from the inhabitants of small towns and workers in luxury trades who blamed the shortages on 'the maximum'. Even the Parisian market women, who had been staunch supporters of the revolution, resented interference in their trade and maintained women from the Society of Revolutionary Republican Women had tried to get them to wear hermaphrodite clothing—the red pantaloons and red woollen bonnets of liberty that had become the revolutionary insignia; saying this marked full citizenship which would compel them to bear arms and was contrary to their rights as women, they pelted the women from the revolutionary women's club with their produce in the autumn of 1793.

These economic divisions among women who supported the French Revolution were accompanied by many political disagreements. Olympe de Gouges believed in constitutional monarchy and was guillotined in 1793 as a suspected royalist. To the left of those who supported a constitutional monarchy, two factions, the Girondins and the Jacobins, were in conflict with one another and women were involved in the factional combats. Several women who played a prominent part in the revolution, including an ex-courtesan Théroigne de Méricourt, were associated with the Girondins. In 1792 she demanded a woman's battalion to fight in the revolutionary wars against the European rulers who opposed the revolution.

The Jacobins were to the left of the Girondins. However, their leader, Robespierre, a follower of Rousseau, hated politically active women. Nonetheless the Jacobins needed the support of the sans-culottes women of the people, who were pressing for price controls. The women's club Society of Revolutionary Republican Women included Pauline Léon and Claire Lacombe, who supported the Enragés, a group to the left of the Jacobins who were demanding stricter price controls.

The Jacobins came to power in 1793 amid war paranoia and economic dislocation. Locally the sans-culottes were asserting their power against old enemies. Political and economic grievances mixed with personal grudges. Spontaneous acts of violence were part of a decentralized terror. Women were no exception. The Jacobin women flogged Théroigne de Méricourt as a reactionary and she subsequently went insane. Robespierre sought to bring the terror under his control and institutionalize it as part of a centralized state. As soon as he believed himself secure he turned away from his left-wing supporters. Eventually he was defeated by the right. After he fell the poor starved and women such as Pauline Léon and Claire Lacombe were imprisoned.

Women were caught up in a maelstrom of events. Mary Wollstonecraft, who was sympathetic to the Girondins, was horrified by the terror.

However, despite divisions, lack of support, and dreadful circumstances, women, even briefly, made momentous claims to enter the institutions of learning, to gain employment, and even to go to war. Poor women did not only protest over bread prices they began to assert the right to intervene in the economy; they were after all "the people." An example of this active role in politics, which was an aspect of the idea of popular sovereignty, is well illustrated by the response of a cook, Constance Evrad. When asked why she participated in a demonstration in Paris in 1791, she replied that the aim was to organize executive power differently. After centuries of absolute monarchy, a cook had got hold of the idea that she should be part of a political battle to force the king to accept limits to his powers through a constitution.

Despite differences between women in social circumstances and politics, the revolution opened up a public sphere of action for women. Although the concept of women's rights as women certainly appeared, there is another strand of women's mobilization as revolutionaries. They asserted their rights not so much in relation to men as in a new relation to politics through a public identity as citizenesses and patriots. They demonstrated for popular sovereignty, imposed their economic demands, fought in the revolutionary wars—though they were never given their own battalion. Some of their loyalty to religion became secularized; market women now ceremonially gave the offerings they had previously presented to the Virgin Mary to the war effort.

The exceptional circumstances of the revolution pulled women toward a public sphere of action. Olympe de Gouges noted that this had unexpected consequences even by 1791, because of the peculiarities of women's oppression. She said women had exercised power in the Old Regime in a hidden manner by ruling "the weakness of man."[4] The revolution had done away with this "nocturnal administration" leaving women who were formerly "contemptible and respected"[5] now "respected and scorned."[6] These were dubious gains.

Nonetheless, as the boundaries between personal and public shift, Olympe de Gouges' extraordinary Declaration surfaces,

> In this contradictory situation, what remarks would I not make! I have but a moment to make them, but this moment will fix the attention of the remotest posterity.[7]

So the statement of women's rights to enter the public sphere emerges just when older forms of personal, sexual power have been weakened.

As the old social order and its rituals and symbols were assailed, new meanings were marked by clothes, customs, moral assumptions, pageants, and even deities. As fear fed the terror, details of personal life could have serious consequences. In 1793 a woman served her guests white cheese in the form of a heart and was accused of secret royalism because it was said the king's heart was white.

When Claire Lacombe clashed with a Jacobin François Chabot she denounced him in the Society of Revolutionary Republican Women as a man of dubious patriotism. The former secret power of women is disdained. Instead the revolutionary women transfer the traditional role of women as guardians of morality into the public arena. They assert their authority as guardians of revolutionary purity.

François Chabot was trying to marry a rich foreigner. Claire Lacombe stated,

> I saw the . . . companion of his disordered life. Once I was inside his saloon. I saw on the couch a woman scented with musk and a man dressed in a reddish orange frock coat with a very large silver braid on the collar.[8]

Anyone wearing musk perfume in the room must have been feeling distinctly uncomfortable.

The Jacobins were not impressed by these claims to patriotic virtue. Arresting the male leader of the Enragés in September 1793, they turned on the left-wing women's club and suppressed them urging women to be simple in their appearance and to become diligent housewives—shades of Rousseau. The Goddess of Liberty a female symbol was launched, only to be rapidly ousted by the masculine Supreme Being—which could be accommodated more easily with the Catholic church, still powerful among the peasantry.

Women continued to be honoured in patriotic festivals but their power was symbolically contained within certain images that emphasized not equal, public participation but a special role as mothers within the family. An interesting personification of the regeneration of France that also expressed opposition to slavery appeared in a festival in Bourg-en-Bresse in January 1794. A white woman was paraded in a cart giving milk to a black child and a black woman nursed a white child. Slave rebellions and the need for black allies forced the Jacobins to accept emancipation in February of that year.

Prices mounted and there were shortages. The crisis of consumption made it difficult for women to be good housewives and mothers. In 1794 Anne Félicité Guinée, a 24-year-old housewife, queued like other poor women for three days without getting food. She was distraught and indignant to be told by a Jacobin official that she should drink more milk. Who did this man think he was telling her how to be a housewife?

I answered that I had men in my house who worked and that I couldn't nourish them with milk.[9]

She called him an imbecile who wanted to play the despot. Femme Guinée was arrested and kept in prison for six hours. She was accused of being a counterrevolutionary and told she was asking for the guillotine. Furious, she told them, "I preferred death to being treated ignominiously."[10]

This incident shows how the Jacobins' popular support was slipping away. Femme Guinée emerged from jail when the Jacobins were defeated by the right. Unfortunately for poor housewives, the prices soared and speculators thrived. There were two attempts at insurrection, in which women took part, but both were defeated.

Apart from some legal changes and small improvements in education, women had made few gains. They were excluded from even the brief and factional public power that men of varying political views asserted.

Nonetheless not only the assertion of women's rights but a completely new society in which women participated as active citizens was glimpsed by poor women. Cooks, charcoal gatherers, market women, and housewives briefly came to know direct political power. This gave women the confidence to imagine an economy based on need not on profit and the market and Femme Guinée the courage to answer back.

The French Revolution brought together strands of rebellion that were to have a considerable historical resonance.

Women's rights were asserted by a minority of women as part of universal human rights and connected with a movement that aimed to transform society in the interests of the "people." Despite defeat the hope survived.

Among poor women the attempt to limit the profits of traders and speculators indicated a shadowy alternative to the capitalist economy. The sans–culottes women acted not in the name of a concept of female equality but because the revolution changed their customary activities in the family and made the ways of being women they had known all their lives impossible.

Both forms of action shared the radical view that human beings, including those without power and privileges, could and should make changes that would improve society.

They differed, not only because the sans-culottes women did not assume a common condition of all women, but in their approach to the public sphere of politics. Advocates of women's rights argued that reason and rights ought to be genderless. They could not be claimed by men and denied to women. The women of the sans-culottes defended their interests as housewives and mothers. But in the context of revolution the previously personal sphere of domestic life involved not only a change in state policy, but a state that protected a moral economy of need.

4

A NEW MORAL WORLD: EARLY RADICALS, COOPERATORS, AND SOCIALISTS

In 1818, the women of a small Lancashire town in the North of England, Blackburn, made a Cap of Liberty out of scarlet silk. They described it as "the emblem that has ever been held sacred to the people."[1]

They were members of the newly formed Female Reform Society, one of several set up to campaign for the extension of the franchise. An archaic system of representation excluded even prosperous business people. Radical reformers argued for universal suffrage, though this was often assumed to mean manhood suffrage.

Members of the Female Reform Societies believed that parliamentary reform would help to solve the economic distress caused by the long war against France and the new factory system. They took part in a demonstration at St. Peter's Fields, Manchester, for manhood suffrage in August 1819. Soldiers charged the demonstrators; eleven people died, two of whom were women. Hundreds were wounded.

A widespread movement for radical reform developed in which the memory of this unjust attack lived on. They called it the massacre of Peterloo, in ironic parody of the British victory against the French at Waterloo. Along with the vote, freedom of the press, the right to knowledge, including birth control, and humane care for the poor combined with trade union organization and the creation of cooperative communities as a demonstrable alternative to capitalism.

These were times when the economic organization of society was changing rapidly. Some radicals who opposed the cruel consequences of industrialization were prepared to envisage the extension of democratic rights to all the unenfranchised and argue that profit and privately owned capital could not secure human well-being.

Others however, such as James Mill, believed change should be restricted. In 1824 he said that women and working class men had no claims to the vote—their interests could be safeguarded by husbands and fathers and people of the middle rank. Both gender and class were thus reasons for exclusion from any say in government.

William Thompson, a radical landowner from Cork in Ireland, wrote a reply, Appeal of One-Half the Human Race in 1825. He was influenced by his companion Anna Wheeler, a socialist and a believer in women's rights.

William Thompson's book not only argued that women should have the franchise, a demand that was still impossible for Mary Wollstonecraft in the late eighteenth century. He also made a connection between the emancipation of women and the economic organization of society. Thompson believed that immediate reforms were necessary to secure more equality but that a cooperative society alone would mean that women would be truly equal. Under capitalism, when they had children, they were necessarily economically dependent on men.

Thompson's "Appeal" did not just take on politics and production. He pointed to inequalities in marriage.

Each man yokes a woman to his establishment and calls it a contract.[2]

He argued that men's power in society defined morality and culture.

He has a system of domineering hypocrisy he calls morals.[3]

The emancipation of women involved political democracy, a co-operative economy, and a challenge to male power in the household and in institutions such as the law. It also meant contesting the power to define the values of society.

The movement for the emancipation of slaves had a tremendous impact on early radical arguments for women's rights. Olympe de Gouges had made the connection during the French Revolution. It was also important in the United States. If rights were universal and all human beings capable of reason how could slavery be justified?

Thompson was aware that the conditions of slaves and the situation of women differed, yet he noted a similarity, not in the external forms of bondage, but in internal attempts at control. Slave-owners imposed their own definition of "nature" on their slaves. This concept of the slaves' character was based in fact in the selfishness and ignorance of the owners but it was presented as common sense. The Appeal thus took up the struggle against the cultural power of the rulers of society. The emancipation of women involved a redefinition of human nature.

In this early radical milieu the movement of ideas was international. Anna Wheeler was in touch with thinkers in France, who were arguing that political reform was insufficient. Production should be communally owned and all personal relations should be seen as part of the project of social transformation.

Charles Fourier, the French socialist who invented the word "feminism," argued that the degree of women's freedom decided the extent of social progress. Women's emancipation was thus linked to the idea of progressive social reform and historical change.

Followers of another early French socialist Saint-Simon linked progress with the old Christian heresy of a woman messiah. Père Enfantin gained a following that included a young Parisian working woman Suzanne Voilquin, whose father had been active in the French Revolution. Enfantin said in 1834 that the new society was to be created by a woman redeemer, La Femme Libre, or La Mére, who would unfold a new morality, develop new feelings, and transcend the Christian denial of the flesh. "Woman" symbolizing animality and fertility as well as love would complement the "masculine" principles of aggression and competition ascendent in a male-dominated capitalism. His ideas enabled Suzanne Voilquin to realize unfulfilled capacities for thought, feeling, and independent action.

At first sight the Saint-Simonians seem a cranky lot, rushing off to Egypt in a disastrous expedition to find the female Messiah. In a round about way though, they addressed a crucial question relevant not only to the emancipation of women but to any attempt at radical social change. How were new values to be developed as a means of making a new moral world? Was it enough to simply change the external institutions? Woman's role as a redeemer involved women as agents of change.

Robert Owen, who started off as an enlightened factor owner, contributed to another strand in radical debate. He believed firmly that by changing the external environment a new human character would develop. He came to the conclusion that the family cultivated selfish, individualistic characters. He was less concerned with the unequal power relations between men and women in the home than with the family as a place where children were brought up in a possessive manner.

He had turned his cotton mills in New Lanark, Scotland, into a project for social welfare in 1812. The changes Owen envisaged were imposed from above. In contrast, political radicals campaigning for the vote argued that democracy had to come first; then people could decide how they wanted society to change.

Owen decided that old habits and customs held too much sway in Britain. He bought land in the United States and formed a community called New Harmony. Things did not go according to plan. Women, especially, resented the rules Owen imposed, which communally educated children away from the family.

New Harmony, however, inspired a young British radical Frances

Wright to set up a community of freed slaves in Nashoba near Memphis in 1827.

Frances Wright combined ideas of universal rights, which echoed the French Revolution, with a moral opposition to slavery, which had been a theme of radical abolitionists. She also held ideas, common among enlightened thinkers and radicals and socialists of the 1820s, about sexual feeling. Frances Wright declared in her "*Explanatory Notes Respecting the Nature and Objects of the Institution of Nashoba*" in 1827:

> Let us not teach, that virtue consists in crucifying the affections and appetites, but in their *judicious government*.[4]

To contemporaries such ideas were explosive when they were expressed by a young woman who openly scorned convention, dressing in the androgynous smock and floppy trousers adopted by "the Saint-Simonian women." Advocacy of free unions was bad enough, but when they developed between black and white people at Nashoba, rumors of brothels and orgies began to surround the place. This was hypocrisy of course, for white Southern slave-owners forced black women to bear their children.

Nashoba failed, but many other utopian communities were formed in the United States in which the liberation of women and sexual equality were inspirational ideas. There was a difference in emphasis among reformers in the United States and Europe. In the United States, during the first half of the nineteenth century, the abolition of slavery, women's rights, vegetarian health cults, and spirituality combined with the emancipation of labor in a vision of the "perfectibility" of all aspects of human existence. In European radicalism, the attempt to give industrialization a cooperative rather than competitive framework along with the struggle against class oppression—in production and in communities was a priority.

One cooperative scheme put forward by John Gray in the 1820s actually tackled the inequality created by the way tasks were divided between men and women. His *Lecture on Human Happiness* proposed a plan to London cooperators in which women not only had equal rights in the government of the community but were allowed time to exercise these rights, by distributing domestic tasks such as cooking, washing, and heating equally.

Seven Owenite communities were established between 1820 and 1845. Owen did not question women doing the housework but he did try and lighten their task. He believed the resources of society should be used in activities that had been seen as personal.

One side of this was technological innovation. Why confine this to production? In one community, Queenswood, in 1841, the kitchen was designed carefully and was full of ingenious gadgets. A little train took the dishes of food into the dining room and returned the empty plates to the kitchen when the meal was finished.

Another element was social reorganization. Owen's earlier interest in education and child-care as a responsibility of the whole society rather than just the individual parents meant that the Owenites were pioneers in establishing schools from infancy. Against the rote learning that prevailed at that time, they educated children through play and through activity.

Followers of Robert Owen saw trades unions as a means of changing society. The Grand National Consolidated Union was concerned not only with economic conditions. A general strike of the working class was to transform state and society.

Women formed unions and set up female lodges. Although women were being drawn into the factory system through the textile industry, many women worked as outworkers making lace and straw bonnets. Work and pay were chancy affairs and the straw-bonnet workers put great stress on the social side of unionism. The union was to help them when they were sick and enable members to have decent burials. It was also to be responsible for the education of infants and adults alike. It was thought that education should be controlled by the working classes themselves in order to safeguard its independence from employers, clerics, and philanthropists.

The war and the factory system had an effect on workers who were still engaged in older forms of production. Clothing workers were facing a reduction of pay as "slop work" of inferior quality became more common in the 1830s. Skilled tailors began to argue that women should be banned from the industry as they took work away from men and accepted less money.

There was a furious controversy in an Owenite trade union paper The *Pioneer,* edited by James and Frances Morrison. Women workers indignantly asked about women who had no man to support them. The *Pioneer's* editors, who printed Mary Wollstonecraft's writing in the paper, had an enlightened approach, arguing for equal pay regardless of gender and insisting,

> the low wages of women are not so much the voluntary price she sets upon her labour as the price which is fixed by the tyrannical influence of male supremacy.[5]

In one women's trade it was actually men who reduced wages. A straw-bonnet maker complained that men trained by the women were undercutting them, offering to take work home and work at lower rates. She said the women discovered "these men were more tyrannical than their former masters."[6] The straw-bonnet makers distinguished between men who were undercutting them and men who were their allies. Part of their commitment to trade unionism was "protection of our noble brothers in the union."[7]

They encouraged other women to disregard setbacks and defeats and exert their utmost efforts to change society, "put our shoulder to the wheel."[8] They had a touching sense of their historical significance, not as individuals like Olympe de Gouges, but collectively.

> Children yet unborn must have to remember, there was woman as well as man in the union.[9]

Owenite women, thus, were both part of a common project of emancipation and had their own viewpoints as women. They were not prepared to accept male trade unionists who blamed the slop trade on women working. They were exasperated at cooperative schemes that put a double load of work on them domestically as well as in production.

They did not always agree, even among themselves, especially on matters of personal morality and sexual freedom. Some Owenite women argued against marriage and for easier divorce. Information about birth control was being published by radicals and it was being argued that reason could be applied to passions such as jealousy and that women had as much right to sexual pleasure as men. But some Owenite women were wary of free unions, for women were still much more vulnerable than men economically, socially, and culturally. In their opinion faithful husbands were more important than fancy freedoms.

So in planning the transformation of all human relationships, the early radicals encountered a problem. Who exactly was to decide the shape of the new moral world?

The scope of their vision of how society could be changed remains impressive. In the early stages of "the industrial revolution" it still seemed that an entirely new way of developing human and natural resources could be devised democratically. Because they were optimistic about making a completely new society they were extremely radical in their views on how women's lives could change. If not only all external institutions but human character was "perfectable" and progress was on their side what could prevent women gaining political, economic, and social freedom?

Unfortunately it proved to be easier said than done.

5

THE ABOLITION OF SLAVERY AND WOMEN'S EMANCIPATION

In 1773 the first book by a black woman ever published appeared in London. Its author, Phillis Wheatley, was a 19-year-old slave, who wrote poetry from Boston, Massachusetts.

Her work contributed to a movement, which was victorious in 1807 to end the British slave-trade. The struggle against slavery in the West Indies and in the United States continued. Black women took part in attempts at violent rebellion in both the Caribbean and the United States. They also developed ways of resisting the sexual advances of white owners and made painstaking efforts to educate themselves.

Maria Stewart, a free-born black woman, became the first American woman to speak in public on civil and women's rights in 1832. She based her arguments not on the secular radicalism of Frances Wright, but on the moral responsibilities of women as mothers, drawing on religious precedents of black women preachers and on charitable organization by black women and using scripture to justify her right to speak out. Maria Stewart combined moral agency with the enlightenment conviction that external circumstances decided character. She appealed to black women to use their own talents and educate their people:

> never will the chains of slavery and ignorance burst, till we become united as one and cultivate among ourselves the pure principles of piety, morality and virtue.[1]

The struggle for social emancipation was thus integrally linked for her as a black woman with mutual self-emancipation.

The abolitionist movement, which gathered strength in the 1830s, included both black and white men and women. In 1833 delegates met in Philadelphia to form the American Anti-Slavery Society. Three women attended the convention as observers and a few days later 20 women met and established the Philadelphia Female Anti-Slavery Society. They included Sarah Douglass, Harriet Purvis, and Sarah and Margaretta Forten, who were to play an important role in the movement as black women leaders. Lucretia Mott, a white Quaker, was also in the Philadelphia group. She was to be a leading campaigner for abolition and for women's suffrage, while also being sympathetic to the cause of labor and supporting a cooperative sewing shop in Philadelphia in 1850. Sarah Douglass brought two sisters into the movement from a slave owning family in the South, Sarah and Angelina Grimké.

The women organized many petitions and meetings. They spoke out against slavery, justifying their public action by citing both the Bible and natural rights. A nonconformist Christianity thus combined with the traditions of the enlightenment.

In 1837, Angelina Grimké challenged the conservative writer

Catherine Beecher, who did not approve of women taking part in the antislavery movement. Catherine Beecher thought American women could become powerful by concentrating on motherhood and domestic life. However, Angelina Grimké stated that women had rights as citizens. Women should,

> have a voice in all the laws and regulations by which she is to be governed, whether in Church or State, and the present arrangements of society, on these points are a violation of human rights, a rank usurpation of power, a violent seizure and confiscation of what is sacredly and inalienably hers.[2]

So a claim for women to be represented in government grew out of the movement against slavery.

In 1840 conflict about women's public role came to a head at the World Anti-Slavery Convention in London, where the American women delegates included Lucretia Mott and Elizabeth Cady Stanton. The antislavery leader, William Lloyd Garrison, sided with the women and the movement split on the issue.

In 1848, with the support of the black leader Frederick Douglass, Lucretia Mott and Elizabeth Cady Stanton called the Seneca Falls Convention to demand women's rights. They paraphrased the enlightenment arguments of the American Declaration of Independence, asserting

> that all men and women are created equal; that they are endowed by their Creator with certain alienable rights; that among *those* are life, liberty and the pursuit of happiness.[3]

This universalist argument claimed that women, like black people, had a right to equality. Individuals should be able to decide their own destinies and develop their abilities. Every person should have the same rights as citizens. Once artificial impediments were removed differences between people would diminish. Every individual was equally entitled to belong to a common humanity. Theoretically there were no boundaries; practically, however, these did exist.

Most of the delegates to the Seneca Falls Convention were leisured, white, middle-class women. They forgot to invite "The Female Reform Association," the first trade union of factory women in the United States, formed by self-educated workers in the Lowell mills, which campaigned for women's rights along with the 10-hour day, temperance, the abolition of capital punishment and slavery.

The mill women welcomed Seneca Falls in the paper 'Factory girls' Voice. They had developed their own critique of the cult of true womanhood. In 1846 in the *Voice of Industry* "An Operative" compared slavery to women's subordination in marriage. She challenged the hypocrisy of a domestic sphere as a means of controlling women.

Man forms our customs, our laws, our opinions for us.[4]

It was not then just a matter of gaining equal access into the public sphere but of challenging relations of power in society, which defined women's place.

Woman is never thought to be out of her *sphere*, at home, in the nursery, in the kitchen over a hot stove cooking from morning till evening—over a washtub, or toiling in a cotton factory fourteen hours per day. But let her for once step out, plead the cause of right and humanity, plead the wrongs of her slave sister of the South or of the operative of the North, and even attempt to teach the science of Physiology, and a cry is raised against her "out of her sphere.[5]"

When male hecklers tried to break up a Women's Rights Convention, "Sojourner Truth," an itinerant preacher born into slavery as Isabella Baumfree, bellowed, in response to a clergyman who had said women were too weak for equal rights:

The man over there says women need to be helped into carriages and lifted over ditches, and to have the best place everywhere. Nobody ever helps me into carriages or over puddles or gives me the best place—and aren't I a woman?[6]

Sojourner Truth claimed equality precisely because she was already in the public sphere of work. Nor had she known womanly privileges in the personal sphere—bearing the lash as well as a man and seeing most of her 13 children sold into slavery. Unlike white middle-class abolitionists, Sojourner Truth was not entering the public sphere through the movement. As a poor black woman the division of public and personal spheres, which was being developed as a cultural ideal for the middle class, simply did not apply to her situation.

White women at the Convention feared that if Sojourner Truth spoke their cause would be associated with "abolitionists and niggers."[7] In fact, she saved the day for them. One of them recorded that they responded to her intervention with "streaming eyes and hearts beating with gratitude,"[8] as Truth demolished the clergyman's claim that because Jesus was a man, men were superior. Where had Jesus come from in the first place? "God and a woman—*man* had nothing to do with it.[9]

The abolitionist and women's rights movement included instances of black and white women working together and bravely facing hostile mobs. But the few black women who were acceptable in the abolitionist groups tended to be from wealthy, educated backgrounds. Indeed there had been an argument at the first national Anti-Slavery Convention of American Women in 1837 about whether black women could be delegates.

Besides public discrimination there was also personal condescension. Harriet A Jacobs, author of *Incidents in the Life of a Slave Girl,* was exasperated by the novelist Harriet Beecher Stowe's fear that she would be spoiled if she went on a speaking tour in Britain. "Mrs. Stowe thinks petting is more than my race can bear."[10]

However, at black conventions women had to struggle to be heard. Although Jane P. Merritt and Mary Ann Shadd Cary, two leaders of the Underground Railroad, which brought slaves to freedom at great risk, did manage to gain a hearing in 1849 and 1855, in this period the movement was fiercely militant. Black men were asserting a manhood humiliated through slavery. Some men saw this as being patriarchal heads of their families and assuming the political leadership of the black movement. This led to a resistance towards women playing an equal part even though women's support was needed by the black cause.

During the Civil War black women such as Harriet Tubman and Sojourner Truth bravely risked their lives. Others organized welfare groups, for example, Elizabeth Keckley formed the Contraband Relief Association in Washington, through a black church, to help freed slaves. Women thus supported the war both by assuming men's roles and acting from women's domestic position.

After the war, in the South, black women did not want to work in the cotton fields. The cotton owners tried to starve them back to work. Labor unions excluded black people and there were violent attacks by white gangs.

Against this background women had a difficult decision. Should they support the Fourteenth and Fifteenth Amendments, which gave black men citizen's rights but defined these as exclusively male? Abolitionists claimed it was "the Negroes' hour."

Sojourner Truth had decided not to support the amendment. She said in 1867

> There is a great stir about colored men getting their rights, but not a word about the colored women . . . and if colored men get their rights and not colored women theirs, you see the colored men will be masters over the women, and it will be just as bad as it was before.[11]

Frances Ellen Harper was prepared to criticize the behavior of some black men toward women but she was more suspicious of an alliance with white women and by 1869 Sojourner Truth had become convinced of the need for black unity.

White women themselves were divided; Lucy Stone and Julia Ward Howe argued that the enfranchisement of black men was a first expedient step, whereas Elizabeth Cady Stanton and her friend Susan B. Anthony saw both these amendments as a betrayal of women's contribution to abolition. They formed the all women's "National Woman Suffrage Association" in 1869 and produced a journal called *The Revolution* financed by a wealthy backer, George Francis Train.

Some black male leaders thought it was wrong to separate black and women's enfranchisement. Charles Remond, for example, said,

In an hour like this I repudiate the idea of expediency. All I ask for myself I claim for my wife and sister.[12]

Expediency appeared to be justified, when, in 1870, the Fifteenth Amendment was adopted and black men won the vote. However it left a bitter legacy that was to mark the history of American radicalism.

Stanton and Anthony now focused on gender as the crucial oppression. They took very radical positions on women's freedom. In the journal *Revolution* they not only demanded the franchise but criticized marriage and women's working conditions. However, the millionaire George Francis Train was for labor but was hostile to the black cause. In the 1860s Stanton and Anthony themselves questioned the worthiness of black men and poor foreign immigrant men to vote in contrast to white women. The universal claim to the suffrage as a right began to shift toward the more conservative idea that some people were morally or intellectually entitled to vote. The assumption was that the white, middle-class automatically fulfilled these criteria.

In the late 1860s Stanton and Anthony tried to make an alliance with The National Labour Union. They succeeded in raising the issue of equal pay but were challenged by male trade unionists for encouraging women to strike break and sacking a woman typographer from *The Revolution* for organizing workers.

Lottie Rollins reasserted the universalist argument in 1870 at the founding meeting of the South Carolina Women's Rights Association in Columbia.

We ask suffrage not as a favor, nor as a privilege, but as a right based on the ground that we are human beings and as such entitled to all human rights.[13]

It was the first address by a black woman to be published on suffrage apart from those of Sojourner Truth.

Less abstract arguments for equality came from a woman delegate from Newport, Rhode Island at the National Colored Labour Union meeting in Washington. Black male workers challenged the discriminatory policies of white unions but forgot women's special problems.

Black women were confined to jobs such as domestic service and washing. They were excluded from the skilled women's trades, such as millinery, dress making, and tailoring, or from respectable occupations, such as being shop assistants. She pleaded

> When you mount the chariot of equality, in industrial and mechanical pursuits, we may at least be permitted to cling to the wheels.[14]

Equality then was not simply an abstract principle and a moral right, it meant tackling specific relations of power in society that decided who was to do the worst jobs for the least pay.

On the whole, the early campaigners for both black and women's emancipation stressed that external circumstances caused inequality. This did not mean they thought external change was enough. There was also an emphasis on self-emancipation among black women and in the writings of white suffrage advocates such as Stanton and Anthony.

Margaret Fuller expressed a differing approach. In the 1830s and 1840s she was observing women active in abolition with admiration. However, the meetings she went to were quieter: a circle of about 30 women in a Boston parlour speaking on "What is Life." She was the first American woman literary critic and was connected to transcendentalists such as Ralph Waldo Emerson who emphasized individual self-fulfilment as the ideal of life. Transcendentalism had ambiguous political implications. Self-fulfilment could imply either personal cultivation or public action.

In *Woman in the Nineteenth Century* in 1844, Margaret Fuller criticized the French Revolution for being concerned only with the external obstacles to happiness. She stressed the need for internal psychological and cultural change. Inequality was not only a matter of institutions, it also involved attitudes. She compared men's contempt for women and children to the acceptance of slavery.

Like Catherine Beecher, Margaret Fuller did not base her arguments for improving women's position on a concept of universal rights. She thought there were distinct masculine and feminine natures and that women needed to seek autonomous self-fulfilment on the basis of difference. Unlike Beecher, she gave this difference a radical, transformatory potential. Difference did not imply inequality. Instead of being led by men the development of the feminine side of society would bring into being a new culture. She was rather vague about what these female characteristics were: electrical, intuitive, spiritual, love, beauty, and holiness. Women were transcendent high mindedness personified. The aim of emancipation was not power but growth.

Fuller was influenced by Fourier and by European romanticism and nationalism. She visited France and Italy in 1847–50 when both countries were seething with revolution. European intellectuals, the Polish poet Adam Mickiewicz and the French woman novelist George Sand, challenged her American transcendentalist dismissal of passion.

In Italy Margaret Fuller fell in love with a young republican revolutionary Ossoli and bore him a child. They died tragically in a shipwreck journeying back to the States. Friends such as Emerson tried desperately to save Margaret Fuller's reputation—ironically as she had sought to live for truth.

The first organized movement for women's rights thus came from the movement to abolish slavery. Both movements were inspired by the universalist case for equal human rights. Both included moral and Christian strands, legitimating radical action by Biblical quotations. True, the abstract principles of equality were not the daily lived reality of relations within these movements. Nonetheless, abolition and women's rights organizers broke down many conventional barriers to the public participation of black people and women. Both movements had an international impact.

The arguments and divisions continued within subsequent radical movements in the United States. Should moral principle or strategic expediency guide political action? Was race or gender the crucial issue? Were black people or women the agents of social transformation? Were individual human rights to be the basis of change or were there social and economic relationships that could not be solved by abstract equality? Should the emphasis be on changing external institutions or changing the individual?

Yet another division was already beginning to crystallize. Was the case to be made for women's emancipation on the basis of women being the same as men? Whether this was seen as the abstract appeal to a common humanity or as Sojourner Truth's experience of doing the same work and suffering the same hardships. Or should women's biological or cultural difference be presented as a force for change? There were several aspects to this; one was indicated by Maria Stewart—women's moral sense as mothers, whereas Margaret Fuller expressed first a transcendentalist idea of women as intuitive, and then, influenced by romanticism, asserted passion.

The romantic movement sought to bring reason and feeling, the desire for knowledge and the free expression of sensual love into harmony. Like the enlightenment, romanticism had ambivalent meanings for women. It was sometimes mined for arguments to keep women in the place men created for them. But it was also a means of seeking emancipation for women on terms rather different from individual equal rights.

6

CLASS AND COMMUNITY: WOMEN AND THE CHARTIST MOVEMENT

In 1838 the women of a small town Elland, in the North of England, held a meeting to protest against the New Poor Law. They decided to appeal as women to the young Queen Victoria. They told her of the cruelty of the new act, which refused the poor any relief in their own homes, herding them into grim workhouses where families were split up and a harsh discipline imposed on paupers. They called the workhouses, "Bastilles"[1] after the prison in France that had been besieged by the Parisian crowd in the revolution.

They justified their intervention in public matters, interestingly, not as individuals but "as part of the community."[2] They also argued as mothers with special family responsibilities, saying it affected women more to be separated from their children. The Poor Law Act also prevented women doing their duties as wives and "helpmates."[3]

The vote was seen as the key to abolishing the hated law and this brought many women into the Chartist movement. When the People's Charter was launched in 1838 it demanded universal manhood suffrage; but there were Chartists who believed in universal suffrage and others who argued for unmarried women at least to have the vote. However, like James Mill, many Chartists presumed men could be trusted to safeguard women's rights. There was also a practical difficulty. The inclusion of women from the propertied classes would have made the social and economic aims of the Chartist movement even more difficult. So some Chartist women and men decided that economic change took priority over universal suffrage.

However, this did not prevent Chartist women from taking an active part in the movement and having a strong sense of their rights as working class women.

In 1839, members of the Female Political Union of Newcastle-upon-Tyne, quoting Shelley, challenged the exclusion of women from the public sphere of politics.

> We have been told that the province of women is in the home, and that the field of politics should be left to men; this we deny, the nature of things renders it impossible.[4]

They added that the economic hardship of the working class meant that women could not avoid politics:

> For years we have struggled to maintain our homes in comfort, such as our hearts told us should greet our husbands after their fatiguing labours. Year after year has passed away, and even now our wishes have no prospect of being realised, our husbands are over wrought, our houses half-furnished, our families ill-fed and our children uneducated—the fear of want hangs over our heads, the scorn of the rich is pointed towards us, the brand of slavery is on our kindred, and we feel the degradation. We are a despised caste, our oppressors are not content with despising our feelings, but demand the control of our thoughts and wants.[5]

The source of their misery was thus the collective oppression of class, which made their womanly activities impossible. This was not simply economic but a denial of their humanity—and an appropriation of their thoughts and desires. They are aware that their struggle is part of a wider movement including the emancipation of the slaves,

> but we have learned by bitter experience that slavery is not confined to colour or clime.[5]

Government was in the hands of the upper and middle classes. The democratic extension of the franchise would enable working class men to remedy the injustices of class. The women's public political activity is not for their rights as individual women in relation to men, but as part of a class and a community who suffer collectively.

Chartist women, especially in the early years of the movement, demonstrated, held meetings, and went on strike. Besides this action in the public sphere, they also politicized the personal world of sexuality and domesticity. They declared they would love only Chartists. Thus the women of Ashton-under-Lyne announced in 1839,

> We are determined that no man shall ever enjoy our hands, our hearts, or share our beds, that will not stand forward as the advocate of the rights of man.[7]

Chartist women took pride in naming their children after Chartist leaders, like the militant Feargus O'Connor.

"What is the child to be called?"[8] the registrar of births asked Mrs. King of Manchester in March 1841. "James Feargus O'Connor King"[9] she replied to the horror of the registrar, who asked, "Is your husband a Chartist?" "I don't know but his wife is"[10] was her quick response.

From the mid-1840s there are less frequent references to women acting in large numbers in the Chartist press. It is not clear whether this was because the movement was becoming more formal and less spontaneous or whether it was part of a deeper social change in which a place for respectable working class women was being made that excluded them from public life. By the mid-nineteenth century women had a proportionally smaller part in the full-time workforce. They had been excluded from many trades and domestic service was their main source of employment. It was also becoming a mark of respectability not to go to public houses. Indeed Chartist women were often temperance supporters.

However, individual women speakers do emerge in the later years of Chartism and a year before their last great petition for manhood suffrage was presented by the Chartists in 1848, a middle class Quaker supporter of the movement, Anne Knight, had produced the first leaflet for women's votes. She had been at the World Anti-Slavery Convention in 1840 when women had demanded the right to speak to a mixed audience. She also had contact with the French socialist women

Even after the petition of 1848 was rejected, Chartists continued to organize. In 1851 a Women's Rights Association was formed in Sheffield, insisting that

> the voice of woman is not sufficiently heard, and not sufficiently respected, in this country.[11]

Interestingly, they echoed Fourier's argument that women's emancipation was a necessity for the whole society because "the test of enlightenment and civilization"[12] was "the estimation in which woman is held."[13]

Catherine Barmby, who had also been involved in the Owenite movement, put the early socialist concept of woman's mission as the bearer of alternative values of love and cooperation. Women's difference did not imply inequality, it was a crucial element in a new social order. She had argued in the early 1840s for women's societies and a women's journal.

By 1852, when the Chartist movement was in decline, the Secretary of the Sheffield Women's Rights Association, Abiah Higginbotham, wrote to the Chartist leader Ernest Jones, supporting his criticism of Chartists meeting in public houses. She thought that Chartist women could "erase"[14] the "stigma"[15] that "the folly of our brothers"[16] had cast on the cause, which should be taken away from the "pothouse."[17] Chartist women could exercise their moral influence both "out of doors"[18] and in the home by educating children in radical ideas. Change in the home was thus linked to the public sphere. This association petitioned the House of Lords for the inclusion of adult women in the suffrage.

Chartist women initially expressed their grievances as women within the working class. They complained not because they wanted a new way of being women but because they could not behave as they felt they should in relation to their families. They had a strong awareness of their rights, but as gendered members of a class.

However, there is a kind of contagion in democratic movements and some Chartist women came to argue that women were a vital force in the social movement. They should not just participate but moralize and improve public life. This meant that they too should have the power of the franchise.

7

WOMEN IN REVOLUTION: NINETEENTH-CENTURY FRANCE

In 1832 a journal appeared amid the revolutionary agitation that brought a constitutional monarchy. It was called *La Femme Libre* and was produced by a group of working women who were familiar with the ideas of the French Revolution and of Mary Wollstonecraft as well as those of socialists like Saint Simon and Fourier. It had the motto,

Liberty for Women, liberty for the people by a new organisation of household and industry.[1]

These connections were to be asserted again in the revolution of 1848 and the 1871 Paris Commune. The liberation of women was assumed to be linked to the people's cause. The new society was to transform both the conditions of production and the circumstances of daily life in the family and community.

Suzanne Voilquin, a seamstress influenced by Saint Simonian social-ists' idea of women as the agents of a new era of cooperation and love, worked on the journal. When she married her husband had syphilis; she left him and trained as a midwife to support herself independently. Desirée Veret, a milliner, also wrote for *La Femme Libre*. She went to London and mixed in Owenite circles where she met her husband Jules Gay. She returned to France in 1837 and wrote an article on association for Fourier's socialist journal in 1841. Jeanne Deroin, another self-edu-cated seamstress, was also associated with *La Femme Libre*.

All three continued to make connections between women's eman-cipation and socialism. Their vision of socialism was based on coopera-tive association and involved a struggle against the power of men in the family as well as both employers and male workers in production. They believed that women's liberation was inseparable from the eman-cipation of the working class.

Flora Tristan, an engraver, was influenced by Mary Wollstone-craft. She knew too of the work of Anna Wheeler and visited Britain meeting Owenites and Chartists. In the 1840's there was an ongoing debate about the means by which society would be transformed; ideas were being developed internationally. In 1843 Flora Tristan proposed an international working class organization, the Universal Union of Working Men and Women. She argued that class combination would be the key to changing the whole basis of society. Flora Tristan, like Marx, said the working class had to emancipate themselves.

The concept of emancipation had been adopted from the move-ments to abolish slavery. European socialists did not see this as a struggle by the slaves themselves as much as a movement of white people to emancipate others. The emancipation of the working class in contrast, then, was to be a movement of self-emancipation. Flora Tristan was concerned about the oppression of women, but she thought their freedom would follow from the working class ending the power of the capitalist system.

She died on a speaking tour, exhausted and isolated in 1844, just four years before a combination of workers and the radical middle class overthrew the corrupt monarchy of King Louis Philippe in the 1848 revolution. In 1848 adult male suffrage was introduced and slavery abolished in the French colonies. Once again the people were declared sovereign. Women were quick to point out that if the "people" were sovereign this should include women. Women could not rely on men to make laws in their interests.

The women's arguments were ignored, but again women formed clubs and produced journals in which they argued for women's emancipation and insisted that the process of revolutionary change had to include them. Among these journals was *La Voix des Femmes*. It included a middle-class woman Eugénie Niboyet and Suzanne Voilquin, Jeanne Deroin, and Desirée Gay. The journal was committed to self-emancipation, encouraging education, training, and women gaining confidence through participation in politics. It included extensive proposals for changing production and daily life.

Workers were pressing for "the right to work"; there was also opposition to the growth of subcontracting in the clothing industry, which cut rates by putting work out to home workers. The men persuaded the government to set up National Workshops. Women workers, led by Desirée Gay, agitated for workshops for women and then protested against the low pay, bad conditions, and lack of workers' democracy in these.

Women workers did not simply say homework should be banned. It was a vital means by which women with children could support themselves. Instead, they proposed that homework be paid the same rate as work in the workshops. They also demanded state child-care, laundries, and restaurants, along with training for women workers.

They began to form their own cooperative associations to secure employment, improve conditions, and enable them to run their workplaces democratically. These cooperative associations extended beyond the workplace. They provided housing and welfare services and they imagined communal housing with gardens and schools and health services for workers on a large scale. Suzanne Voilquin developed an idea through her Association of Midwives for a social fund to maintain and care for poor mothers-to-be.

Jeanne Deroin was 43 in 1848. Small, pale, and thin she hurtled herself into a round of meetings and organizations, leaving her children with a friend. Her thought was infused with the importance of self-emancipation, reflecting her own struggle to write and think. She believed that change in the relationships between men and women in the family was necessary; the man could not be a tyrant in the home while advocating working class emancipation and motherhood should be freely chosen. She also argued that women needed to be included in the sovereignty of the people and required a new cooperative system of production and distribution; thus change had to be personal, domestic, political, and economic.

Some male socialists like Pierre Joseph Proudhon were maintaining that women should not be part of the public sphere of politics and work but have a special personal place as mothers. Jeanne Deroin took issue with these ideas and contributed her own theory of the necessary agency of women, which involved dissolving existing boundaries between personal and public life. Women's experience as mothers was a vital contribution to the socialist project. Public politics were to be both entered and transformed. She believed that mothering carried values very different from those that prevailed among men. A new cultural synthesis was necessary for women and men. Citizenship and law could not be defined only in male terms.

She also tackled the financial and economic structure of society. Working class women who formed associations found it difficult to obtain credit and gain access to markets. Also their social needs made it hard for them to make profits. Jeanne Deroin envisaged financial institutions sympathetic to poor women's needs and developed an idea for a federation of associations. Richer workers could help the poor and there was to be training and advice on marketing. A commission would monitor which goods were in demand and set prices.

Though the workers were defeated in June 1848, associative schemes and journals persisted. The women were preoccupied with both the question of agency and the process of transition. What values and structures would enable people to move from a capitalist to a cooperative society?

In August 1848 Desirée Gay formed a new journal *La Politique des*

Femmes in which a distinct consciousness of working class women emerges more clearly than in *La Voix des Femmes*. Political defeat resulted in economic hardship and working women and the "socialists" reject the condescension of "the Lady" who seeks to justify the harsh treatment of the working class.

This little group anxiously debate an alternative solution. The idea that women's experience is valuable in developing a strategy appears in a more specific and concrete form. A character called "The Socialist Woman" asks for their help and opinions. But the working women ask, "What opinion? We know nothing.[12] The Socialist Woman refuses to accept this reply.

> ' " How come? You don't know how you feed your children, care for your husbands, how you work, think, observe and you don't have enough common sense to distinguish between right and wrong?"
> The women—"Oh yes, this we know."
> The Socialist Woman: "All right then, that is all that is needed. We shall find ways and means to look after our household and family collectively, so that we are able to form an association to build up shops and workshops. We shall be so persevering that they finally will have to respect our wishes and demands."[3]

Jeanne Deroin put herself forward as a candidate to the National Assembly in 1849 after pleading with the novelist George Sand and the socialist teacher Pauline Roland to step forward.

> It was because I had the conviction that it was necessary to strike at every closed door that I did it.[4]

However, reaction was closing in around them on all sides. Louis Napoleon took power in a coup and Jeanne Deroin's federation was deemed subversive. The men in the federation asked her not to say it had been her idea. They thought it would damage their cause if a known supporter of women's rights was the instigator.

From their prison cell Jeanne Deroin and Pauline Roland wrote in support of both the Sheffield women reformers and the American Women's Suffrage Convention in 1851, regretting the silence in the

French assembly on women's rights. Liberty, Equality, and Fraternity were not enough:

> only by the power of association based on solidarity—by the union of the working classes of both sexes to organise labour—can be acquired . . . the civil and political equality of women and the social right for all.[5]

Jeanne Deroin went into exile in Britain where she produced yet another journal *L'Almanach des Femmes*. When she died in 1894 William Morris, the socialist and artist, paid tribute to her. Suzanne Voilquin emigrated to a Fourierist community in Louisiana. Desirée Gay went first to Switzerland and then to Belgium. The ideas of the working class women thinkers were almost entirely forgotten as the causes they espoused fragmented.

Marx and Engels took up some of the ideas of the French labor movement in the Communist Manifesto. But the role of women as active agents and the problem of how to move from one culture to another fade in significance before the idea of the working class chained to capital in relentless struggle.

Fourier's idea of women as an index of the progress of freedom in society does appear in Marx's writing. When American feminists got the National Labour Union to vote for equal pay for equal work in 1868 Marx wrote off cheerily to a friend in the States.

> Great progress was evident in the last Congress of the National Labour Union in that among other things it treats working women with complete equality—while in this respect the English and the still more gallant French are burdened with a spirit of narrow-mindedness. Anybody knows, if he knows anything about history that great social changes are impossible without the feminine ferment. Social progress can be measured exactly by the social progress of the fair sex.[6]

The idea that there was an inherently progressive tendency in history influenced not only Marx but many nineteenth-century thinkers, liberals as well as socialists and advocates of the rights of women. Emancipation was thus presented both as an outcome of social development *and* as the conscious action of human beings.

In contrast to Proudhon's insistence that socialism would return women to the home, Marx took the view that paid work meant women would be drawn into the proletariat.

French women such as Jenny d'Héricourt and Juliette Lambert in the 1850s and 1860s opposed the French socialists who followed Proudhon but, at the First Congress of the Workers' International in 1866, the French labor movement was still saying woman's place was in the home. However, a woman bookbinder, Nathalie Lemel, in the First International, revived Jeanne Deroin's idea of a federation of associations. Women workers also set up cooperatives in service work, baking, and catering.

In 1869 an Association for the Rights of Women was formed demanding civil rights for women, access to secondary and higher education, the right to work, and equal pay. Among the signatories were André Léo and a rebellious school teacher, Louise Michel. André Léo had been exiled after Louis Napoleon's coup. She was the author of several novels about women's position in the family and conscious of the significance of culture and language in maintaining subordination. "Language is reactionary"[7] she exclaimed in 1869 because women were defined by male terms in political discourse. She believed women suffered a double oppression in the family and at work. She thought women's oppression would not be automatically solved by socialism. It was necessary to work for both causes.

André Léo and Louise Michel were both active in the Commune of 1871 when again barricades, clubs, and a popular literature emerged. Wall posters and newspapers called women to meetings and again to form cooperatives. Again the need for welfare and the reorganization of child-care was asserted by the women. A women's organization emerged. The "Union des Femmes" was linked to Marx's First International. But many women such as Louise Michel participated simply as individuals.

Some men like the bookbinder Eugéne Varlin supported the women and in Bordeaux Leo Frankel compared women's oppression to slavery. But even in the Commune, despite their heroic role, women encountered opposition. In 1871 André Léo reflected sadly that the whole history of revolutions in France had been to disregard women's demands and drive them toward reaction and the Catholic church. She insisted that revolution had to include the abolition of inequalities of race and sex.

After the defeat of the Commune Louise Michel was deported and imprisoned. André Léo and another socialist Paule Minck were exiled. The triumphant politician Adolphe Thiers announced that socialism was dead. He was wrong; but a period of reaction followed the defeat that was hostile to all egalitarian ideas.

However, in 1878 an International Women's Rights Congress was held in France. The link to revolution had gone. They demanded the right to work, equal pay, the abolition of state regulated prostitution, and the closing of brothels.

8

EQUALITY AND INDIVIDUALISM: HARRIET TAYLOR AND JOHN STUART MILL

Harriet Taylor wrote a series of articles in the Westminster Review in 1851 with the liberal philosopher John Stuart Mill on "*The Enfranchisement of Women*" in which they took a stand against claims for a special mission of women. They were challenging the position of some radicals, for example, Anne Knight, the abolitionist and Chartist who had argued, like Jeanne Deroin, that women's experience as mothers was necessary for political reform, along with less radical versions of woman's mission appearing in both religious circles and in literature. Sarah Lewis had published *Woman's Mission* in 1839 and women were at once elevated and confined in works such as Tennyson's *The Princess*.

Echoing Marion Reid's 1843 "*Plea for Women*," Harriet Taylor and John Stuart Mill rejected presenting women as "a sort of sentimental priesthood."[1] Harriet Taylor's writing was influenced by the women's rights meetings in the United States. American women were pointing the way by demanding education, equal participation in work, and an equal share in making and administering laws through local and national government. She argues that equality and democracy are the keys to emancipation for women. Harriet Taylor engages with both abolitionists and Chartists, acknowledging their contribution to democracy but pointing out the exclusion of half the human species.

Harriet Taylor, like Mill, was active in middle-class radical circles. They became close friends and companions and married when her husband died. His *The Subjection of Women* was published in 1869, though written a decade earlier, and Mill paid tribute to Harriet Taylor's influence on his ideas.

British society had changed from the early 1850s when the rebellions of the Chartists and the European revolutions of 1848 were still in the air. Mill accepted the existing structure of society as established, if needing a few modifications. He saw Victorian Britain as exemplifying rational advancement and at times invoked progress as somehow historically inevitable. Modern ways were assumed to be enlightened and women's subordination was an ancient survival that was to be swept away. Like Marx, Mill incorporated Fourier's idea of historical progress—society cannot develop fully without the emancipation of women. Both he and Harriet Taylor had been greatly influenced by utopian socialism.

Mill refuted claims that women were inherently inferior. In the tradition of the enlightenment he argued that external factors determined character.

What is now called the nature of women is an eminently artificial thing.[2]

Indeed he believed that this constructed femininity restricted not only women but men. Rational men would gain from the emancipation of women. He did, however, believe that women's natures differed in some ways from men but believed these differences would enrich the public sphere of politics.

Mill criticized both the laws that kept women subordinate and the political system that excluded them from the franchise. He took up the argument that William Thompson had had with his father James Mill, coming out on the side of Thompson. The rights of women could not be included in the rights of man. Mill spoke passionately against the domestic coercion and violence of men toward their wives as proof that men could not be trusted to be guardians of women's interests. However, Mill did not advocate universal suffrage but equal voting rights with men. This would have favored rich and middle-class women.

Though he argued women should be free to compete for public office and enter professions, he was less committed to women's right to work than Harriet Taylor. He assumes that married women would not work. So unlike Thompson and Owen he did not concern himself with how, if women were to be active in the public world, children were to be cared for. He also disregarded contemporary circumstances. Many working class mothers *had* to contribute to the family income. Mill put his case for emancipation in middle-class terms and even within those limits he was cautious about women's employment opportunities.

His caution may well have been tactical. Even as a young man his interest in utopian socialism and radical causes like birth control had been tempered by his assessment of the prospects of reform. He said in 1832 that when trying to "persuade the English" it was important to make a proposal that did not appear to be part of any system and of telling "them only of the next step they have to take."[4]

In *The Subjection of Women* Mill was very clear that the next step for middle-class women was entry into education, public office, and political rights. But this clarity had a price. It left many questions that had been discussed extensively by earlier radicals and socialists unanswered. Mill's approach concentrated on women's political rights. He did not explore how these might involve changes in the economic organization of society.

He was part of a radical middle-class network within the intelligentsia that included a group of women from religious, professional, and radical backgrounds who were campaigning for women's rights. In 1858 the *English Women's Journal* was launched by Bessie Rayner Parkes and Barbara Leigh Smith Bodichon. It advocated employment opportunities and training for women. It did take up the problems of women in the working class and also pointed out that many mothers had to seek employment.

In 1859 a Society for Promoting the Employment of Women was formed. The improvement of education was seen as a key issue. Schools and colleges were set up by Emily Davies, Miss Buss and Miss Beale, and Anne Jemina Clough. Elizabeth Garrett (later Anderson) followed the American Elizabeth Blackwell into medicine.

Though it appeared that women in this milieu were demanding equal access to the opportunities of the men of their class, there were complex strands within the egalitarian arguments for emancipation.

Anna Jameson had an important influence on Bessie Parkes and Barbara Leigh Smith. She argued the expansion of women's public sphere should be based on the "communion of labour," of complementary male and female responsibilities and a single moral standard.

Varying emphases on equality and difference led to arguments about whether middle-class women's education should be the same as men's or whether there should be special standards for women.

However, the main contention of this activist middle-class group and of Mill's politics was the claim for equal access. In 1865 Barbara Leigh Smith, Elizabeth Garrett, and Emily Davies started a Women's Suffrage Committee and launched a petition that Mill presented to parliament. Among the signatories were 25 Irishwomen including a Quaker Anna Haslam. In Ireland as well middle-class women were struggling for better education and the opening of professions.

In 1868 the National Society for Women's Suffrage was formed. The following year Elizabeth Garrett's young sister Milicent, recently married to the blind radical economist and liberal MP, Henry Fawcett, heard Mill moving the amendment to the 1867 Reform Bill, which was to extend the franchise to some male workers. Mill's amendment sought to omit the word man and substitute the word "person." It failed, but it asserted the universalist principle that human beings had the same claims to all rights.

Milicent Fawcett, who was to become a leader of the liberal wing of the suffrage movement, was profoundly moved by Mill's speech, which she described as "a masterpiece of close reasoning, tinged here and there by deep emotion."[6]

Mill's opponents often accused him of being a reasoning machine, which always upset him, although it is true that he probably underestimated the emotions that his reasoning for women's rights evoked. The approach he took to women's emancipation strongly asserted that reason was on the side of rights as if that settled the matter.

The passion in Mills' writing was in his commitment to the freedom of the individual. The romantic idea of self-realization and the individual woman's right to develop all her capacities influenced his liberalism. This concern about the individual explains some of his reservations about the democratic implications of women's rights. He was anxious that exceptional individuals be allowed to develop and was fearful that a democratic consensus would inhibit their freedom. So he wanted emancipation for exceptional women of the liberal intelligentsia; he was not really concerned about women in the working class. The idea that they might have understandings and needs that involved changing the political and economic system was outside his concept of equality. Though Harriet Taylor's enthusiasm for cooperative association modified his emphasis on individualism to some degree, Mill's project of emancipation related to middle-class women from educated backgrounds who were constrained by the parasitic idleness of gentility and wanted to play a more active role in society and politics.

In Britain the initial impact of his book was within the small group of the radical intelligentsia. However, it was to have a tremendous international influence. It went immediately to the United States, Australia, and New Zealand and was translated and published in France, Germany, Austria, Sweden, and Denmark. In 1870 it appeared in Polish and Italian and was being excitedly discussed by young Russian women studying abroad. By 1883 the Swedish translation had reached a group of Finnish women who studied the book in Helsinki. In Japan, Fukuzawa Yukichi opposed Confucian ideas about women's role in his book *The New Greater Learning for Women* in 1897. He argued for liberal reforms for women's emancipation on the lines of Mill's approach.

The rights of the individual were extended beyond Mill's arguments for women's emancipation in the Campaign against Contagious Diseases Acts, which began in 1869. The Acts had been passed to curb venereal diseases among the armed forces; they meant that women could be stopped on the streets and forcibly searched for venereal disease in hospitals. Josephine Butler, who came from a radical, anti-slavery family, led the Campaign. Suffrage supporters were divided on the issue and it was seen as rather scandalous that middle-class women were discussing sexuality and the body in public and encouraging prostitutes to resist.

Josephine Butler's campaign was supported by radical working class men because any working class woman could be stopped and forced to undergo the humiliation of an inspection. They saw it as a violation of working class rights.

Arguments about the inviolability of the person can be traced back to the seventeenth century; Josephine Butler adapted these radical ideas about individual rights to resist what campaigners saw as the invasion by the medical profession and the state of women's bodies. They argued that compulsory examination was a violation of women's rights over their persons. One campaigner described it as "espionage of enslaved wombs."[7]

The campaign had repercussions in Australia, Ireland, and later India, because the British tried to impose the Acts in the colonies. Josephine Butler formed an International Abolition Federation and supporters of women's rights in France, and Denmark debated and split over the issue of state regulated prostitution.

Individual rights over one's body had already appeared in the case among early nineteenth-century radicals for birth control and in Jeanne Deroin's insistence that motherhood should be voluntary. Voluntary motherhood could mean, in fact, either the right to celibacy or the use of contraception and was connected to a wider health movement. In the United States, there was interest in alternative medicine and by the 1870s sexual hygiene was being linked to woman's "right to her own body"[8] and "control of one's person."[9]

Still within the terms of the radical commitment to individual rights, free thinkers asserted the right of working class men and women to knowledge and kept alive some of the traditions of the Owenites and Chartists. A secularist, Harriet Law, was a popular speaker in Britain and the only woman on the General Council of the First International. She argued for women's emancipation and was joined on secularist platforms by Annie Besant, who campaigned for birth control and criticized marriage.

Women in the 1870s were thus pushing the individualism in Mill's arguments beyond the claim for equal entry into the men's world. They were saying realization of oneself is not just a matter of an independent franchise but involves a connection between one's body, sexuality and fertility, and conscious reason and control.

There was also a growing recognition among British and American liberals in the 1870s that the assumption that all individuals were free to maximize their opportunities was far from reality. The Campaign against the Contagious Diseases Acts made middle-class reformers aware of conditions among working class women. They felt morally driven to seek change. Involvement of women in the investigation of conditions through the Social Science Associations in Britain and the United States also emphasized the limits of free competition. It seemed to present an alternative of a rationally planned harmonious society.

Harriet Taylor had foreseen this need for intervention. "So long as competition is the general law of human nature, it is tyranny to shut out one half of the competitors."[10] Liberalism's commitment to individual freedom could then extend to the argument for state intervention to secure the competitive parity of otherwise unequal individuals. For this reason the cause of state education in Britain had liberal backing.

When the new system of state education was introduced liberal and radical women participated in the School Boards, which determined educational policy. Helen Taylor, Harriet's daughter, won a place on the London School Board in 1876, upsetting both the local Liberals and the Garrett feminist circle by developing a base in trade unions and radical working men's clubs as well as in the Irish community.

Involvement in local government was to be extremely important for women's entry into a wider political sphere. It included women of every political persuasion—socialists, radicals, and conservative. There were not only party political differences but various approaches to women's public role. Some women in local government felt they brought women's values into public institutions, such as the poor law and working class education. They argued that home economics for working class girls would enable them to be better wives and mothers.

Others who supported egalitarian policies applied their ideas to the working class. When Lydia Becker laid the foundationstone of a new school for the Manchester School Board she told the assembled worthies,

> She did not know why cooking was considered an exclusive subject for girls. If she had her own way every boy in Manchester would be taught to mend his own socks and cook his own chops.[11]

However, democracy could be at odds with the views of radical middle-class reformers. Helen Taylor decided to argue for cookery lessons for girls on the School Board not because she believed in a different education for girls, but because many working class parents approved of the subject as practical and useful.

II

CHANGING PERSONAL LIFE

THEMES FOR DISCUSSION

- ★ The meaning of the word "reproduction."
- ★ The idea of women owning their own bodies.
- ★ The meanings of sexual emancipation.
- ★ The best way to organize domestic life.
- ★ What kind of society would result from making the whole world homelike?

9

SENSUOUS SPIRITS: VICTORIA WOODHULL AND TENNESSEE CLAFLIN

In 1870 the New York Herald published the First Pronouncements of Victoria Woodhull.

> While others of my sex devoted themselves to a crusade against the laws that shackle the women of the country, I asserted my individual independence; while others prayed for the good time coming, I worked for it; while others argued the equality of women with men, I proved it successfully engaging in business.[1]

It was not exactly modest, but it was perfectly true; Victoria Woodhull had an uncanny ability to somehow personify as an individual, political and social causes.

She and her sister Tennessee Claflin came from a poor family of wandering clairvoyants and medical showmen. This was not the respectable educated establishment that had claimed the suffrage through the abolitionist movement. It was that other America, surviving by their wits and living in hope of a perfect world.

Victoria Claflin married at 15 and became a mother at 17. She left her drunken husband, supported the family as an actress, and met a spiritualist and advocate of free love, who was involved in a range of reforming causes, Colonel Blood. Again Victoria Woodhull had fallen for a man she had to support. Through Tennessee Claflin's friendship with Cornelius Vanderbilt who was old and bored and amused by the two sisters, Victoria and Tennessee turned into financiers. They started investing despite the suspicion of the banking world. The newspapers were fascinated and celebrated the "Bewitching Brokers."

Clairvoyance was in the family and in 1867 Victoria Woodhull joined the Spiritualist Association. The origins of spiritualism in the United States are not completely clear. One strand was the Shakers, a religious group that had been led by Mother Ann Lee. Other influences came from the American Indians who also practiced herbal medicine and it is possible that Afro-Americans brought spirit-possession beliefs.

Spiritualism also absorbed radical ideas of universal salvation. It gave those who failed to perfect their souls in this world a second chance. The millenarian faith in women's mission was there too. Spiritualists believed the emancipation of women would harmonize a world divided between the Father God and the Mother Nature. When the two principles were in union men would lose their compulsion toward aggression and women would find equality through love and reason.

The Spiritualist Association was an organization with thousands of members. They had had links to abolitionism, William Lloyd Garrison for example was a spiritualist. They also advocated marriage reform, free love, and women's rights. Some members believed in vegetarianism and homeopathic medicine and others in currency reform. Some were sympathetic to socialism.

Victoria Woodhull and Tennessee Claflin started their own journal, *Woodhull and Claflin's Weekly*. It discussed dress reform, communal living, free love, abortion, the suffrage and women's employment, serializing the French novelist George Sand and The Communist Manifesto.

Victoria Woodhull combined an irresistible attraction toward scandal with a cool intelligence. In 1870 she went to the Women's Suffrage Convention in Washington and argued that the Fourteenth and Fifteenth Amendments, which had enfranchised black American men, gave women the right to vote by stating that everyone born or naturalized in the United States was a citizen with citizens' rights. She called on women to take direct action and simply vote at the polls. She thus linked constitutional rights to direct action—an important connection in American radicalism.

A young student at Howard University's Law School, Mary Ann Shadd Cary, heard Woodhull's speech and decided to act on it. She wrote a statement to the Judiciary Committee of the House of Representatives, pointing out that as a taxpayer she had the same obligations as black men. Also the Fourteenth and Fifteenth Amendments said that all blacks were citizens with the right to vote. While demanding that "male" be taken out of the Constitution, she based her claim on citizenship. In 1871 she successfully registered to vote, one of the earliest women to test Woodhull's case.

Some American suffrage campaigners were embarrassed by the flamboyance of Woodhull and Claflin as protagonists of women's rights. They also were wary of them as two socially dubious adventurers. But Elizabeth Cady Stanton became their staunch supporter giving them a shield of approval.

We have had women enough sacrificed to this sentimental, hypocritical prating about purity.[2]

Thus declared radical and respectable, Victoria and Tennessee joined Section Twelve of the New York branch of Marx's First International. In contrast to the Spiritualists, the First International in the United States was a tiny organization. However, this did not prevent it from portentous theoretical disputes.

In 1870 a struggle was going on about whether the eclectic, individualistic traditions of American radicalism, currency reform, women's rights, and personal liberation were to define the politics of the International. A marxist of German origin, a veteran figure in the 1848 revolution, Friedrich Albert Sorge was trying to preserve his European based socialism against the Americans. Influenced by secularism and a materialist, spirits were anathema to him. As for free love and women's rights, he wanted to recruit Irish working class Catholics to the International. Woodhull and Claflin's influence in Section Twelve exasperated him.

Victoria meanwhile had presented herself as a candidate for the presidency of the United States. She persisted in making speeches on free love. She and Tennessee marched at the head of a group of fifty thousand protesting the execution of the defeated French Communards, holding a banner "Complete Political and Social Equality for Both Sexes."

Friedrich Albert renewed his efforts. "Universal suffrage cannot free us from slavery,"[3] he declared, and concluded that women's role was as auxiliaries to the proletariat—no doubt hoping this would contain the two heterodox women leaders of Section Twelve.

The task of the workers is to draw women into the social struggle for the liberation of the workers and therewith mankind.[4]

This was emphatically rejected by the American radicals who supported Woodhull in Section Twelve. They produced their own First International manifesto declaring its goal to be the political and social freedom of both sexes.

The argument between the two factions hinged on what came first.

The extension of equal rights of citizenship to women must precede any change in the relations between capital and labour,[5]

maintained Woodhull's ally William West.

It was a curious replay of the argument about strategic priority and agency that had taken place in the abolitionist movement. But this time class rather than race was presented in opposition to gender. Suspicion of immigrant men also resurfaced, and Woodhull's supporters demanded the expulsion of "aliens" from the First International.

The New York branch was completely split. Sorge complained furiously to Marx. The Conference of the International voted against "the women first" tendency and Woodhull was expelled. Undaunted, she called on Communists around the world to replace Karl Marx with Victoria Woodhull. She gained some sympathy from workers who wanted a more federal structure and opposed Marx's centralized control.

Marx was convinced that class conflict was the key to change and women's rights were a secondary issue. However, he thought the Germans were too sectarian and isolated within their own immigrant culture. He also disagreed with the German Marxists' dismissal of education as a force for change.

In complete contrast, the American faction stressed education and changing consciousness. Class was merely an element in a wider movement for universal justice. They did not accept the idea of a necessary conflict between capital and labor and the German Marxists' materialism and insistence on working class emancipation was incomprehensible to them.

The German Marxists for their part stressed those aspects of Marx's thought that saw consciousness as arising directly from material life. Marx himself avoided a simple materialism in which consciousness was an automatic reflex that could be reduced to determinate components. Although giving great weight to material circumstances, he also stressed the capacity of human beings to make their own creative intervention for change and he recognized that ideas and culture interacted with material existence.

This dispute, which originated among a handful of people, had much wider implications. It contributed to a sharp polarization over agency and a deterministic materialism shaping Marxist socialism. The brief connection between millenarian radicalism's emphasis on self-emancipation and the Marxist commitment to social transformation of the state and ownership of capital was severed.

Victoria Woodhull was more successful with the Spiritualists who elected her as President of their Association. She also had the backing of a group of reformers in her claim to the Presidency of the United States.

However, she was drawn irresistibly not only toward factionalism and fame but more fatally toward scandal. She decided to reveal in the *Weekly* that the respected preacher Henry Ward Beecher (brother of Catherine Beecher who could not abide Victoria) was having an affair with the wife of Theodore Tilton, an abolitionist and supporter of women's suffrage.

The religious reforming intelligentsia and supporters of women's rights were thrown into confusion. The Beecher sisters were divided. Theodore was completely dazzled by Victoria; even Henry Ward proved susceptible. The *Weekly* claimed it was exposing hypocrisy from a high-minded position.

However, in 1865 and 1872 laws had been passed that made it illegal to send anything through the mail that could be described as obscene. A young, dry goods salesman Anthony Comstock decided that *Woodhull and Claflin's Weekly* was indeed obscene and obtained a warrant. Under this law Woodhull and Claflin were arrested and this turned into a civil rights case.

Eventually the jury found them not guilty. Elizabeth Cady Stanton declared triumphantly that they had struck a blow at priesthood. But the trial had dragged on and Victoria was becoming weary of personi-fying causes. She lacked Cady Stanton's extraordinary stamina. Also she was not, like her, secured by a respectable marriage and as she grew older she became tired of keeping Colonel Blood.

She began to argue that women's redemption was to come through purity and in the 1880s she married a British banker and went off to live a relatively sedate life in an English village with him.

It seemed like a complete reversal from the woman who, in 1871, had horrified German working class Marxists and Catherine Beecher alike by announcing,

> I have an inalienable constitutional and natural right to love whom I may, to love as long, or as short a period as I can, to change that love every day I please.[6]

But it was not such a total turn about as it appeared. The claim to free love had been made in the context of an ascendent progress toward perfectibility in love. Victoria Woodhull was heading toward a transcendent zone.

> Promiscuity in sexuality is simply the anarchical stage of development wherein the passions rule supreme. When spirituality comes in and rescues the real men and women from the domain of the purely material, promiscuity is simply impossible.[7]

This was yet another version of the argument that progress was inherent in history and was to culminate in relations of harmony and a perfected humanity.

The free lovers of the 1870s retained the conviction that progress and history were on their side and in the tradition of the enlightenment had faith that reason could liberate sex. But for them it was not a matter just of changing external institutions such as marriage. They were materialists in their conviction that the body and control over reproduction could be perfected. Whole grain diets, therapeutic baths, alternative health, and closer links with nature were part of boundless transformation. But unlike radical materialists such as Owen's son Robert Dale Owen and the secularists, the free lovers envisaged human relations changing sexual experience rather than contraceptive technology being the means to greater control.

Like other strands in American radicalism there were both individualistic and communalistic polarities among free lovers. For 30 years John Humphrey Noyes maintained an authoritarian form of communalistic free love in the Oneida community. He was opposed to permanent coupling and believed in eugenic breeding. He developed a form of birth control by having the men learn to constrict the seminal ducts during intercourse thereby preventing ejaculation. This took time to perfect so the older men slept with younger women and the young men who still ejaculated had intercourse with women who were past childbearing age. Noyes called his system "male continence" and believed it made a higher form of sexual love, based on the interchange of magnetic or electric influences between men and women possible.

Noyes' ideas of changing sexual relations were adapted by sexual reformers in the late nineteenth and early twentieth century and connected with interest in erotic writing from the East. There was an unease developing about the mechanical materialism that had had such an influence during the nineteenth century.

But the free lovers also drew on enlightenment ideas about nature and on the radical tradition of individual self-ownership. Tennessee Claflin thought contraception was disgusting and unnatural. Control over reproduction was interpreted in terms of voluntary motherhood. Love could not be free unless women could say no. Self-ownership and free love consequently denied male marital rights. Because no person could be the property of another, radical advocates of women's rights argued that unwanted advances by the husband were rape. There was thus convergence between some free love arguments and women's rights.

Elizabeth Cady Stanton held separate women-only meetings to talk about "the gospel of fewer children and a healthy, happy maternity"[8] in the early 1870s. This was all the more impressive coming from a ceaseless agitator and mother of seven in a time when childbirth was hazardous. Even the more conservative feminists in the Association for the Advancement of Women believed in 1873 in "Enlightened Motherhood." One aspect of enlightenment was voluntary motherhood. Control over one's body and fertility could mean the possibility of a more erotic sensuality or the transcendence of physical desire altogether.

In the early twentieth century these two definitions were to part company, not only in the United States but in many other countries. One wing of the feminist movement was to argue that women were more pure and less driven by sensual lust. Women's mission was therefore to redeem man to a deeper spirituality. In rebellion against the role of pure redeemer, young feminist rebels reasserted the ideas of the radical birth controllers, advocating contraception as a means of control over reproduction, which could enable women to enjoy sex without fear.

Social purity feminism was to assert women's moral leadership because it assumed that women already possessed alternative values that were superior to men's. The social improvements that women would bring were simply counterposed to what existed. The case for womanly values was not linked to a wider process of social transformation in which women were active agents in changing both themselves and society.

Victoria Woodhull's spiritualism, however, still retained some connection between self-emancipation and women as the agents of new relations between human beings—albeit on a spiritual plane. A synthesis of opposites was to create a new mystical unity. Addressing a spiritualist meeting at Vineland, north of New York, on the "*Scarecrows of Sexual Freedom*" in 1872 she said,

In a perfected sexuality shall continuous life be found then shall they, who in ages past, cast off their mortal coils be able to come again and resume them at will; and thus also shall a spiritualized humanity be able to throw off and take on its material clothing, and the two worlds shall be once more and forever united. Such to me, my brothers and sisters, is the sublime mission of Spiritualism, to be outwrought through the sexual emancipation of women, and her return to self-ownership, and to individualized existence.[9]

It was a cheery message; the spirits were to become flesh and the living and the dead would find one another. The boundary between matter and spirit dissolved, women's sexual emancipation bringing both perfected social relations and an autonomous individuality. Sensuous existence thus reached its fullest expression in transcending the material. It suggested unrevealed potential in human capacity rather than the achievement of external goals.

Victoria Woodhull's vision belonged not to any philosophical system or theory of politics but echoed Christian heresies of the middle ages and the extreme radicals of the seventeenth-century church. It was a heterodox, spiritual, radicalism that presented a relevant metaphor to an era that was beginning to express angst about materialism and yet was incapable of breaking from it.

Interestingly Woodhull, the individualist par excellence, like Cady

Stanton and Mill, also hankered after communalism. Individuality could be realized through new forms of association. In 1873 the *Weekly* announced the establishment of a women's community outside Boston. Aurora Village was to have a cooperative laundry and a domestic school for instruction in homemaking.

10

TRANSFORMING DOMESTIC LIFE: COOPERATIVES AND THE STATE

Both a political emphasis on women's equal access to the public sphere and a vision of spiritual transcendence disregarded a most pressing material dilemma. If women were to play a large part in society and also develop their potential as individuals in the fullest sense how was housework to be done and children cared for?

Rich women of course could evade the problem to a large degree by employing servants. However, many women who tried to change their lives and society did not accept this as a solution. They believed it was necessary to change how domestic work was organized and develop new ways of bringing up children. The problem was how?

The ideas of the early socialists in France and Britain about communal living and cooperatives influenced the women's rights movement in the United States. In her speech in 1848 at Seneca Falls, Elizabeth Cady Stanton criticized the isolated household and argued that cooperative living on the lines of Fourier's communities was the answer. Many utopian communities were formed in the United States. However, they were often somewhat factious and inclined to collapse. Also not everyone wanted to live in a community.

Women who could not afford servants and had never heard of either women's rights or Fourier's communities developed their own informal networks to help each other with housework and child-care. They also met for social and practical reasons in isolated communities in the countryside. One very creative activity was the "quilting bees." Quilts were not only warm, they were works of creative craft skills.

There were also cooperatives providing services needed in the home. Although by the 1860s the utopian impulse to transform the household and production was receding in Europe, it was revived in the United States, where the trade union movement was interested in cooperatives, both in production and in services.

In the late 1860s Melusina Fay Peirce, a descendant of the seventeenth-century rebel Anne Hutchinson, decided the time had come to apply cooperation to housework. After the Civil War land prices were high and apartment houses were being built. These grouped people together for practical, economic reasons. Why not take this a step further and establish cooperative housekeeping?

Melusina Fay Pierce worked out that women could earn their own living and learn how to organize themselves through cooperative housekeeping. Their husbands would pay them and cooperation would improve the efficiency of domestic life.

She was interested in how technology could be applied to cooperative housework and change the conditions of work. She saw domestic transformation also as having implications for architecture, design, planning, and the use of the environment.

Indeed she believed these changes within the household and community were the most important for women. Rather than campaigning for the vote she advised women to set up their own communities to deal with education, health, and welfare. Direct action in the community would have more impact than political rights.

Melusina Fay Peirce's ideas aroused considerable interest in the United States. They also were discussed in Britain by cooperators, though they were inclined toward shops rather than production by this time. From the 1840s the Christian Socialist movement had encouraged workers to set up cooperatives at work and had criticized competition and individualism. They were wary about women's political rights but interested in improvements in the community and in cooperative housekeeping. Melusina Fey Peirce also had an impact in architectural circles. E. W. Godwin, a well-known British architect, produced elaborate plans for a cooperative home in *The Building News* in 1874.

Theories are all very well. The real challenge is how to put them into practice. The snag in Peirce's scheme was the husbands, who proved very reluctant to pay their wives or other women to look after them and their children. Cooperative housekeeping floundered for lack of finance and Peirce's conviction that the way forward for women was to reform housekeeping, thus strengthening women's values, and purify society, remained untested.

Another advocate for domestic change, Marie Stevens Howland, viewed these ideas of women's moral mission with derision—the conceptions of hypocrites and prudes. She was not a dependent middle-class housewife, but knew what it meant to earn a living. As a young woman she had worked in the Lowell textile mills in Massachusetts. Like many of the early women factory workers in the United States, she combined a contempt for the snobbish attitudes of many middle-class women toward working women with a determination to better herself through education.

On arriving in New York, she met the radicals, anarchists, and free lovers who were to influence Victoria Woodhall. She became convinced that not only should housekeeping be cooperative but that children should be brought up communally. In American cities, employed working-class mothers had to take their children with them to work, tie them to the bed or leave them alone, or let them roam the streets. She understood why the women had to work and was aware of the consequences for children.

In the early 1860s she visited a Fourierist community in Guise, France. She returned, inspired not only by the centrally heated apartments and design of interior courtyards but by the educational methods in the nurseries and kindergartens. The approach was that learning should be fun. She noted a circular structure fitted with toys and games that helped children to learn to walk. Instead of being kept under strict control children were encouraged to develop a wide range of their faculties through play.

The transformation of domestic life was partly material—creating a new living environment. It also involved the development of alternative relations and culture.

When Marie Stevens Howland came back to the States she continued to write and speak about cooperative living and communities. But she wanted to show that her ideas could work. With the help of a sympathetic engineer she prepared elaborate plans for a colony, Topolobampo. She laid out different kinds of housing—apartments, cottages, and houses—and there was to be cooperative housekeeping along with cooperative stores and factories.

Topolobampo was in reality never to be as grandiose as the plans; nor was it really a success, though her ideas about cooperative housekeeping were taken up by more conservative women in the temperance movement, women's clubs, and the campaign for women suffrage, as a form of self-help for women.

In 1871 Victoria Woodhall published an article in her *Weekly* that had been written by Steven Pearl Andrews in 1855, "*The Baby World.*"

> There is wealth enough now to house the whole people in palaces if they rightly knew the use of it. The big houses are going to be built. The Baby World is going to exist. The Grand Domestic Revolution is going to take place.[1]

It never did of course. Though Karl Marx had lived in a commune when he and Jenny first married, he spent his life trying to maintain a conventional middle-class household and was preoccupied with the conflict between workers and capital rather than the "Baby World" and central heating.

However, other strands in the socialist movement did get excited about the domestic revolution. Marie Stevens Howland's vision of transforming the lived environment may not have succeeded in her colony, but it served as a bridge between early nineteenth-century community building and attempts to change existing urban life. She had an influence on Ebenezer Howard and Raymond Unwin in Britain who designed a Garden City at Letchworth. Unwin was an ethical socialist close to the Fabians who believed in gradual reform. The workers' movement in Europe took up the idea of cooperative housing. This began to get local and state funding in the twentieth century.

The reorganization of housework was a theme in a famous utopian novel by Edward Bellamy *Looking Backward* in 1888.

' "Who does your housework, then?" ' asks the hero Julian West who wakes up in a socialist Boston in the year 2000.

"There is none to do," said Mrs. Leek, to whom he had addressed this question.'[2]

The trick was that the state provided families and individuals with food, housing, and even help with spring cleaning. Every aspect of life was organized. Bellamy believed in efficiency and social security but had little sympathy for democracy and freedom. His ideas were extremely attractive to middle-class men and women in professions, concerned about the sprawling chaos of the new urban America and profoundly uneasy about the immigrant working class.

William Morris was horrified by Bellamy's state socialism and wrote "*News from Nowhere*" in protest. But the idea that the state should provide services to households and welfare in the community began to replace the earlier conviction that voluntary association should be the means of socializing domestic activity. Bellamy had a considerable influence in America. After the failure of her marriage in the early 1890s Charlotte Perkins Gilman began her public career in one of the clubs that developed from the publication of Bellamy's book. She was mainly interested in the position of women and the need for more scientific care for young children. She rejected the socialism of both Marx and Morris with its stress on class struggle and inclined to the evolutionary gradualism of the Fabians, Beatrice and Sidney Webb.

She had spent part of her childhood in a community and disliked it very much. She thought the answer to domestic labor was apartment houses providing services—cooking, cleaning, child-care—to enable the women residents to combine their professions with motherhood. She was keen that these should be on a business basis and was interested in how technology could be applied in domestic work.

In Charlotte Perkins Gilman's scheme for socializing domestic life there are obvious class differences. The working class women are doing the domestic services for professional women on a collective rather than an individual basis as servants. She was quite able to accommodate to a system in which some people had the chance for self-expression at other's expense, believing that some races, for example, had not evolved sufficiently for democracy.

Encouraged by Beatrice and Sidney Webb, she published *Women and Economics* in 1898, believing that economic independence was more important for women than the vote and that it was unjust that men could combine home life, love, companionship, and fatherhood with active citizenship, while women had to choose to live alone or give up any public role with motherhood. Her argument was that women were holding back evolution because of their confinement in the household and absorption in mothering. *Women and Economics* pioneered a critique of conventional, male-dominated, economics for ignoring the contribution of women to wealth through domestic labor.

Her amusing utopian novel, *Herland,* published in 1915, about an all-woman community built around maternity and maternal values, explored the question that had troubled Jeanne Deroin. How could society evolve from male-dominated capitalism into a socialism that would emancipate women? Her utopia suggests that if mothering and the values associated with caring for children were to expand into a larger sphere in society, they might provide a basis for a transition from the present to the future.

Curiously she rejected Marx's ideas on the grounds that his thinking was deterministic for her writing emphasizes not the importance of women developing their confidence through organizing, which is part of Melusina Fay Peirce and Marie Stevens Howland's domestic transformation, but a deterministic evolution to state socialism in which the home is made efficient and scientifically managed.

Some socialist strategies for changing domestic labor were to be on these lines. When state welfare was introduced early in the twentieth century in Vienna by Social Democrats, working class women were terrified of the supervisor of the public laundry who timed them as they did their washing. The authoritarian aspects of state welfare assumed that working class people were ignorant and had to be reformed despite themselves.

A more democratic cooperative approach to welfare emerged in a movement of women started by a middle-class liberal in Britain in 1883. Alice Acland helped to found a "Women's League for the Spread of Co-operation." This became the Women's Co-operative Guild, which in the twentieth century gained thousands of members. They campaigned for healthy food, women's health, cooperative laundries and wash houses, as well as stores. They imagined community cinemas, investigated maternity conditions, and campaigned for birth control and abortion.

The Women's Co-operative Guild stressed mutual development, self-emancipation, and participation in local democracy. But they also tried to shift public resources in various ways toward the needs of working class women. They emphasized the conditions of housewives because many married working class women did not have paid work. But they also argued for equal pay in cooperative enterprises and demanded the vote.

From the late 1880s middle-class women who investigated working class living and working conditions were horrified by the circumstances of family life. In both the United States and Europe eugenic ideas about breeding were influential—there was a panic that the white Anglo-Saxons were being overtaken by other races and that working mothers created feeble "stock." Moreover, because the environment of working class women in factories and workshops was appalling, some feminists and reformers argued that it would be better for married women to stay at home and look after their children. Instead of trying to change the conditions of housework it was claimed that it would be better to pay women enough money to support themselves and their children. This money payment was to come from the state and was initially called "Mothers' Pensions." In a modified form these were to be pioneered in Australia in the 1920s.

After World War II many European countries did introduce a child benefit, though it was not enough to make women independent of men. Instead it supplemented the family income and was paid for from taxes.

The "domestic revolution" remains incomplete though schemes that seemed utopian have been partially adopted.

11

MORAL UPLIFT, SOCIAL PURITY, AND TEMPERANCE

The Irish feminist Anna Haslam reflected in 1914 that the fight for repeal of the Contagious Diseases Acts in Ireland,

> threw the suffrage movement back for years, we were all so absorbed in it.[1]

On the other hand, in the long run, the campaign, started by Josephine Butler, certainly mobilized many women and provided an impetus for suffrage demands. The problem was that differing assumptions and approaches to women's emancipation were becoming evident around issues of social purity and women's difference, which created conflicts and arguments internationally. For instance, the Danish Women's Association in the mid-1880s was deeply divided over state-regulated prostitution and whether women should enjoy the same sexual freedom as men. The International Abolitionist Federation argued that women should introduce a higher moral standard rather than seek equality with men. They wanted prostitution abolished.

Social purity campaigners sought to protect women and children from male sexual desire. They also tried to tackle domestic violence and sexual coercion. Their cause of moral reform came to be based on rather different principles from Mill's arguments for equal rights. Josephine Butler's approach had been based on the freedom of the individual. There was a certain common ground possible at first because her campaign was inspired by liberal arguments about individual autonomy. But social purity also involved state intervention. After the Contagious Diseases Acts were repealed, in Britain, campaigners went on to expose child prostitution and white slavery, securing the passage of the Criminal Law Amendment Act in 1885, which raised the age of consent for girls to 16.

A shift from merely safeguarding individual rights was evident. Sometimes this meant a defence of the state as a moral entity above the freedom of individual, for the Act also gave the police powers to close houses where couples lodged who were not married. It thus increased the extent to which the state could intervene in the personal life of working class women. Unrepentant prostitutes and incorrigibly sexy girls also gave the social purity reformers problems. They advocated an all-embracing version of women's moral superiority. What were they to do about "fallen" women who resisted rescue? They could see them as victims or decide that the fallen had to be forced to be good.

The National Vigilance Association succeeded Josephine Butler's Campaign and the people it persecuted were often working class women. Josephine Butler opposed this. She did not believe in the compulsory implementation of virtue.

Temperance was another important moral movement among women in many countries in the late nineteenth and early twentieth centuries. In the mid-1870s a spontaneous temperance campaign sprang up among women in the western towns of the United States. Frances Willard was drawn into the Women's Christian Temperance Union (WCTU) and became its president in 1879. In 1883 she succeeded in winning support from the WCTU for women's suffrage and set about remaking the suffrage movement's image, which, because of Victoria Woodhull, had acquired a scandalous reputation.

Curiously though, some of her arguments for temperance echo Woodhull's preoccupations. She wrote in 1883,

> The WCTU stands as the exponent, not alone of that return to physical sanity which will follow the downfall of the drink habit but of the reign of a religion of the body when for the first time in history shall correlate with Christ's wholesome, practical yet blessedly spiritual religion of the soul.[2]

Also, while the WCTU was moral and respectable, it was capable of militantly, unladylike behavior. It took direct action against drink; temperance supporters assembled outside saloons with pictures of suffering women and children, picketing entrances. They were sometimes involved in scuffles with the men they tried to prevent from entering and the women were taken off by the police. Occasionally the women even entered the saloons and broke glasses and bottles with axes or hatchets.

Frances Willard brought the Protestant missionary fervor of rural America to women's rights. She also was very impressed by Bellamy's state socialist ideas.

In Australia, the Women's Christian Temperance Union was formed, first in Victoria, and then spreading to other states. It joined with suffrage societies under the leadership of the United Council of Women's Suffrage to launch a petition in 1891 for the vote.

The temperance and suffrage organizations in Australia were not linked but they worked closely together on many issues. The movement for temperance was concerned with a personal, moral reform, but opposition to drink was also seen as connected to social reforms and to political power; temperance thus formed a bridge between women's domestic activity and the public sphere.

In Canada, the Women's Christian Temperance Union argued

that prohibition would save society from domestic violence, family breakdown, crime, and political corruption. At first it concentrated on recruiting members and getting people to sign temperance pledges and petitions; by the 1890s it sought to influence local government, but members found it difficult as women to speak before all-male town councils. Their failure to influence local politicians convinced many of the women that if they had the vote they would be more successful.

In Japan in the 1880s women were not allowed to attend political meetings. However, the Women's Christian Temperance Union was established in 1886 and was a permitted form of activity. The moral sphere thus gave women a limited leeway.

Instead of seeing women's domestic experience as limiting, Frances Willard asserted the positive values of the home. She linked this version to women's contribution to reforming society as a whole.

> Were I to define in a sentence, the thought and purpose of the Women's Christian Temperance Union, I would reply: *It is to make the whole world HOMELIKE.*[3]

Willard maintained that women

> will come into government and purify it, into politics and cleanse [it] . . . for woman will make home-like every place she enters, and she will enter every place in this round earth.[4]

This version of women's role as redeemers had a powerful appeal to small town and rural women in the United States, who viewed the economic and social problems of the cities with horror. It was also influential in Australia and Canada. The Canadian socialist Nellie Letitia Mooney McClung argued for prohibition, changes in the laws affecting women and children, protective factory legislation for women, compulsory education, and prison reform.

In the early 1900s she said,

> Women have cleaned up things since time began; and if women ever get into politics there will be a cleaning-out of pigeon-holes and forgotten

corners, on which the dust of years has fallen, and the sound of the political carpet-beater will be heard in the land.[5]

Making the world home-like could involve women demanding political power, arguing for social reform and even socialism.

However, it had an appeal that could be also defensive and conservative. The homelike values were sometimes asserted against an amorphous danger that lurked in the big Northern cities among immigrants and aliens, or among black people in the south. In the United States in the 1890s white people were not only using economic force to make black southerners accept segregation. In 1892 Ida B. Wells, a black journalist, revealed how lynching was being used as a means of intimidation. She courageously investigated the charges of rape, which had been brought to justify lynchings, and showed them to be false.

She criticized Frances Willard on a speaking tour in Britain, quoting an interview Willard had given to the *New York Voice*, a temperance paper. Willard had described "great dark-faced mobs"[6] multiplying like "locusts"[7] and habitually in the "grog-shop"[8] in the southern states. Echoing the fears of the upper class white southerners who had entertained her, and who were also members of the Women's Christian Temperance Union, Willard declared the safety of women, children, and the home was "menaced."[9] Lady Somerset, the temperance leader in Britain, was furious and tried to stop Ida B. Wells from speaking, but Wells gained influential support in Britain.

Strengthening home life was nonetheless extremely important to black women reformers who, exasperated with discrimination in the working class and in the temperance and suffrage organizations, formed the National Association of Colored Women in 1896 in the United States. It was headed by one of the earliest graduates of Oberlin College, Mary Church Terrell. However, the home had a rather different meaning because slavery had wrenched families apart and black women were sexually stereotyped by whites.

Mary Church Terrell said,

We believe we can build the foundation of the next generation upon such a rock of morality, intelligence and strength that the floods of proscription, prejudice and persecution may descend upon it in torrents and yet it will not be moved.[10]

The consolidation of the home thus was to be part of the struggle to overcome race oppression and reform society. The motto of the National Association of Colored Women was "Lifting as We Climb." The educated women shared some of the experiences of poor black women and worked to set up kindergartens, nurseries, schools and colleges, and homes for the aged and inform. They taught domestic science and black history. Their aim was education for both survival and aspiration. A comparable movement emerged in Jamaica. Mrs. James McKenzie was secretary of the Kingston Branch of the Pan African Association in 1902 and an activist for women's rights.

The white suffrage movement in the United States in the 1870s did not argue in terms of universal natural rights but shifted to arguments of expediency. The conservative leader Carrie Chapman Catt said that women's suffrage would be a bulwark against the votes of men in the slums and ignorant foreigners. The vote should be limited to those who were educationally qualified.

Even Elizabeth Cady Stanton decided that it would be dangerous to enfranchise illiterate women in 1895. Her daughters, Harriet Stanton Blatch and Susan B. Anthony disagreed, but Stanton's arguments won the support of the National American Woman Suffrage Association.

One of the problems of arguing that political representation should be based on virtue was who decided the criteria? In 1893 Fanny Harper had asked why white women thought people who had blood on their hands from lynching were fit to govern. Another dilemma that was to trouble liberal reformers was how to balance the freedom of the individual with the imposition of improvement by the state. The old argument about strategic priority also resurfaced in a new context. Both Stanton and Anthony saw women's suffrage as a panacea from which other reforms would follow. Compromises were thus tactically necessary. They had after all been campaigning for half a century. But what about poor and working class women, black and white. Could they justifiably feel secure that privileged white middle-class women could be trusted with their needs?

III

POLITICAL MOVEMENTS AND SOCIAL ACTION

THEMES FOR DISCUSSION

★ The difference between ideas for women's emancipation based on the individual and those based on a collectivist viewpoint of the nation, society, class, or race.

★ The significance of the state for women's movements.

★ The impact of wider movements for social change on women's position.

★ How class and race differences might affect the aims of women's emancipation.

★ Birth control and workers control: the strengths and snags in this dual vision of emancipation.

12

NATIONALIST MOVEMENTS AND WOMEN'S PLACE

Daniel O'Connell, the Irish nationalist leader, was persuaded by American women supporters of abolition that women should be admitted to the World Anti-Slavery Convention in London in 1840. O'Connell was also an admirer of the work of Mary Wollstonecraft and William Thompson and was impressed by the women's rights meeting at Seneca Falls. His vision of Irish nationalism was socially and politically moderate and he was certainly not an ardent supporter of women's suffrage. But he was sympathetic to movements of reform, even though the mass appeal of his ideas was dependent on the Catholic church.

Nineteenth-century nationalist and anticolonial movements retained some of the reforming ideas of the enlightenment and the French Revolution. In some cases they advocated the sovereignty of the people and argued for progress and modernization. Nationalist men were sometimes prepared to embrace the emancipation of women within this modernizing project.

However, there were diverse strands within nationalism, which also contained an organic, antimodernist approach to culture. Some nationalists were suspicious of western radicalism and liberalism, including the emancipation of women. For example, Nikolai Strakhov, a Russian conservative nationalist, grumbled about the impact of John Stuart Mill in the early 1890s. In his view the Westernized intelligentsia were merely chasing another imported fad. Revivalism and reform were both features of the nationalist project.

Whereas certain forms of nationalism were open to international influences, others sought to develop their ideas behind barriers. One reason for this ambiguity was that nationalist thinkers in colonial countries confronted Western dismissals of their cultures as uniformly backward; equally problematic was the orientalism that romanticized them as "exotic" or "natural."

One aspect of nationalism was the creation of an idea of a common culture as a people. Women's roles were pivotal in male nationalists' constructions of a national tradition that presented definitions of what should be conserved and what should be made anew, but the progress of the nation was invested with differing meanings for women than for men, by the reformers as well as the revivalists.

The new culture frequently involved a redefinition of the spheres of the public and the personal. For instance, when Greece won independence in 1830, a middle-class leadership used the language of Western liberalism. An urban life developed in Athens, similar to that of the cosmopolitan bourgeoisie in Western cities. However, the cafés, theatres, clubs, and restaurants were male public spaces. The creation of this modern public sphere was a surface phenomenon. Greek middle-class women were detached from the male defined project of modernization; their confinement and lack of power within hierarchical families and exclusion from production were actually intensified after 1830.

Western education for a national elite, however, was an aspect of modernization that could have a radical significance for women who themselves began to challenge personal life. For example, a privately educated Ottoman upper class woman Fatma Aliye Hanim opposed polygamy in a book called *Nisvan-i Islam* (Muslim Women) in 1891 and attracted the attention of the censor. Some reformers and nationalist men supported education because they endorsed women's rights on a liberal basis and believed women should have access to the public sphere. Others saw education as necessary so that women could be better wives to national leaders. The aim was to reform domestic life in order to complement the new world outside.

In countries as diverse as India, Egypt, and Turkey in the second half of the nineteenth century newly established girls' schools were appearing for middle-class and upper-class women. Education could mean access to employment and the public sphere. Privileged women who had servants in Argentina, Chile, and Uruguay were entering professions toward the end of the nineteenth century. Similarly in India and Sri Lanka women were becoming teachers and doctors.

The modernizing element in nationalism was linked to women's emancipation in a special dynamic in which the main focus was on transforming public aspects of the lives of privileged women and creating a new realm of reformed domesticity. But the new woman in the home was to complement rather than challenge the nationalist man in the family. Liberal nationalist men were inclined to argue that although they needed to take from the West some elements of modernization in order to oppose colonial rule, it was also necessary to safeguard a national tradition. The peculiar coincidence, of course, was that the interests of men and the nation converged in masculine definitions of both modernization and tradition.

Along with the readjustment of public and private, nationalists were recasting not only womanhood but manhood. Several conflicting concepts of manhood appear in nationalist movements and dissatisfaction with the prevailing forms of masculinity could contribute to a search for a new woman. Deniz Kandiyotī notes that in Turkey, for example, nineteenth century "Modern men often felt alienated from Ottoman patriarchal structures which curtailed their own freedom considerably."[1]

Just as westernization was not homogeneous but contained several political strands, the shaping of national identity varied historically. Because there were disagreements not only about the emancipation of women, but about what kind of gender relations should be the means of shaping the nationalist project, nationalist and anticolonial movements opened an important theoretical space for questioning women's position and prevailing religious doctrines which legitimized subordination.

The West was not the only source for ideas about emancipation. A convergence of western and eastern reforming strands appeared in India in the early nineteenth century. The social reformer Raja Rammohan Roy, a Bengali, had been influenced both by European radical ideas of individual freedom and by his knowledge of Hindu law. He not only supported education but tackled issues such as women's right to own property, widow burning (Sati), and polygamy.

Whereas some strands of nationalism and anti-colonialism were determinedly secular others sought to purify religious systems of beliefs that they saw as oppressive. In early nineteenth century India, for example, Roy began a movement to reform Hinduism. Later, Muslim religious reformers were to support various degrees of emancipation; for instance, Syed Ahmad Khan, who pioneered Muslim higher education, advocated a modern education for both men and women and opposed the seclusion of women (purdah).

In Egypt in the 1870s Sheik Mohamed Abduh, who believed Islam should be guided by a spirit of rational enquiry, said the Muslim religion was not hostile to women's equality. He was also concerned that national development was being impeded by women being kept back. He argued their rights should not be given but restored. His disciple, a lawyer, Qasim Amin, produced an historical explanation that made a reformist interpretation of religion possible. In 1895 he maintained that it was not Islam but customs "which prevailed in nations conquered by Islam"[2] that were responsible for women's seclusion.

Of course these reformers had adversaries, but their arguments created a basis for an historical approach to religious laws. The reinterpretation of religious beliefs combined with secularism in nationalist movements as a means of contesting divine authority for women's subordination.

Nationalist and anticolonial movements of course also utilized western ideas though advocates of women's emancipation were particularly likely to face the accusation that they borrowed ideas from the oppressor. Although it is true that enlightenment ideas about individual freedom did have an international impact, there were histories of rebellious and powerful women in many countries. There was also intellectual questioning; for example, in the eighteenth century China had had a literary genre that was critical of the position of women.

Moreover movements of resistance were never hermetically sealed. Indian reformers in the early nineteenth century followed the antislavery literature. Irish and Indian movements against the British influenced one another from the late nineteenth century. Egyptian feminists read about both legislative reforms in Turkey and the European suffrage movement in the early 1890s. Eastern reformers also affected Westerners.

Eastern women moreover were radicalized not simply by ideas, but by the extreme contradictions facing privileged women. Questioning arose from their own lives not just the examples of others. It was frequently not a matter of following western women's movements but of creating a completely new synthesis in which emancipation combined with antiimperialism.

Huda Shaarawi, an upper-class Egyptian woman, read and discussed in the harem two works written by Qasim Amin, *The Liberation of Women,* published in 1899, and *The New Woman,* published in 1900. After her marriage Huda Shaarawi pioneered public lectures for women. When the nationalists created the Wafd (delegation) to speak for the nation she became president of the Wafdist Women's Central Committee and played an active role in the revolution against the British in 1919.

One of the first Indonesian women to put forward ideas of women's emancipation, Raden Adjeng Kartini lived within similar contradictions. The daughter of the Regent of Jepara, she left school at 12 and longed to study like her brother in Holland, but her father would not allow her to go. In the 1890s she corresponded with a Dutch

socialist and feminist, eagerly seeking news about the women's movement and enthusing about a novel by Cecile van Beek en Donk, *Hilda
Van Suylenberg,* which described a single mother deciding to bring up
her baby alone.

Kartini, however, married the Regent of Rembang and despite her
opposition to polygamy became one of his wives. Marriage did not
prevent her work. She set up a school and continued to oppose both
colonialism and women's oppression. She did not focus only on entry
to education and work. She was critical of Muslim laws that deprived
women of rights in marriage.

However her interest in some western ideas did not mean she
thought European culture was superior. She argued for a selective
approach, writing in 1902,

> we do not expect the European world to make us happier. The time has
> long gone by when we seriously believed that the European is the only
> true civilization, supreme and unsurpassed.[3]

Nationalism and antiimperialism pulled women into public action
because they were needed by the nation. Their emancipation was less an
individual right than a public duty. The individual was to find realization
through the nation. Nonetheless in the process some men and women
questioned the domestic and sexual control of men over women.

However, nationalist movements had a profound ambiguity about
the proper place of women. The exceptional circumstances of struggle
required a break with custom. The enlightenment heritage sometimes
envisaged women educated and engaged in production. Yet the creation of a nation involved also the legitimation of continuity. A simpler
age of handicrafts and wifely devotion was invoked, a moral past that
had also been an element in both enlightenment nostalgia for a golden
age and the French Revolution.

Frequently women's participation in times of crisis threatened the
boundaries of the men's ideal of the customary woman's role. In
the Independence struggle against Spanish colonialism that ended in
victory in 1824, women played an important part in several South
American countries including Argentina, Venezuela, and Peru. They

were involved in intellectual defiance and in the political salons of the conspirators. Women went to jail for distributing revolutionary literature. Women defended cities and became soldiers in Bolivar's rebellion. After independence though they returned to their former lives. In 1826 Bolivar warned his sister Maria Antonia, "not to mix in political business nor adhere to or oppose any party."[4] In his vision of national independence, "a woman ought to be neutral in public business."[5]

Anna Parnell in Ireland became the leader of the Ladies' Land League in 1881 and encountered a similar response. The sister of the MP Charles Stewart Parnell, she came from a Protestant landed family. Her American mother was, however, fiercely opposed to British rule.

In 1879 depression and widespread social discontent in the Irish countryside resulted in an alliance between her brother, Parnell, and Michael Davitt, leader of the Fenians, who advocated physical force rather than constitutional pressure. Fearing another famine, they defended tenants from eviction and demanded peasant proprietorship.

This strategy of direct action against the big landlords was met with sentences of imprisonment. The male leaders were in danger of all being in jail when Michael Davitt decided they should bring in the women. The men were reluctant, but Davitt prevailed, declaring,

they are in certain emergencies, more dangerous to despotism than men.[6]

The female reserve against despotism was given little choice in the matter. Davitt simply decided Anna Parnell was to be the secretary of the Ladies' Land League without even consulting her.

The Times in London sneered,

when treason is reduced to fighting behind petticoats and pinafores it is not likely to do much mischief.[7]

In fact, the women's organizing proved they were able to create a formidable opposition. They walked about the country at all hours encouraging an increasingly militant peasant resistance, distributing the paper *United Ireland,* and defying the British government. They sought to create an opposing national culture by encouraging home manufactures and teaching children Irish history. They thus combined a male and female role in a movement that not only shook Ireland but also had a decisive impact on many English radicals, for whom the "Irish question" helped to force a break with the liberals.

Parnell, however, found himself in agreement with the British government; both were resolved to get rid of the women. The British offered compromises; in 1882 they released prisoners and introduced some rent protection. With the men back there was conflict with the Ladies' Land League. The women had become accustomed to an autonomy that the men would not tolerate and the Ladies' Land League was disbanded. When Davitt was asked in New York about women's contribution he said, they "contented themselves,"[8] with doing "charitable"[9] activities.

In the mid-1880s when the young Maud Gonne tried to discover what had happened to the Ladies' Land League she had difficulty. She was told by Tim Harrington that it "did too good work and some of us found they could not be controlled."[10] This issue of the autonomy of women's organization in relation to men in nationalist movements was to recur.

Maud Gonne was to be involved in another assertion of women's contribution to the nationalist struggle. In 1899, when Queen Victoria was to visit, Maud Gonne, along with other Irish women, organized an alternative Patriotic Children's Treat. Thirty thousand school children demonstrated holding green cards proclaiming "No Flunkyism."[11]

This dramatic mobilization created an opening for a new women's organization, Inghinidhe na hEireann (Daughters of Erin). Commitment to political independence combined with the encouragement of economic independence through home manufactures. Inghinidhe also fostered a conscious national culture that shaped a new sense of Ireland's Celtic past, in which goddesses and queens played a heroic part and resilient continuity found an image in the old women of legend. Indirectly Inghinidhe contributed to the development of a national theatre; Yeats wrote *Kathleen ni Houlinan,* in which Maud Gonne acted.

Inghinidhe na hEireann became part of Sinn Fein in 1908. Rejecting both the parliamentary road and the suffragist insistence on women's demands having priority, the strategy of nationalism first, subordinated women's political rights to the general issue of sovereignty. Women supporters of Sinn Fein argued that the spirit of self-reliance gained in a women's movement on Sinn Fein lines would ensure that with independence from the British, women would be granted political rights.

There were clear strategic conflicts between Sinn Fein women and the suffrage movement. For nationalists the Irish suffrage movement was merely another branch of the British movement. On the other hand, for some feminists the self-reliance fostered by Sinn Fein was wrongly posited on assumptions of women's domestic sphere. Hanna Sheehy Skeffington, co-founder of the Irishwomen's Franchise League in 1908, criticized the Sinn Fein approach because it did not free women as individual citizens, recognizing them in their role only as mothers and housewives.

Ireland's partial independence as a nation did bring universal suffrage in the South, but these arguments about strategic priorities have continued to this day in the North.

Autonomous women's groups and feminists linked to nationalist movements in the late nineteenth and early twentieth century brought their own aspirations to the nationalist project in India as well as Ireland. They adopted varying strategies over time and differed from country to country in how they sought to shape a new place for women in the nation. These have been cultural as well as political. In nineteenth-century and early twentieth-century Ireland and India alike issues of language became important elements in nationalist movements. Honor Ford Smith describes the continuing significance of language in the context of a later anti-colonial struggle against British hegemony. "In the 1930's . . . Una Marson the Jamaican black nationalist and feminist writer made several attempts to organise women into an active force in the nationalist movement through cultural expression."[12] Marson's play *Pocomania* brought Creole ('Patwah' dialect) to drama and "showed the effect of African religious ritual on the black middle class identity."[13] A conscious cultivation of a new culture drew on tradition to find new meanings.

But nationalism was not only cultural and social. Nationalist political assertions of popular sovereignty stimulated demands for the suffrage by women. In 1905 the Asociación Feminista Filipino was organizing for votes for women. In two Scandinavian countries, Norway and Finland, where women got the vote before World War I, nationalism, popular sovereignty, and women's rights are linked to the theme of moral redemption by nationalist women from the 1880s. In Norway, amid anti-Swedish agitation, propertied women got the vote in 1907 and universal suffrage was gained in 1913.

In Finland, liberal women were active in the nationalist movement first against the Swedes and then against the Russians. Finnish feminism in the 1880s was influenced by both J. S. Mill and Josephine Butler, agitating not only for equal legal rights, access to education, and employment but also equal moral standards. In the 1890s, feminists reached out to peasant women, developing welfare groups, schools for poor children, orphanages, libraries, knitting schools, and health care. The Finnish peasantry were by no means a conservative force in society. Free thought became a popular alternative for women as well as men to a Lutheranism that seemed too compromised by its identification with foreign rulers.

As large paper mills were established they employed a predominantly female workforce and by the 1900s working class women were taking part in strikes in mills and factories where they were the majority of the workforce. Their militancy was not confined to wages but extended to opposition to male sexual power in strikes against sexual harassment. Women workers began to create their own welfare groups, which included working class housewives. Their movement consequently bridged work and community. Within these networks a working class feminism developed that recognized that rights and needs were linked. They debated universal suffrage along with wages, employment protection, maternity leave, allowances, children's shelters, education, prostitution, and sexual morality. Political citizenship was thus an integral aspect of economic and social citizenship.

There was conflict between the working women and the middle class because middle-class feminists did not give much support to the economic battles or the struggles against sexual harassment at the workplace. Also the middle-class women demanded not universal suffrage but votes for propertied women.

In 1905–1906 Finland was in uproar. A general strike against the

Russians encouraged the mobilization of working class women, who joined unions, petitioned, and demonstrated in a human chain around the Diet of the Four Estates when it discussed parliamentary reform in May 1906. Their agitation resulted in a motion for universal suffrage, which the Tsar, who also faced insurrection in Russia, was forced to accept. It became law in October 1906.

Finnish women immigrants to Canada and the United States took this tradition of democratic participation backed by women's social networks with them. Within the socialist movement their awareness of emancipation created a journal *Toveritar* (Woman Comrade) in Oregon in 1911, with a former woman member of Finland's Diet as its first editor.

The Finnish women's combination of assertion in the public sphere and political and social organization within women's groups was aligned with a movement of popular nationalism.

In Eastern Europe the fusion of women's suffrage and nationalism was less successful, though it did emerge in the early 1900s in Czechoslovakia and Hungary, where the theme of moral reform appeared.

Hungarian nationalism, however, was based on the Magyar nobility, who suppressed other nationalities to safeguard their position. Opposition to the rule of the Hapsburg dynasty and Austria never took on a mass popular basis. Leadership of the suffrage movement developed in Jewish liberal circles outside official nationalism. Rosika Schwimmer, from a free-thinking Jewish family, linked the emancipation of women to internationalism. She was interested in social and economic changes as well as the vote, translating Charlotte Perkins Gilman's *Women and Economics* and also campaigning resolutely for peace.

World War I transformed the meaning of nationalism for many European feminists. The international organization of women for peace and the transcendence of nationalism became the ideal for the feminist left in Europe and North America. However, women's part in many struggles against colonialism persisted in other parts of the world and within these some of the contradictions apparent within nineteenth-century nationalisms were to reappear, including the complex dynamic between personal and public emancipation and the differing perspectives of women of various classes.

13

SOCIAL REFORM:
PROTECTION BY THE STATE

In the last quarter of the nineteenth century the liberal conviction that equal rights in conditions of free competition were the means to create a good society was losing its hold—even in Britain. Social reformers questioned how equality of opportunity could exist when individuals were placed at such unequal starting points. This seemed especially pertinent for those women who faced not only obstacles of gender but of class.

One consequence was a change in liberal attitudes to trades unions. The social liberal theorist of industrial relations, Arnold Toynbee believed that unions would be less disruptive if they were legally recognized. In the first half of the century, combination had been seen as akin to subversion; Toynbee's new liberal approach presented unions as a legitimate way of countering the power of capital—especially necessary for vulnerable groups such as women. Not only could unions benefit from incorporation, the state's powers to intervene in industry could be developed. Existing protective legislation had set a precedent, restricting the rights of employers through limiting hours.

In the same period the emphasis on working class organizations providing their own welfare services shifted toward demands for social welfare from the state. This had a specific meaning for working class women who, because of low wages and caring for husbands and children, were often dependent on the state if the men were out of work or ill.

Attitudes to state intervention changed gradually. There was a protracted argument among liberals, socialists, and anarchists about whether the state could be helpful among women in the trade unions. Women social reformers and feminists were caught up in these wider political debates and also had disagreements among themselves about whether women should seek special protection at work or be workers on an equal basis to men.

In 1874 Emma Paterson formed the Women's Protective and Provident League, later called the Women's Trade Union League. Arnold Toynbee and leading craft trades union men attended the founding meeting.

Emma Patterson came from a middle-class family, but had been apprenticed as a bookbinder and married a cabinet maker. She had worked for both the Working Men's Club and Institute Union and the Women's Suffrage Association where she had helped Emily Faithfull campaign for women's printing societies.

A visit to America in 1873 had enabled her to see successful unions of working women, for example, the Parasol and Umbrella Makers' Union and the Women's Typographical society.

The aim of the League was to prevent wages being reduced but to discourage strikes. Like Arnold Toynbee, Emma Paterson hoped to settle grievances through arbitration. In the tradition of Harriet Taylor's liberalism she believed equality of opportunity required "the combined action of workers themselves"[1] to offset the employers' superior advantages.

She stressed the self-emancipation involved in organization and its democratic potential, insisting that through unionization women gained a means of making their views known. Their mutual association was necessary not only to bargain with employers but to find a voice in the trade union movement.

Some male craft trade unionists supported the League; however, others believed women should not work and said protective legislation should extend into workshops and outwork at home. Emma Paterson opposed this protective legislation because she argued for women's right to earn a living. A member of the League, Mrs. Mason from the Leicester Society of Seamers and Stitchers, an organization of outworkers, argued it was an intrusion by the state upon individual rights. She said in 1877

> it would be as reasonable to pass a law to enable inspectors to visit their houses, and see that their husbands were out of bed instead of laying there until what they called luncheon time, as to have these laws for inspecting the work of women.[2]

A leading craft trade unionist, Henry Broadhurst opposed the League's case that women's unionization was the answer not state intervention:

> they knew it was very natural for ladies to be impatient of restraint at any time, and therefore they might imagine the uneasiness which would be created when the law of the factory prescribed rules and regulations. They (the men) had the future of their country and children to consider, and it was their duty as men and husbands to use their utmost efforts to bring about a condition of things, where their wives should be in their proper sphere at home, instead of being dragged into competition for livelihood against the great and strong men of the world.[3]

This combined the assumption that women's interests were best represented by men with an ideal of woman in the home. Such a division between personal and public spheres was a common theme in

Victorian literature. It was becoming a mark of respectability in skilled working class families for the man to support the woman. Women were regarded as exceptions, outside economic and political concepts of the virtues of competition.

In opposing the extension of protection, Emma Paterson challenged this exclusion of women from economic affairs and trade union politics. The League, however, was unsuccessful in opposing the Factory and Workshops Acts and pragmatically Emma Paterson changed tack, to campaign for women factory inspectors to safeguard the interests of women workers. Finally, in 1893, the first women factory inspectors were to be appointed.

There were important changes occurring not only in the relation of the state to workers but in the actual forms and functions of trades unions. Apart from the textile industry, women's employment was frequently in small units or at home. Even the factories where they worked were frequently unorganized. Women's jobs often changed and employment was on a casual basis. The League was linked to cooperation, rather like the French women's associations in 1848; it included a cooperative store and a cooperative society of shirt-makers. A range of social institutions strengthened its members' commitment to unionization: a half penny bank, a women's labor exchange, a workers' restaurant, a seaside house, a swimming pool, and a circulating library. Emma Paterson faced a persistent contradiction, the low wages and sporadic employment of her members could not possibly finance these social projects—however valuable they might be to women workers. Despite her wishes the League was dependent on middle-class philanthropic support.

Emma Patterson died in 1886, just as a new vision of trade unionism was emerging. In the late 1880s a wave of unrest among unskilled and semiskilled workers created a militant "New Unionism" in which many women workers were active, including the Bryant and May match girls whose strike revealed the terrible consequences of an illness from phosphorous called "phossy jaw." It was difficult, however, for women to sustain their membership in the new unions even though these were more democratic and committed to equality than craft unions because women workers were often more likely to be replaceable. Thus the emphasis on bargaining for better pay and conditions with employers was harder to put into practice.

An important principle of equality was established in 1888 when Clementina Black, a socialist, got the Trades Union Congress to support equal pay for equal work. But resolutions were not effective without action. Led by the liberal Lady Dilke and influenced by the impact of new unionism, the Women's Trade Union League continued to try and organize tailoresses, mantle makers, milliners, dressmakers, cigar makers, bookbinders, shop assistants, and even the rag sorters. Unlike Emma Paterson, Lady Dilke believed that women's workplace organization should be complemented by protective legislation.

This acceptance of state intervention became common among both liberal and socialist middle-class women organizers and investigators of working conditions from the 1890s, though there was still some opposition among liberal feminists such as Milicent Fawcett and among anarchist women, who stressed the emancipatory aspects of organization.

In 1890 Clementina Black devised a new means of combining the powers of the local state in an attempt to improve women's wages and conditions. She persuaded the London County Council to extend existing powers to prevent insanitary conditions and outwork through its fair wages ruling. Under pressure from trade unions, the Council had agreed they would only give outwork to firms paying decent wages. As there were no fixed union rates for women clothing workers this set another precedent, the local state was to decide what was a "living wage." Clementina Black defined a decent wage as one "at which the woman employed can live in health and reasonable comfort."[4] She invoked the social needs of women as a basis for the wage rate.

The "fair wages" ruling of London's local government was taken up by national government departments. The principle of public bodies giving out contracts to employers who paid fair wages was established. But in practice there were loopholes. Many women workers continued to work in the sweated trades, in nonunionized clothing factories or doing work at home.

Women workers themselves varied in their attitudes to protective legislation and state intervention. Fear among factory workers that it would destroy their livelihoods had receded. By the 1890s the cotton workers had discovered that limits on women's hours had tended to lead to men also working less. A canvass of 67,500 laundresses in 1891 by the League showed that a majority of 66,000 wanted to be included in the new Factory and Workshops Bill.

In 1894 Ada Nield Chew, who worked in a clothing factory in Crewe in the North of England, wrote to the Crewe Chronicle,

> Now I wonder if the Government of this country know (or care) that those on whom the real business of executing their orders fall are "sweated" thereby. And is the Government so frightfully poor that it cannot afford to pay a living wage to those who make the clothing of our soldiers and policemen.[3]

When she was sacked for taking this public stand Marx's daughter, Eleanor Marx, came and spoke in her defense; Ada Nield Chew was to become active in both the socialist and suffrage movements. Socialists advocated legal intervention to protect workers and changing attitudes to the state were evident in the demands of new unionism from the late 1880s: the eight hour day, equal pay, and welfare provision. Liberal and socialist women did not agree on the extent to which the middle class and working class could work together, but in practice there was a certain convergence on the state. Moreover, new unionism, especially in relation to women, relied on moving middle-class public opinion. Middle-class moral concern about the conditions of women workers radicalized many women and led them to support trades unionism and campaign against "sweated" work. They found a common ground in pressure on the state.

In the United States an alliance of women trade unionists, suffrage, and church groups developed in Illinois in the late 1880s. In 1888 a series of investigative reports headed "City Slave Girls" appeared in the *Chicago Times* revealing the terrible wages and conditions of women in small workshops and at home working for subcontractors. Like the social purity campaigns, opposition to sweating was presented in terms of the protection of women and children.

For six years this cross-class alliance combined a mix of feminist, radical, and socialist demands. They effectively used a combination of investigation, publicity, and pressure on the state for legislative change.

Like Josephine Butler, they opposed the sexual double standard, which blamed women but not men for prostitution. Also like her they took social purity to mean improvements for women not coercion, opposing laws that gave the police powers to round up and arrest homeless women and children suspected of prostitution and demanding why there should be only "Erring Women's Refuges." Surely the erring men needed reforming too.

They campaigned for laws to protect children and also for public education. They tried to improve sanitary conditions in cities and helped to set up public wash houses.

Tension developed around the demand for an eight hour day. The socialist women in the Alliance, Elizabeth Morgan and Fanny Kavanagh, thought trade unions should extend their role from the workplace and exert pressure for social and political reform through the state. However, manufacturers were furious when the state of Illinois introduced the eight hour day. It was one thing for the local middle-class women to support social reforms and quite another to restrict capital directly.

Dissident voices in the workers' movement in Chicago were the anarchist women Lucy Parsons and Lizzie Swank, who opposed the socialists' readiness to ally with the middle class and campaign for legislative measures. They thought gains from the state would not serve workers' interests. They wanted the campaign for an eight hour day to be one of direct action by workers and not through the state.

The practical reason for the shift toward making demands for state intervention were obvious. Middle-class women reformers and working-class organizers often despaired of working-class women in the chaotic slums of large cities organizing themselves. But in retrospect it is possible to see that this strategic change contained problems. Pressure on the state tended to reduce the emphasis on the self-emancipatory aspects of democratic organization. It also transferred control over the definition of social need. It was invariably middle-class reformers who decided that other women needed protection. The de-

mand for protection from the state and strategies that sought to combine unionization with state intervention at work assumed that every
individual had an equal say in state policies. The state floated benignly
above society in a neutral space. Anarchist and some socialist women
contested this view of the state, which they saw as expressing ruling
class interests. Some reforms were beneficial but others could overlook
the actual needs of poor women. There were examples of both effective
alliances and of tension between working-class and middle-class
women.

The emphasis on protection by the state raised the basic issue of
women's right to representation. By the early 1900s many women
who had struggled for social reform and the protection of women
workers were arguing that if women had the vote it would be easier
to get these reforms. So, by a roundabout route, some women who
had seen social and economic reform as a more urgent priority than
political rights reappear in the suffrage movement. The feminist movement in the 1900s thus found itself with a confused heritage of arguments for individual equal rights and for the special protection of
women as a sexually and economically vulnerable section of society.
There was also to be disagreement on whether the acquisition of
political power by privileged women would necessarily tackle the
social problems of the poor.

14

WELFARE AND
SOCIAL ACTION

Liberal concepts of individual rights were of such fundamental significance in the case for women's emancipation that the painful transition
to social liberalism necessarily affected feminism. The argument about
whether women needed protection or independence was only part of
it. Against Mill's model of society as composed of competing atomistic
individuals, John Ruskin argued for an organically connected society.
His vision of the economy as a household meeting welfare needs
inspired some women committed to social service. For example, Ruskin's ideas appealed to the housing reformer Octavia Hill, a close friend
of suffrage campaigner Sophia Jex Blake, much more than arguments

for individual political rights. She believed women should exercise public duties not claim rights.

Ruskin's stress on social need made possible a critique of the brutal consequences of the market. But the emphasis on planned welfare subordinated individual rights. The price of social security was high.

In 1870, for instance, he wrote to Octavia Hill advocating that the state should fix rents and also establish a fund

> to employ, compulsorily if needful, all idle persons at a fixed rate of wages, adequate to the maintenance of themselves and their families by wholesome food and in wholesome lodgings.[1]

A less authoritarian approach to welfare planning was developed by the social liberal philosopher T. II. Green, who stressed the importance of personal action by the upper classes to prevent class conflict.

Leonard Montefiore, a friend of Arnold Toynbee, was inspired by Ruskin, Green, and American utopian communities when he founded the Settlement Movement in East London in the 1870s. Upper middle-class professionals settled in the slums and combined social projects with research and personal interaction. The settlements were to be a practical means of putting into practice ideas developing in social science of the benefits of a planned, rational society. They also answered powerful personal needs.

The drive toward social action was partly influenced by a crisis of faith. Biblical criticism was making it impossible for many educated Christians to accept the scriptures in a fundamentalist sense as the word of God. Salvation through works provided a welcome relief from doubt for many liberal Christians.

There was an element of fear of the working-class poor concentrated in large cities. Images of themselves as social missionaries or colonizers of savage, barbaric terrain were borrowed from the Church and from imperialism. All the more urgent when the working class had the vote and began to demonstrate against unemployment or for shorter hours.

There was a self-consciousness and insecurity among members of the socially concerned, liberal intelligentsia. Neighborliness and personal friendship between classes were important to them. They did not only go to purify "the other." They wanted workers to show affection and in some cases saw themselves as learning from the working class.

These concerns affected men and women alike but the settlement movement presented a secular means by which women could enter public space from which they normally would be barred. An opening was possible too because the settlement movement was characterized by a yearning to be redeemed through service; service was acceptable for women, as was the human contact.

Settlement work for women thus was another means of translating skills in personal relations into the public sphere. Teaching and nursing were just opening up to middle-class women but were still not really for educated upper middle-class women. The settlements brought freedom to work and live in parts of the city that otherwise would have been outside the bounds of middle-class life. Volunteers might come dressed up in fashionable finery but the settlers discarded gloves and hats. They developed a style for middle-class young women that despised showiness, was unconventional, and yet still respectable. The call of social service brought fulfillment and freedom. It was both womanly and adventurous.

Honnor Morten trained as a nurse and then started a settlement in Hoxton, North East London. Housework was done communally and the aim was to reduce class division. It was all rather daring and fun. She delighted in disturbing the local curate with her unorthodox views on God and the display of a Botticelli painting, Chianti, and cigarettes.

Honnor Morten went on to work for physically handicapped children and was responsible for introducing nurses in schools. Settlers' proximity to working class life enabled them to identify needs and take action for reform. They set up girls' clubs and educational classes of all kinds for women. They pioneered services for children, nurseries, and model schools for handicapped children. Many of their voluntary projects were adopted by progressive local councils and thus came to be funded by the state. Their inventiveness ranged from holiday camps for slum children to temperance music halls.

Women settlers themselves often went on to serve on school

boards and local government; they took the knowledge they had gained in settlements and the policy proposals that emerged from their attempts to improve conditions.

Charlotte Despard was widowed early in the 1890s. Horrified by the conditions of children in Wandsworth, South London, she opened her house and formed the Despard Clubs, rounding up children for holidays in the country at her family's country house in Esher. She had a similar approach when she served in local government, first as a Poor Law Guardian and then on the School Board. When the Board said that money could not be legally spent on school dinners, Charlotte Despard, who had become a socialist, simply provided the saucepans, stove, tables, and benches herself.

Jane Addams, a suffrage and temperance reformer, influenced by the British settlements, formed Hull House in Chicago. Believing in combined middle-class and working-class action for social reform Jane Addams settled in the immigrant area of Chicago in 1889 and began to draw together a group of professional middle-class social reformers. Instead of charity they used the methods of social science to investigate conditions. Idealistic university trained women saw themselves as advocates of the poor. They also learned from the circumstances that surrounded them.

When Mary Kenney, a young skilled bookbinder of Irish descent, was campaigning for better sanitary conditions at work, Jane Addams invited her to dinner. She was reluctant initially to go because she found the middle-class club women snobbish. Her mother insisted she should give Jane Addams a hearing.

> You can't judge without knowing her and she might be different from the other club women. It's condemning you are.[2]

Jane Addams offered the bookbinders a meeting place and said she would help leaflet for a trade union meeting; Mary Kenney decided her mother had been right and she became closely involved with Hull House.

The settlement helped workers to help themselves by organizing. They also campaigned for legislation. Mary Kenney was joined by

Florence Kelley in a campaign on sweated labor. Florence Kelley had been involved in a reforming alliance in Philadelphia, which resembled the Illinois Women's Alliance. A friend and translator of Engels' work, she was a strong supporter of protective legislation. Kelley and Kenney used their knowledge of the local community to bring homeworkers' conditions to the attention of investigators and journalists. Encouraged by a reforming governor in Illinois, Altgeld, their efforts contributed to the 1893 Factory Act, which declared that tenement houses could be searched and goods exposed to contagious diseases destroyed. Fear of a smallpox epidemic had aroused middle-class support for the anti-sweating campaign. However, while poor women needed to earn a living, it was difficult to end sweating by legislation. Moreover, local manufacturers combined to undermine the law.

Besides campaigns the settlers took direct action to meet needs. Aware of the problems of working mothers, a nursery and kindergarten were started, followed by the Public Kitchen in 1894. Settlers studied nutrition and introduced healthy diets; however, immigrant families preferred their own food and the kitchen turned into a coffee house for busy settlers.

A more successful form of prefigurative self-help grew out of a strike meeting. Jane Addams said it became clear from discussions among women workers from a shoe factory that

> the strikers who had been easily frightened, and therefore the first to capitulate were naturally those girls who were paying board and were afraid of being put out if they fell too far behind. After a recital of a case of peculiar hardship one of them exclaimed: "Wouldn't it be fine if we had a boarding club of our own, and then we could stand by each other in a time like this."[3]

They set up a self-governing project for cooperative living, the Jane Club. It was cheap, independent, and, unlike charitable housing schemes, fun. Off they went to dances together, checking their escorts' hat bands and cigars for the union label.

Hull House thus was the base for a combined strategic offensive against differing, but interconnected aspects of women's oppression. It linked a commitment to women's rights with an awareness of women's needs. Instead of equal opportunity they stressed self-organization, the professional skills of social scientists, and protection from the state. They put into practice Frances Willard's idea of making society home-like. This commitment to social reforms for women has been called "social feminism."

For the settlers the ability to investigate, take action, and influence public policy was empowering even though women could not vote in most U.S. states. Communal living and personal networks strengthened their inner resolve—the bonds were both of friendship and erotic love. Jane Addams, like Lilian Wald, another settlement organizer, was a lesbian—America owes its early reforms for children to two lesbian women.

Settlement work could be sometimes discouraging—the sheer extent of material deprivation and suspicion and resistance from slum women could make settlers despair. In Britain many women turned toward campaigning for legislation and became involved in local government. Some went into the socialist movement.

An interesting question is why reformers in Britain were able in the early twentieth century to secure some welfare reforms. In the United States, it took longer and welfare was more piecemeal. The answer seems to be that in Britain outside pressure combined with some support within the Liberal Party, who introduced welfare policies in the early twentieth century. Germany had developed state welfare but, lacking a strong individualist liberal tradition, had a conservative and philanthropic women's movement. In France the bitter memory of the Commune made it difficult for left-wing women to work with middle-class liberal reformers. There were sharper lines between a militant labor movement and a feminist movement that was mainly concerned with equality. Demands for protective legislation and state welfare took longer to crystallize.

The strength of social feminism was its capacity to confront the immediate needs of women and seek practical reforms. It was innovative and resourceful in combining a range of strategies. It challenged liberal approaches to women's emancipation that emphasized rights and ignored material needs. However, its weak points were revealed when conflict was too deep to be glossed over by sisterly contact. The reforming intervention of concerned middle-class women had its limits, for not all women were prepared to accept their ideal of the wholesome planned society. In the United States racial and ethnic inequalities were pervasive and as problematic as class. Black women club members developed their own welfare services and, because of racism, conceptualized social intervention differently. As Rosa Bowser wrote in *The Woman's Era,*

The race rises as individuals rise . . . and individuals rise with the race.[4]

This interaction was rather different from the white middle-class reformers who went to redeem the poor and found personal strength through social action.

15

SOCIALISM, WOMEN, AND THE NEW LIFE

Women who became involved in the revival of socialism that occurred in many European countries and in North America in the 1880s saw the new movement as both the solution for the wrongs of society in general and the means of women's emancipation. Socialists argued that liberalism's emphasis on political and legal rights ignored the necessity of the social and economic means to exercise democratic freedoms.

Whereas some socialists, both revolutionary and reformist, stressed the scientific understanding of society to assess the possibility of change objectively, others argued that the action of human beings would be decisive in deciding the odds. Some socialist groups tried to influence capitalist institutions from within; some organized themselves, waiting for the predicted crisis of capitalism; others tried to change people's consciousness. A powerful current among these argumentative pioneers was a vision of socialism that was not restricted to political power or public ownership of the means of making wealth. Socialism was conceived as a process of cultural transformation that was to create new relationships between people.

Tom Maguire, a socialist in West Yorkshire who had been a member both of William Morris' revolutionary Socialist League and the Independent Labour Party that worked for gradual reforms, described the movement as "a living thing entering into all the ways of life—as a great ideal."

Socialism was both a means of tackling the immediate practical problems of life and an aspiration to another way of living—another way of being human. Socialism thus offered women a solution to their own oppression and the injustices that they could see in capitalism in the future. It also brought more immediately an engagement with a collective project through which the individual changed. Socialism provided not only a means of ending all forms of oppression, it also psychologically enabled women to find a new sense of self.

This crucial link between self-emancipation and social emancipation was a feature of the socialist revival in general. It was powerful in Britain, where not even the hard headed Fabians completely evaded the enthusiasm for the new life, and where the marxist leader of the Social Democratic Federation, H. M. Hyndman, was plagued with what he described as "faddists."

Becoming a socialist could be akin to conversion in the 1880s and early 1890s. Katherine St John Conway in Bristol was moved by the demonstrations of women cotton workers as part of New Unionism among the unskilled and semiskilled. When she went to find the Bristol socialists, a Christian socialist, Robert Weare, gave her a book by Edward Carpenter, *England's Ideal*. Returning to her lodgings, her life appeared in a new light. She was ashamed of her aspirations to refinement and her middle-class privileges. Instead she found companionship and "the cause."[2]

Commitment had rather different meanings depending on class.

For thoughtful and rebellious working class women such as the "Crewe factory girl" Ada Nield Chew and a young cotton worker Selina Coombe (later Cooper) in Nelson, Lancashire, socialist groups were a means of gaining education and contact with a wider intellectual world.

The socialist movement offered an entry into a public world of meetings, speeches, organization, and social life that was adventurous compared to women's ordinary lives. But again class was a factor. Katherine St John Conway, Carolyn Martyn, Enid Stacey, and Margaret McMillan were middle-class women speakers who became national figures. Selina Cooper, in contrast, became a well-known local figure through the Social Democratic Federation, the Independent Labour Party, and the Women's Co-operative Guild. It was harder for married working-class women to tour the country.

Regardless of class, however, socialism provided an alternative culture. Many young socialist women belonged to the Clarion cycling club—an organization that combined propaganda with social activities—and would go off with the men to speak in villages and small towns. The Clarion's horse-drawn vans provided socialists with a working propagandist holiday. When Katherine St John Conway married Bruce Glasier they set off together in one for their honeymoon.

Socialism involved women not only in socially daring propaganda but in legal defiance. When Liverpool police tried to stop Enid Stacey speaking in 1895 she clung to the railings. When they dragged her away she appeared on the roof of a tramcar to address the unemployment demonstration. The socialist battle for free speech in Manchester also drew in Emmeline Pankhurst, who was later to be a leader of the suffrage movement.

The sense of being a small band of pioneers contributed to a need for personal fellowship within the movement. This created the means by which women could use existing female skills in a wider context. Women in all the socialist groups were important in this internal life of organizations, transferring their domestic skills into political organizing. Northern working class women, for example, prepared the hall with pride for the founding conference of the Independent Labour Party in Bradford in 1893. Fundraising, rambles, picnics, concerts, and socialist Sunday schools were all seen as within women's sphere. Some women combined several forms of activity. Marx's daughter Eleanor was a prominent organizer, speaker, and writer in the Social Democratic Federation and the Socialist League, but she also organized parties for children—a demanding job as she had to cater for unknown quantities.

There was both a special place for women *and* an ideal of equality between men and women socialists that could sometimes challenge relations and identity. Isabella Ford came from a Quaker upper middle-class family in Leeds. Her mother had been involved in the agitation against the Contagious Diseases Act and she and her sisters had been involved in the educational movement in Leeds among middle-class women. Contact with women workers in Bradford and Leeds who were forming unions and striking made her increasing critical of the Liberals who were closely involved with the local employers. She was a friend of the socialist writer Edward Carpenter and in the late 1880s began to help Tom Maguire and other Leeds socialists in organizing women workers, finding their new unionist arguments of equality attractive. She was to join the Independent Labour Party because it stood for equality between the sexes. She saw this not simply as an abstract item in the political program but as part of the life of the organization.

> My last doubts were removed after a visit to a Labour club in the Colne Valley, where the men had been giving a tea party to the women, and had poured out the tea, cut the bread and butter, and washed everything up without any feminine help and without any accidents! A party, that included the education of men which hitherto had been so much neglected, as well as the education of women, that gave one such skill and dexterity, and the other wider and true views of life, was the party for me I felt and I joined it.[3]

Edward Carpenter had abandoned a career as an Anglican curate and gone to live in the North of England, lecturing first in an adult education movement and then for the early socialist groups in the 1880s. He was ecumenical, involved with the Fellowship of the New Life, which sought personal perfection, the Fabians, which split from it, the Social Democratic Federation, the Socialist League, the Independent Labour Party, and anarchists and syndicalists. His writings on socialism wrestled with materialism and the means of breaking from it to create a new consciousness and new social relations. More interested in beauty and nature than political economy he was sceptical about "civilization" and critical of the complicated needs that industrialization developed. Influenced by Walt Whitman and Eastern religion, he advocated the simplification of life and opposed a parasitic dependence on the labor of others—including servants.

Two Bristol socialist women Helena Born and Miriam Daniel, who had become socialists in the New Unionist organization of working women, were inspired to live according to Carpenter's simplified domestic aesthetic.

He was one of the earliest advocates of homosexual rights and from 1898 lived openly with his lover George Merrill. Edith Lees, a lesbian friend who married Havelock Ellis, commented on the division of domestic labor between the two men.

> His belief is that what a woman can do a man can always share. He has realised the truth that no occupation is a sex-monopoly but a chance for free choice and the division of labour.[4]

There was discussion of sexuality and questioning of marriage among socialists. In the 1880s Eleanor Marx became friends with the young South African novelist Olive Schreiner and they talked eagerly about their sexual feelings as women. Olive Schreiner was also friendly with Edward Carpenter and the early sex psychologist Havelock Ellis. It seemed as if sexuality would be part of the process of change. Socialism was not only a rebellion of the intellect but of the heart, spirit, and body. Edward Carpenter was a powerful inspiration with his conviction that the individual liberation of needs and feelings could combine with social liberation.

For some early socialists not only relationships but gender identities would change with socialism. Helena Born spoke on women to the Bristol Socialist Society in 1889 saying that socialism would mean a different masculinity and femininity.

> Genuine comradeship is possible only if the man becomes more effeminate
> or when the woman to some extent rationalises her costume.[5]

This was consistent with Carpenter's view that middle-class men's upbringing made them incapable of being open to feeling. Not only women but men were formed by society's conventions.

The issue of free unions was again being discussed in advanced circles and in the socialist movement. A modification was the democratization of marriage. When Katherine St John Conway married Bruce Glasier, she put some unconventional terms to him:

> What does a poet think of a woman with ink on her finger and a hole in
> her stocking? . . . What would he say to a woman who would sooner eat
> bread and butter and drink milk or buy fruit than cook it. . . . Again what
> would a poet say to a woman who *liked* earning money.[6]

These hopes that socialism would make new men and new women by democratizing all aspects of human relations continued the optimistic enlightenment, faith in reason, and perfectibility as applying both to individuals and external institutions. The connection between personal and political emancipation assumed there was a fit between subjective responses and conscious commitment to concepts. This proved to be overly simplified and the democratization of sexual relations faced many obstacles. One was most basic and obvious, women's equality often conflicted with men's interests and material comforts. It also involved more than an effort of will or shift in consciousness. It required profound changes in the division of labor in the home and at work and in the whole social system of authority.

Nor was it clear how socialists' visions of emancipation really fitted the everyday lives of working class men and women. Once the small socialist groups sought to gain electoral appeal it became evident that the mass of people, women as well as men, tended to prefer improvements to their existing situation to speculative ideals of what might be.

The gap between aspiration and actuality resulted in a tension within a movement that aimed to prefigure a better future. For example, the Independent Labour Party (ILP) in Leeds was so preoccupied with its faction fights in 1895 that Tom Maguire was left to die alone of pneumonia without food or fuel.

The disconnection had a special significance for women. Hannah Mitchell, a northern shopworker, was wary about marriage because she had seen her mother being crushed by housework and her family. But young men and women in the local Independent Labour Party "were talking of marriage as a comradeship, rather than a state where the woman was subservient to and dependent on the man."[7]

Working class women, like Hannah Mitchell, could not evade the division of domestic tasks that was possible for those middle-class socialists who had servants. She was confronted with the split between rhetoric and reality and reflected bitterly,

> Even my Sunday leisure was gone for I soon found a lot of the socialist talk about freedom was only talk and these socialist young men expected Sunday dinners and huge teas with home-made cakes, potted meats and pies exactly like their reactionary fellows.[8]

Though the hopes of integrating new ways of relating in the here and now were frequently disappointed, the assumption that cultural transformation was part of the socialist movement was vital for women. The utopian impulse to prefigure the future in the present enabled them to challenge the power of the men to decide what the movement was about, and to resist when self-interest halted the extension of democracy in the everyday life and policies of organizations.

The unequal situation of men and women in paid employment was another awkward issue. Men in the trade unions argued women lowered the wages of organized male workers. Some believed the solution was to raise the male wage so they could all support their families.

Isabella Ford had considerable experience of the problems of organizing working women and insisted on the right of married women to work. Many socialist women as well as men believed that mothers should not work because they would bear and rear sickly children. While Isabella Ford thought women were best suited to caring for children, she did not see why women should be confined to the home. Women should have a choice.

The Fabians encouraged middle-class women to study working-class conditions, but Isabella Ford's practical organizing experience led her always to stress the need for women workers' independent action. Investigators had to learn first-hand, "from the actual workers' own stand point."[9] This insistence on the democratic process meant she sought to combine the power of self-organization with pressure on the state. She was unusual in not accepting state intervention unless it was clear that specific groups of women workers believed legislation would be beneficial.

Local government provided a context in which middle-class socialist women could exert pressure for the redistribution of public resources toward women and children. This combined democracy and social need but tended to shift the argument about the changes necessary for women's emancipation away from the unequal relations within the working class to the wider social inequalities that a combination of class and gender oppression created.

Involvement in local government was partly a pragmatic response to desperate hardship. In Bradford, Margaret McMillan and Fred Jowett of the ILP tried to develop a cross-class alliance in local government to improve the conditions of children from 1894. They secured school baths and medical inspection. In 1894 Emmeline Pankhurst was nominated by the ILP in Manchester by a progressive alliance that campaigned for free education, free preschool breakfasts, and equal pay. From 1894 working-class women were able for the first time to serve in local government. Ada Nield Chew quickly became a member of the Crewe Board of Guardians, one of the first of a new kind of Labour woman councillor who knew the problems faced by working class families.

Local government meant women could use domestic skills in a public context and provided the means of mobilizing women. A strength of this practical socialism in which women played an important part was its attention to detail and its record of small but visible successes. Selina Cooper, for example, managed to double the butter allowance of 25 children in the Burnley workhouse in 1901.

The Women's Labour League was formed in 1906 and became affiliated with the new Labour Party in 1908. It continued the campaign for school meals and concentrated on other community needs such as housing. The idea of changing domestic life persisted in demands for changes in the built environment. Ada Nield Chew in 1913 proposed building houses without private kitchens and in 1915 an experimental communal kitchen was actually set up by the League.

Some years earlier Isabella Ford had advocated cooperative housekeeping, while acknowledging that one of the obstacles was the suspicion of working-class women. Wartime experience of communal washhouses and restaurants convinced a member of the League, Averil Sanderson Furniss, that working-class women preferred the work being "done by highly skilled people and not by providing appliances which each in turn may use."[10]

The shift was similar to Charlotte Perkins Gilman's rejection of communalism, but led not to the demand for private household services, but for local councils to provide municipal resources to help women. This change in approach was to influence the later demands for welfare. Women not only demanded amenities they questioned planning priorities. After World War I Hannah Mitchell became a councillor and wryly noted there were even male and female parks. Her male colleagues wanted tarmac and bandstands; she argued for flowers, rest, and a place to drink tea while children could play.

The emphasis on social demands in the community was partly in response to women's needs. But it implied a view of women's situation that differed from the liberal emphasis on individual rights. The popular speaker Enid Stacey, who was involved in both the ILP and the Fabian Society, had argued in 1897 that socialism overcame the limited insistence on the individual rights of a "middle class spinsters"[11] fighting for an equal livelihood against men. It could speak to "the wife and mother"[12] and show how she could fulfil her "duties"[13] better through "her freedom as an individual and her equality as a citizen."[14]

Women's social citizenship as an ideal influenced many women in the reformist socialist camp after the utopian élan of the 1880s began to fade. It made possible an alliance with social liberals and with feminists who were committed to social reform. It solved the problems in demanding equality when working class men's lives were obviously less than idyllic. It also provided a means of raising issues that an egalitarian perspective missed because of women's differing biological and social circumstances.

However, it shelved the question of what should be done about the inequality of men and women within the working class and indeed within socialist organizations. The creative pioneering work in local government was both vitally important for women in the here and now and indecisive about how socialism was to change women's position in relation to men.

It was extremely difficult to hold together the recognition of difference with the demand for equality—especially as the hope of a fundamental transformation of society grew faint. The assumption that self-emancipation and the socialist movement went together and that the liberation of the working class demanded the liberation of women were also to have a bumpy ride. Margaret McMillan was to comment tersely in her biography of her sister Rachel, who pioneered children's nurseries,

> The Independent Labour Party was not formed to champion women. . . . It took that battle in its stride, and might drop it in its ardour. It was born to make war on capitalism and competition.[15]

Having argued that socialism overtook liberal feminism's preoccupation with individual rights and antagonism between the sexes, both reformist and revolutionary socialists faced considerable difficulty in tackling the very inequalities within their own organizations that prevented a challenge to the male-defined orientation of socialist theory and practice. Their conviction that women could gain emancipation only through a movement to transform the whole society made them often dismissive of the need to work within movements for specific reforms like the suffrage. At the same time the ideal of equality between comrades made many of them suspicious of separate women's groups within parties, which they suspected institutionalized their secondary status.

All the socialist groups, however, were affected by the militant suffrage movement that emerged actually from within the ILP in the 1900s. Equality, political rights, and the gaining of confidence through struggle were to be renewed among socialist women as a result. But the existence of an autonomous movement also brought real dilemmas. Did they support the militants' criticism of Labour men? Did they argue for women's votes even though these would involve a property qualification or did they campaign for adult suffrage? Was the vote as important as economic and social reform and could women's interests be regarded as unified regardless of class? These questions were partly faced as individual conflicts in loyalty but they also raised again the theoretical implications of socialism for women's equality.

16

MARXISTS AND
THE WOMAN QUESTION

In 1895 Annie Sleet exploded angrily in the paper of the British Social
Democratic Federation (SDF) paper *Justice:*

> In the sacred name of justice, I as a woman, demand equality. I am not
> keen on my sex getting into Parliament. As for Female Suffrage I am sick
> of it, it spells to me delusion, snare, cant and hypocrisy. What I want is
> Social Democracy. I had cherished the hope that women's interests were
> safe in the hands of man; it seems so, and so safe, that they hold them
> there and put their hands into their pockets. I also thought that man's
> interests were woman's, and that as his advanced towards the goal of
> freedom so did mine.[1]

Instead she found women "crushed"[2] and "hobbled"[3] by a man-made system.

Part of Annie Sleet's problems were the male leaders of the SDF who were particularly dismissive of women's emancipation. She was not the first or last woman to clash with the male hierarchy. Annie Besant before her and Dora Montefiore later crossed swords with them. However, part of the difficulty also lay with Marx.

Marx's thought could be applied by women to reveal and illuminate aspects of their oppression, but in his own work women's relations to men and women's capacity to shape society and culture are extrinsic. Man in his early thought is the maker of history and woman the passive indices. True women could claim inclusion within the general concept of humanity but woe to any bits that did not fit the male model. Later as the Promethean struggle of the workers against capital consumes him, women are admitted as proletarians but otherwise left dangling. Although Marx was formally committed to the legal emancipation of women and to the right to work, his intellectual passion was not directed toward the relations between men and women, but toward class. When it came to the business of changing society it seemed women's interests were assumed to be safely included with those of men.

Two important books attempted to fill the obvious gaps in Marx's thinking about women's subordination and the means by which it would be overcome.

Woman and Socialism by Auguste Bebel, the leader of the German Social Democrats was published in 1878 and Frederick Engels' *The Origin of the Family, Private Property and the State* followed in 1884.

Like Marx, Bebel defended women's right to work. This was still a controversial issue and involved yet another battle with the French socialist Proudhon, who thought women's place was at home. Bebel pointed out that women's employment would improve workers' living standards and enable women to organize. He argued that legislation should curb the worst effects of exploitation.

Along with Mill, Bebel tended to think most married women would opt for full-time mothering, but he believed women should be able to choose. To make a real choice possible he proposed changes in domestic labor and daily social existence that could help women with household tasks.

Though influenced by Fourier, Bebel envisaged communitarian forms developing within daily life rather than separate communities. There were to be public halls for eating—to cut down on cooking— and leisure would be socialized with public concert halls, theatres, museums, reading rooms, libraries, halls for games, playgrounds, and green parks for the people. These were extensions of the initiatives of 1848 and the Commune and in a modified context were to be the demands of municipal socialism. Indeed in later editions of his work the social benefits of efficient domestic organization predominate over their emancipatory aspect for women.

Bebel wrote sympathetically about the struggles of middle-class women for emancipation and compared women's specific oppression to that of the proletariat. Class and gender thus rode in tandem.

Eleanor Marx, Marx's daughter, reviewed Bebel's book with her lover Edward Aveling in 1885. They agreed with Bebel that the oppression of women was comparable to class.

> Women are the creatures of an organised tyranny of men, as the workers are the creatures of an organised tyranny of the idlers.[4]

The review, which became a pamphlet called *The Woman Question*, argues for emancipation in the libertarian idiom of the revolutionary women in 1848 and the Commune. Women as a group are seen as an active force in the making of socialism. The struggle was against many aspects of oppression, including middle-class women's efforts to enter higher education and secure legal changes. Not only equal access to the public sphere but the challenge to the sexual double standard made by opponents of the Contagious Diseases Act and an end to the hypocrisy that denied women sexual pleasure and freedom are included. Bebel's work is placed in a tradition of writing on emancipation in the widest sense: Wollstonecraft, Shelley, Mill, Ibsen's *The Doll's House*, and Olive Schreiner's *The Story of an African Farm*.

Engels' *Origin of the Family, Private Property and the State* was not translated into English until the early 1900s. But his ideas were summarized by socialists in Europe and the United States. Engels took up an idea Marx had not had time to follow through, stressing that the key to the oppression of women was material and had to be seen historically. He said, "the production and reproduction of immediate life"[15] had to be taken together. By understanding how, as circumstances changed, women's existence altered, it would be possible to find the means of transforming women's position. Engels used the word "reproduction" in a double sense, meaning both the activities involved in enabling life to go on, producing food, clothing, and shelter, and the bearing and rearing of children, which he describes as "the production of human beings themselves, the propagation of the species."[6]

He believed that the forms of social organization including the relations of men and women in different epochs were decided by the stage of development of both production and the family. Women's subordination, Engels argued, had an economic basis. Here he differed from Bebel who had regarded it as partly a result of biology. Engels' interest in origins had a contemporary purpose in contesting the view that women's inferiority was immutable. He supported his theories by drawing on nineteenth-century anthropological work that argued there had been a golden era for women that had been overthrown by men's ownership of private property.

It is an argument that still causes controversy today and is impossible to settle for it is difficult to prove what kind of relationships existed between people in societies before written records exist. The assumption of the nineteenth-century evolutionary anthropologists, who influenced Engels, that there have been universal stages through which every culture passes is, however, an oversimplification, whereas the search for a single cause for women's subordination is historically unverifiable.

The Origin of Family, nonetheless, provided a means of conceptualizing the family as changing over time and in various societies. The liberal tradition of feminism, following Mill, tended to see the family as a given. Engels' writing suggested that the family might well be altered in a future society. Engels also presented procreation not just as a private, individual matter but as an economic force in society.

His economic and social perspective was a useful complement to the abstract assertions of an individual's right to self-ownership, which was the basis of both the feminist case for voluntary motherhood and the freethinkers' demands for birth control.

Unfortunately the two aspects—the individual's control over fertility and the implications of the social organization of child-bearing and rearing—were not integrated. In Engels' writing both the individual woman's needs and the collective action of women become submerged in his analysis of the evolution of the social and economic structures of reproduction and production.

Potentially Marx's theoretical approach could have been reworked to consider women as both active agents and within historically specific social relations. Instead Engels provided a valuable but restricted way of looking at women's predicament that left its own set of problems, which were to be especially acute for socialist women who struggled for birth control and abortion rights. Marxists were frequently to insist that socialism would make these unnecessary by creating sufficient wealth for all children to be wanted.

The Marxist approach to "the Woman Question" brought new insights, but it also cast off earlier understandings of reproductive rights. Similarly Engels' argument for involvement in production did not consider the extent to which male workers contributed to the inequalities of working class women within the workforce or examine the implications of male sexual and cultural control in society, though both of these had been part of the early socialists' critique of women's oppression.

More generally Engels' approach to theory in *The Origins* detached it from personal experience. He was inattentive to the details of everyday life that had illuminated his own earlier work on the condition of the working class. He also implicitly assumed a sexual division of labor. Biological difference between men and women was extended to imply that social differences in male and female activity in reproduction were also natural. He ignored data presented within his own circle that suggested women found some of these apparently "natural" divisions irksome; Marx's own daughters had their share of middle-class housewives' troubles.

In 1881 Jenny, a young mother of three and lacking sleep, wrote desperately to her sister Laura,

I feel wretchedly hopelessly nervous—ill at ease mentally and physically.[7]

A year later she complained,

I hear and see nothing but the baker and butcher and cheesemonger and greengrocer—I do not believe that even the dull routine of factory work is not more killing than the endless duties of the ménage. . . . Some women I know glory in this home drudgery—but we are not all made of the same stuff.[8]

Neither Marx nor Engels was responsible for the dogmatic reduction of their ideas to an infallible system that subsequent Marxists sometimes projected back on to them. They did, however, see themselves at the center of developments on the left and Engels maneuvered resolutely to control the women's movement in Marxist parties in Europe and the United States. He was by no means always successful. The discipline and imposition of lines and programs that Lenin achieved in the Third International was not yet possible. There was in fact a wide range of theories among Marxists about "The Woman Question" in different places in the late nineteenth century and early twentieth century. Leading figures changed their minds, whereas local groups often simply adopted their own policies. Theory and practice alike developed not in the abstract, but in relation to intrigues and factions that were part of general socialist politics in the period.

In France, for example, Marx's son-in-law Paul Lafargue did not accept the need for women to work in paid employment. Indeed he was critical of the elevation of labor in socialism. He stressed women's power as mothers and argued that women socialists should concentrate on creches, better maternity provision, and school dinners instead of demanding the right to work.

In contrast, the leader of the French Parti Ouvrier (POF), Jules Guesde, who was influenced by Marx, argued in the 1870s that woman's place should not be confined to the house but be "everywhere her activity can, and wishes to deploy itself."[19] By 1888 Guesde had altered his position and was regretting the injustice of industrialization in forcing women to work. The only woman ever to rise to a prominent position in the POF, Aline Valette, took the view that socialism should restore women to their proper place, the home.

However, POF's own practice in the Lille textile area was, in the early 1880s, able to combine class and gender and acknowledge women *both* as equals and as a group with a specific predicament. They addressed women as members of working class families, whose collective interests could be served by various forms of mutual aid, such as food cooperatives, savings, and insurance schemes, as well as securing municipal reforms by getting socialists elected locally. They also appealed to women as workers, whose class interests were shared with those of their male workers. However, recognizing that women suffered "a double slavery,"[10] and thus had a differing situation from men, they held women's meetings to discuss domestic and family problems and encourage women to participate in workplace organizing and political activity. Their combined approach to class and gender oppression proved extremely successful, though this was forgotten even a few years later when a socialist woman speaker appeared and bemoaned the conservatism of women.

The argument about how women should be organized tended to polarize around attitudes to women in the workforce. In Germany, Clara Zetkin believed firmly in women's right to work. Not only was it a means by which women achieved economic independence, they could, through organization, improve their conditions and develop confidence. In 1889 she argued that women did not want to separate their cause from male workers by claiming they had different needs. Unlike Bebel she took an egalitarian position. There should be no "special formulas" and "no other protection than that which labour demands in general against capital."[11]

By 1896 she had shifted from this stance and argued for protective legislation and the abolition of domestic production. She also said working-class women had an important role in improving family life and improving the family in "proletarian struggle."[12]

This was partly a pragmatic response to the problems of organizing

German working class women, many of whom were housewives. There was also intensive international pressure for protective legislation from Engels who, in 1891 persuaded her to change her views. In the early 1890s Engels was busy getting Eleanor Marx, Laura Lafargue, and Louise Kautsky to "straighten out"[13] the socialist women's movement in Austria on protective legislation, which became a kind of litmus test in the Marxists' arguments with "bourgeois feminism."[14]

In contrast to her tone in the 1885 review of Bebel, Eleanor Marx, by the early 1890s, was scathing about the egalitarian position of the "bourgeois" feminist Milicent Fawcett who opposed protective legislation. Interestingly, she is equally scornful about an Anarchist woman Edith Lupton, who was trying to organize laundresses into a cooperative, as an alternative to demanding the extension of protective legislation by the state.

Ostensibly the advocacy of protective legislation was consistent with Marx's criticism of abstract arguments of equal rights, which ignored unequal starting points, though it conflicted with his advocacy of universal emancipation for the working class and his suspicion of claims to particularity.

It marked a shift in the thinking of the left. The state was to complement the somewhat fragile organization of working women and might be used as a means of banning the sweated labor of home workers. The organized female proletariat, for both Eleanor Marx and Clara Zetkin, were defined as factory workers, even though the majority of actual women workers were not included in this category. In contrast, the Austrian women Social Democrats were persistently pragmatic and heterodox, extending the concept of the proletariat to include domestic servants, who they organized into an association that merged with homeworkers in the early 1900s.

Not only was an argument taking shape about the role of the state in relation to women and with it a particular definition of the working class, the Marxists were involved in a furious conflict with the anarchists over the campaign for the eight hour day. The anarchists were against trying to influence the state and change laws. The Marxist ferocity over protective legislation partly derived from the wider conflict.

There was also a sectarian desire to control the socialist women's movement by detaching it from feminism. Engels' denunciations of American feminists who had merely said working class women should decide whether protective legislation was in their interests sparked off a general attack on any alliance between socialist women and feminist movements. His informant on the "drivel of the swell mob ladies"[15] was none other than Victoria Woodhull's old opponent, Sorge.

The separation suited Clara Zetkin in Germany where the illegality of socialist organizing and the conservatism of the feminists had created a rift. But in many other countries socialist women supported feminist demands and even in Germany there was to be a continuing connection between some feminists and socialists.

Certainly conflicts of interest arose between working-class and middle-class women. In France, for example, at a feminist congress in 1900, the delegates split on the issue of a minimum wage for domestic servants, which would have hurt the pockets of the bourgeoisie. In Russia there were extreme differences in political perspective.

There were nonetheless possibilities for alliances between feminists and socialists, for many of their demands converged. Consequently Engels' and Zetkin's strategy caused much needless acrimony, especially in countries such as the United States and Britain, where the feminist movements were larger and included many socialist women. In France the socialist Madeleine Pelletier tried to oppose the separation but it was supported by Louise Saumonau, who denied that problems of gender could divide workers.

In Germany, however, the policy of separation did secure a preeminent position for the women Social Democrats, who became the most important force in the suffrage campaign.

Within the Social Democratic Party, Clara Zetkin fought resolutely against male authoritarianism and patronage. This was not just a matter of political attitudes but of personal behavior. There was no Marxist theory about this. However, relations between men and women were raised by women who complained men joked about "the women's question"[16] or refused to let women take part in the movement.

When Adelheid Popp, a working-class woman who was a leader

of the Austrian Social Democratic women, spent her first day at the offices of the newspaper *Arbeiter-innen-Zeitung,* it was a freezing day. She was keen to show the men she could make a good fire, but she held back, because she knew she would be seen as a female helper.

Women in the British Social Democratic Federation wrote to the party's newspaper *Justice* complaining that men sneered and patronized women when they spoke at meetings. Letters also appeared demanding that socialist men should do more housework, cook Sunday dinners, and mind babies.

In September 1893 "Hopeful" objected to the male definition of culture that was presented by the use of masculine forms to describe humanity in general. "Women feel repelled at the continual sole use of the masculine nouns and pronouns."[17]

An alternative culture emerged informally in assumptions and advice about how a socialist woman should behave. Adelheid Popp, for example, told young socialist women that they should speak up for their opinions in marriage, not regard themselves only as wives, maintain their dignity with employers and male workers, and not bother with frippery such as pierced ears. Marx, of course, had left no clear directions on pierced ears or indeed on personal power in relations between the sexes.

There was persistent confusion over sexuality. Engels had said monogamy would prevail under socialism. However, the here and now was rather more muddled. Unlike the anarchists, the Marxists were officially respectable, but Engels had lived in two free unions; Marx had had an illegitimate child, Freddy Demuth, and Eleanor lived in a free union with Edward Aveling and finally committed suicide when he secretly married. Clara Zetkin also lived in a free union, but took the name of her lover, Ossipand, then lived with, and later married, a man who was 18 years her junior. In Britain, the Social Democratic Federation found itself rocked by a free love battle in 1892, when Edith Lanchester, a middle-class woman, formed a free union with an Irish railway clerk, James Sullivan, and her family tried to get her certified as insane. Eleanor Marx, along with Herbert Burrows, who had helped organize the match girls with Annie Besant, and E. Belfort Bax (who was later to clash with Dora Montefiore on suffrage) organized a public protest and Edith Lanchester was able to live with her lover; their daughter Elsa Lanchester became a well-known actress.

There was never an easy consistency in sexual politics between theory and practice. Nor was there always a clear correlation between political radicalism and openness to sexual radicalism. Thus the Austrian Social Democratic women were cautious on the suffrage campaign led by Zetkin, but there was much discussion of women's health, population, and birth control in Vienna in the early 1900s. Though the Austrian socialists did not include abortion in their program, in 1918 the first socialist government in Austria was to introduce abortion.

Very few socialists in the 1890s were prepared to defend homosexuality, but when Oscar Wilde was arrested in 1895, the German Social Democrat Eduard Bernstein defended him in the Marxist journal *Die Neue Zeit*.

> Although the subject of sex life might seem of low priority for the economic and political struggle of the Social Democracy, this nevertheless does not mean it is not obligatory to find a standard based on a scientific approach to knowledge rather than on more or less arbitrary moral concepts.[18]

Three years later Bebel was a major supporter in the Reichstag of a petition launched by Magnus Hirschfeld and the Scientific Humanitarian Committee to make homosexual relations between consenting adults over 16 no longer a criminal offence.

A "scientific" approach to sexuality was to be one of Marxism's most perplexing quests in the twentieth century, and one that indicated some fundamental dilemmas. Buried amidst all the disagreements were profound ambiguities about whether Marxism should be a total system of knowledge, how to link human action and social analysis, how to recognize existing material reality, and how to find the means by which it could be transcended to create 'what might be.'

17

ANARCHISM AND REBEL WOMEN

Lizzie Swank arrived in Chicago in the late 1870s and supported herself by sewing. She joined the union, the Knights of Labor, where she made friends with a black woman in her local named Lucy Parsons. They both decided working women's interests were best served by the class struggle of workers rather than by legal reforms supported by middle-class women. At a workers' demonstration for the eight hour day in 1886 a policeman was killed and Lucy Parsons' husband, Albert, was one of the men accused of murdering him. He and four others were executed despite international protest the following year.

Emma Goldman, a young Russian Jewish immigrant in the United

States, was deeply disturbed by the executions. A self-taught factory worker, she was to become one of the best known anarchist women agitators and speakers. Emma Goldman's lectures and writings struggle with the polarities of reform and revolution, individualism and collectivism, personal expression and political dedication.

Emma Goldman saw the liberation of women as inseparable from creating a means by which individuality and community could be reconnected. Anarchists were divided between those who stressed the assertion of individual will and those who saw anarchism as a development of mutuality. Emma Goldman was able to absorb ideas of self-development and the collectivist anarchist-communism of Alexander Berkman, who was for many years her lover and companion.

She believed it was important to acknowledge both. For her the essential problem was

> how to be one's self and yet in oneness with others, to feel deeply with all human beings and still retain one's own characteristic qualities.[1]

This was the key for women's liberation, but it applied equally to men; it was a general political project.

Many anarchist women thought the emancipation of women was simply integral to anarchism's rejection of all authority and hierarchy though Emma Goldman was critical of the contemporary feminist movement, she did write and speak specifically on women. Some anarchists rejected all immediate changes as "palliatives"; Emma Goldman did not think all reforms should be dismissed, but she was critical of the emphasis in the women's movements on suffrage. This argument was not new. Louise Michel, the "Red Virgin" who had spent many years in exile for her role in the French commune, supported some feminist demands but would not join the suffrage movement. In 1888 she argued,

> we must not allow ourselves to be duped by the false promises of the suffrage, it is a mirage.[2]

Parliamentary democracy gave workers only the illusion of participating in politics. Instead of representative democracy, Emma Goldman advocated collective direct action in politics and society as well as at work. Some anarchists tended to view "the masses" as hopelessly inert, victims of an overwhelming oppression, only to be roused by heroic and sacrificial action on the part of small groups of conspirators. In opposition to this, Emma Goldman thought that through the new consciousness gained from acting and organizing people would create a democratic society. This direct democracy was the solution for women as well as men.

Within anarchism there was a strong current of self-denial. An important influence was the example of Russian revolutionaries in the last quarter of the nineteenth century. Because they faced the Tsars' absolute power and the lack of any means of legal agitation, they had despaired of rousing the peasantry and tried to overthrow the state by assassination. Women had abandoned experiments in sexual emancipation, their own intellectual development, even their children, to join small revolutionary bands. They were to face death and imprisonment as equals.

When Vera Figner heard that her student friends from Zurich were all in prison in 1875 for propaganda, she was initially torn between her desire to continue her studies and the need to take up her companions' work in Russia. She decided to return and work in the revolutionary underground, declaring,

'Social concerns had gained ascendence over personal ones for good.'[3]

Louise Michel's life was similarly dedicated to the "cause," presenting a model of asceticism. In contrast, Emma Goldman, in the very different circumstances of New York during the 1900s, tried to connect the personal expression of women's rebellion with the transformation of society. Greenwich Village, before World War I, was a center of bohemian and radical dissent. Novelists and journalists wrote about women who rejected marriage and sought sexual emancipation. Their inspiration came from Nietzsche, Sorel, Ibsen, and Edward Carpenter. Dynamic human action was the key to change; the internal realization of the individual was as crucial as the collective movement against oppression. Psychoanalysis, the recognition of sexuality as a force, the questioning of monogamy, the reorganization of domestic life and child-care, and the changing of masculine and feminine identities were all part of this rebellion.

Emma Goldman spoke out bravely for women's sexual freedom, struggling to unite sensuality and autonomy. Passionate and free, she appeared to demonstrate her views; her own life was defiantly unconventional. But inevitably there were strains within this attempt to overcome all boundaries and taboos. She emphasized her own independence in her public writing, but her private correspondence, especially as she grew older, revealed a more vulnerable, dependent self.

Her delineation of sexual emancipation had its own limits in relation to erotic feelings between women. It was very difficult in this period for "lesbian" women to assert their sexual desires and feelings. Indeed the word "lesbian" belongs to a later period. Lesbian sexuality was portrayed in terms of an outcast romantic decadence or enclosed in the intimacies of female friendship in much nineteenth-century discourse. Emma Goldman was overtly supportive of lesbian women's rights, but personally ambiguous about lesbian women. The contemporary early twentieth-century discourse of sexual emancipation focused on heterosexuality. Lesbian sexuality was at best marginal and at worst depicted as an aberration.

There were several different approaches towards women's heterosexuality in Goldman's writing. She expressed the free lovers' concern with control. Women's independence

must come from and through herself. First, by asserting herself as a personality and not as a sex commodity. Second, by refusing the right to anyone over her body; by refusing to be a servant to God, the state and society, the husband, the family etc; by making her life simpler, but deeper and richer.[4]

On the other hand she was determined to assert the importance of sexual feeling. Wryly, in a letter to Frank Harris in 1924, she remembered a clash with the Russian anarchist Peter Kropotkin in London before World War I. Kropotkin said women would be free when they were equal intellectually to men. The 34-year-old Goldman challenged this view.

> All right dear comrade when I have reached your age, the sex question may no longer be of importance to me. But it is *now*, and it is a tremendous factor for thousands, millions even of young people. Peter stopped short, an amused smile lighting up his kindly face. "Funny, I didn't think of that", he replied. "Perhaps you are right after all."[5]

Kropotkin was 58 at the time, Goldman's age when she wrote to Harris. In 1924 she could see the irony.

Goldman was by no means unique in her conviction that the "sex question" could not be ignored. Many women in the 1900s argued sexual relations had to change—though frequently less optimistically than Goldman. Emancipation and eroticism were uneasy companions.

Lou Andreas-Salomé, a writer who knew Nietszche, Wedekind, Rilke, and Freud, returned again and again to the themes of the force of sexuality and women's autonomy. In 1900 she published "Thoughts on the Problem of Love" in the periodical *Neue Deutsche Rundschau* and developed her ideas 12 years later in her book *Eroticism*. She was to be drawn toward psychoanalysis and became close to Freud.

She believed the surrender of sexual union had differing meanings for men and women. Sexual love was a crucial aspect of human creativity, but it also endangered women's freedom. Surrender was thus invested with great significance, but was to be simply an erotic moment. The self was realized and rediscovered—Dionysian ecstasy required a quick get away.

> People who are not faithful do not necessarily desert one person for another, but are simply driven home to themselves and only then make their way back to mankind again, as though from a free universe.[6]

Infidelity for a higher purpose was no betrayal.

> A woman has no other choice than to be unfaithful or to be only half herself.[7]

So as not to be "struck and shattered by one lightning bolt"[8] she had to "renew herself again and again."[9]

Tactical asceticism was another alternative. Madeline Pelletier, the French socialist feminist, said in 1908 that she had decided to remain celibate,

> because under present conditions sexual relations are a source of debasement for the married woman and of scorn for the unmarried.[10]

She did not recommend this as an ideal solution. "It is only the consequence of the unjust situation in which women find themselves."[11]

There was a strand in feminism that far from seeing the assertion of sexual desire among women toward men as liberating believed that the oppression of women was bound up with sexuality. Frances Swiney, a British feminist, agreed with Goldman's emphasis on control.

> Men have sought in women only a body. They have possessed that body.[12]

Like some of the free lovers, she thought the answer was to raise "sex relations from the physical to the spiritual plane."[13]

Unconvinced that this transcendence would be taken up on the Lower East Side, Goldman in contrast, believed, as did the French anarchists led by Paul Robin, that a womans' right to control her own body was best defended by access to birth control. Sexual pleasure was impossible without real choice on fertility. She went to a conference in 1900 and smuggled contraceptives back with her when she returned.

Advocates of birth control were called neo-Malthusians, because in the eighteenth century an economist, Malthus, had argued that the only way to prevent poverty was by reducing population through the sexual restraint of the poor. Marx and Engels had been very critical of Malthus' ideas, and many socialists continued to oppose birth control on the grounds that redistribution of wealth would mean that the working class could have as many children as they wanted.

By the 1900s some socialist women were questioning this attitude;

pointing out that birth control could help working-class families reduce the suffering caused by poverty and enable women to gain more control over their lives. In the Socialist Party in the United States Annette Konikow, a doctor, wrote and spoke in support of birth control. The French Anarchists and a minority among the socialists were arguing for birth control with the slogan "La Maternité est Libre." In 1911 Madame Pelletier's pamphlet *L'émancipation sexuelle* combined feminist, anarchist, and neo-Malthusian assumptions in arguing that the individual woman and man had an absolute right to control her or his own fertility. Sex and reproduction were not inevitably linked; sexuality for men was already separate from "reproductive intent."[14] Contraception and abortion were necessary if women were to enjoy sexual pleasure; along with state support for unmarried mothers, so women could freely choose maternity.

In the United States the Comstock law still made it illegal to send "obscene" material through the post. Putting her theory of direct action into practice, Emma Goldman, with her lover Ben Reitman, decided to challenge the law by distributing a small pamphlet called *Why and How the Poor Should Not Have Children*. It showed the reader how to make home made contraceptives—a "recipe" for suppositaries, how to use a cotton ball dipped in borated vascline, and a douche. Goldman and Reitman went to prison for this "propaganda by deed" amid a blaze of publicity. A lesbian writer, Margaret Anderson, was impressed, declaring in the *Little Review Anthology*

> In 1916 Emma Goldman was sent to prison for advocating that "women need not always keep their mouths shut and their wombs open."[15]

Margaret Sanger, a young nurse in the Socialist Party, was also interested in Goldman's and Reitman's birth control propaganda. She knew of the desperation with which New York working-class women faced unwanted pregnancies. In 1912 she was writing a series of articles in the Socialist Party paper on sex and reproduction under the heading "What Every Girl Should Know." The following year she visited Paris, where she made contact with the French anarchists and syndicalists.

Already drawn toward the anarcho-syndicalist Industrial Workers of the World (IWW or "Wobblies"), when she returned to the States she published an anarchist feminist paper *The Woman Rebel*. "Bourgeois" feminism was denounced under the Anarchist masthead, "No God No Masters." Sanger discovered that there was an American history of birth control among utopian socialists, radical free lovers, spiritualists, and theosophists.

"Workers' Control" as a slogan was in the air, and she transposed the IWW's Anarcho-Syndicalist emphasis on control in production to reproduction, coining the phrase "birth control." She also took direct action against the law by giving advice on birth control and suggesting an abortifacient.

> The working class can take direct action by refusing to supply the market with children to be exploited, by refusing to populate the earth with slaves.[16]

When her case came to trial she decided to flee to England, where she inspired the anarchist Rose Witcop and the socialist Stella Browne. However, Havelock Ellis, the sex psychologist, and some members of the Neo-Malthusian League convinced her the cause of birth control would be more likely to succeed if it was not associated with the left. Oblivious, Socialist Party groups and members of the IWW had embarked on a campaign for birth control in her absence.

In Britain, Anarchist women were also opposed to the vote and rejected "bourgeois" feminism. Lilian Wolfe, for example, left the suffrage movement, disillusioned with the attempt to work through parliament and helped to produce an anarchist paper *The Voice of Labour*. Rose Witcop from the Jewish anarchist movement in the East End of London was connected with *The Voice of Labour* and read Sanger's *The Woman Rebel*. She regarded the demand for "votes for women" as simply agreeing to be ruled by legislation. Anarchist women saw the suffrage movement as an illusion and argued for direct democracy at work and in personal life. Rose Witcop believed, as did other anarchist women, that the state should have no control over people's lives. Opposed to marriage, she lived in a free union with an anarchist-communist Guy Aldred and bore him a son. Increasingly interested in how motherhood could be free, she met Margaret Sanger and spoke with her on birth control. In 1920 she was to publish Sanger's "What Every Girl Should Know," "What Every Mother Should Tell," and "Family Limitation."

Another critic of suffrage as the key to emancipation, Elizabeth Gurley Flynn had spoken with Sanger and with Emmeline Pankhurst's daughter Sylvia at a meeting supporting laundry workers. Sanger and Flynn had then worked together during the 1912 Lawrence textile strike in Massachusetts where the slogan was "Bread and Roses." Mobilization not only overcame the divisions of many differing nationalities among the workers, it also reached out to the community by organizing wives and providing support for the children.

During one of the strike meetings Carlo Tresca, the Italian anarchist labor organizer, had said shorter hours would mean workers could have more babies. Elizabeth Gurley Flynn disagreed. She believed working-class women needed birth control.

Elizabeth Gurley Flynn's parents were socialists. Her father was an Irish republican and her mother was interested in women's rights. As a young woman she read eagerly Mary Wollstonecroft, Bebel, Engels, Kropotkin, and Morris' *News from Nowhere;* she admired Emma Goldman. She was influenced by the Irish writer and organizer James Connolly, a friend of her family's, and joined the anarcho-syndicalist IWW or "Wobblies."

Anarcho-syndicalists stressed action at the workplace. The Wobblies were predominantly male workers, many of them itinerants traveling from town to town and living rough in the search for work. Though some members of the IWW had supported birth control, many men thought women held men back from the Wobbly cause and did not spend much time reflecting on women's emancipation. But they loved and revered Elizabeth Gurley Flynn as an individual exception. She repeatedly confronted their arguments that women were backward and difficult to organize. She told them the IWW should find special ways of organizing women rather than assuming their situation was always the same as men's.

Jane Street, a Colorado domestic worker in the IWW did just that. She recruited maids to a union by putting employment advertisements in a newspaper and collecting information about jobs. By becoming an informal employment agency, she propagandized the maids to join the IWW.

For Anarcho-Syndicalists, workers' control was the means of emancipating workers. They concentrated on production and the economy. Flynn believed this was true for women as well as men, "political emancipation is impossible as long as there is economic slavery."[17] But she realized this was not all women needed. Although dismissive of the suffrage, she recognized the importance of control over fertility for women and was aware that women needed changes in domestic work and life.

Flynn, whose own son was raised by her mother, gravitated toward the strategy of Charlotte Perkins Gilman. Technology and mass production were to modernize domesticity.

> The home of the future will eliminate the odd jobs that reduce it to a cluttered workshop today and electricity free the woman's hand from methods entirely antiquated in an era of machinery.[18]

She differed here from the approach of some anarchists including Louise Michel, who on the lines of Morris' *News from Nowhere* wanted to restore men and women to the home and elevate housework as a skilled craft. In Britain, Lily Gair Wilkinson in her pamphlet *Women's Freedom* in the 1900s opposed feminists who argued for entry into male employment. Emancipation was not to be found by women gaining access to the professions, but in the creation of a "free communal life."[19] Men should also withdraw from such "abnormal occupations"[20] as lawyers "returning to home and garden and field as the true sphere of human life."[21]

Both Flynn, the modernizer, and Wilkinson, the reviver of domestic industry, united however on their castigation of bourgeois feminists. There could be no united sisterhood. Class cut across women's interests. In practice, however, Flynn, like Sylvia Pankhurst, who was also influenced by anarcho-syndicalism, formed links with middle-class feminists to support working women's strikes and campaigns. In the United States the left's response to feminism was deeply affected by the syndicalist rejection of the state. Women in the Socialist Party campaigning for the vote thus often found the right wing of the Party more sympathetic to the suffrage cause; the left supported economic organization and birth control.

The issue of how to relate to the suffrage movement revealed anarchist and anarcho-syndicalist difficulties not only about the state, but on how to bridge the gulf between present and future. Madeline Pelletier broke with syndicalism because of this opposition to women's suffrage.

Anarchism's claim to encompass all aspects of freedom made it peculiarly difficult for women to raise specific inequalities. Lilian Wolfe, for example, worked all her life for the anarchist cause, resisting World War I, living in a community at Whiteways, doing active organizational work, but always in the background.

The rhetoric of freedom disguised an implicit division of spheres in which men prevailed both culturally and theoretically. For example, in Europe, anarchist male culture was based in the cafe's. So women with families were implicitly excluded. In Catholic countries their world revolved around the church, which men denounced as reactionary, without thinking often of the practical needs it served for women and seeking to develop alternatives.

Also anarchist appeals for women to defy convention ignored the realities of the consequences for women. Women who had children in free unions, like Rose Witcop and Lilian Wolfe, faced much greater difficulties than men because of both the economic situation of women and sexual attitudes.

The focus on control over production in anarcho-syndicalism emphasized the dichotomy that had appeared among Marxists. Material life fused with the economic, which came to imply production. Consequently control of the workplace was presented as the means to transform society. This made it seem that women were apart from material existence, and unless they worked for wages had only a supporting role in social change. Hélène Brion, like Madeline Pelletier, a French socialist feminist who inclined to the syndicalist left before World War I, criticized this concentration on work in *La Voie Féministe*. She argued that syndicalism dismissed the oppression of working class women in the family and ignored innumerable forms of sexual and cultural oppression that had a long history of resistance. She reminded them of the utopian socialists Flora Tristan and Jeanne Deroin, the Anarchist-Communist Louise Michel, and the feminist Hubertine Auclert. There was the social purity work of Josephine Butler and Lady Stanton, Elizabeth Garrett's struggle to become a doctor, and the campaigns against widow burning in India and foot binding in China. She observed that many syndicalists retained Proudhon's limited conception of woman as either 'housewife or courtesan.'[22]

A theoretical fragmentation had arisen by the early twentieth century in which an encompassing vision of resistance against oppression, self-emancipation, and social emancipation was difficult. The dynamic faith in action that infused anarchism and syndicalism, as well as some strands of feminism had connected sexual control with women's autonomy internationally. For example, Hiratsuka Raicho's feminist journal in Japan translated Emma Goldman before World War I. But a dualism emerges by which male workers take control over production and women control reproduction. This preoccupation with control touched only the surface of the problem of how women were to redefine erotic union and autonomy.

History is not a theoretically tidy affair. Anarcho-syndicalists and militant suffrage campaigners had divergent aims but converged in their use of direct action: the first for revolution and the second for constitutional reform. The Wobblies thought voting was a waste of time, but they hailed the bravery of the British members of the Women's Social and Political Union when they attacked property and went on hunger strike in prison. In 1911 the Wobbly paper *Solidarity* declared, "They were just like the IWW boys."[23]

Sylvia Pankhurst might have been pleased by this accolade. Undoubtedly, however, her mother, Emmeline, and sister, Christabel, would have felt this was praise they could do without.

IV

POLITICAL POWER: REFORM AND REVOLUTION

THEMES FOR DISCUSSION

* What political representation meant for women.
* The circumstances in which women have taken direct action.
* Is "women's rights" a western idea?
* How has women's emancipation been linked to the transformation of society?
* The practical difficulties that women have encountered in processes of social transformation.

18

THE SUFFRAGE: PATRIOTS
AND INTERNATIONALISTS

In the autumn of 1905 members of the British Women's Social and Political Union (WSPU) were arrested for heckling a prominent liberal Sir Edward Grey at a meeting in Manchester. They wanted to know what the attitudes of a future Liberal government would be to women's suffrage. The new organization had been formed by Emmeline Pankhurst out of the Independent Labour Party (ILP) in 1903. The women who were arrested argued, in the tradition of liberalism, that democratic government must rest on the consent of the governed. Until they got the vote on the same terms as men they would withhold their consent by disturbing the peace. These had been precisely the tactics of both the middle-class and working class agitation for the male franchise in the nineteenth century.

Though the militancy of the "suffragettes," as the Conservative newspaper *The Daily Mail* named them, marked a break with the earlier campaign for women's suffrage, there were many continuities. Militant suffragettes, like the law abiding constitutional suffragists led by Milicent Fawcett, argued for the suffrage in terms of liberal freedom and justice. The assertion of suffrage as a right was frequently bolstered by social liberalism's emphasis on citizenship. Women's duty was to serve "the race," humanity, or the state. Thus women should be fully integrated in the public sphere. The theme of women as moral redeemers resurfaced again both among militants and constitutionalists. The militant wing of the movement, however, brought to the fore those strands of social purity feminism that had emphasized antagonism between men and women and women's superiority to men.

Rebecca West observed that Emmeline Pankhurst's approach was based on the premise

> that sex antagonism was so strong among men that it produced an attitude which, if it were provoked to candid expression, would make every self respecting woman want to fight it.[1]

The suffragettes' strategy certainly revealed derision, contempt, and hostility. The militants' direct action and civil disobedience were met with harsher and harsher measures. Repeated imprisonment and violent forced feeding left many suffering from permanent ill health. Their courage and sacrifice inspired women not only in Britain but internationally. On the other hand militancy also antagonized many women. Nor were men inevitably opponents. Some organized in support of women's suffrage; men also went to prison and one man died as a result of a hunger strike.

The militants were always a minority. The old guard around Milicent Fawcett retained mass support for legal, constitutional forms of organizing and could mobilize huge demonstrations.

In 1907 conflict arose in the Women's Social and Political Union when Charlotte Despard, along with other members, wanted a constitution. They split and formed the Women's Freedom League. The schism was partly caused by opposing visions of how to organize. For Christabel the WSPU should be a disciplined army not an exercise in democracy. Charlotte Despard, who was a socialist, was also unhappy about Emmeline and Christabel's move away from the labor movement.

The WSPU presented labor women with a dilemma. Some working-class socialist women believed in constitutional tactics. Others such as Hannah Mitchell supported militancy but felt betrayed by Emmeline and Christabel's instrumental view of the organization as overriding all individual needs. Also although she was prepared to castigate the attitudes of some socialist men she resented the high-handed treatment of male supporters by the WSPU.

Some constitutionalists as well as militants focused on the unity between women in opposition to men. Others, such as the founder of the constitutionalist "Common Cause," Helena Swanwick, saw the vote simply as a necessary part of the liberation of human beings.

Labor women had to choose between adult suffrage, which the socialists advocated, and women's suffrage, which would have meant the vote for propertied women. Ada Nield Chew decided that adult suffrage would be of more benefit to the working class. But Selina Cooper decided tactically that the more limited demand of votes on the same terms as men was more effective.

Some socialist women found themselves as exasperated by the Labour Party as they were with the Liberals.

> Just as some men go to the public-house and come home to beat their wives, so the Labour Party goes to talk to Mr. Asquith and comes home to beat its principles.[2]

wrote the young socialist Rebecca West, who sympathized with syndicalist criticism of the new parliamentary Labour Party in *The Clarion* in 1912.

Isabella Ford, however, still struggled to maintain a labor suffrage alliance. Not only was it difficult to get socialists to make votes for women a priority, there were very different political conceptions within the suffrage movement about the significance of the demand for the franchise. The escalation of militancy polarized the conflict, making the suffrage appear as an issue that should override all differences and defer all other struggles. The WSPU came increasingly to regard men and women as irreconcilable and presented enfranchisement as a separatist, women-only movement.

However, the vote also became the focus for many hopes of economic and social reform, which required alliances with men. The campaign against sweated women's work, along with the panic against unhealthy motherhood meant that some liberal feminists began to argue for state intervention to fix a minimum living wage and take up demands for child benefits, or Mothers Pensions as they were called, so poor mothers would not be forced to do sweated work. They also helped women workers to organize in unions.

World War I brought greater state intervention in industry. Lloyd George was willing to grant workers welfare in the interests of the war effort. The women's trade union leader Mary MacArthur tried to improve the conditions in industry by working with the wartime government. The needs of the wartime state made it possible to secure reforms that would have been impossible in peace time. This connection between the state and welfare had an important influence on the Labour Party, which was part of the coalition government. After the war many Labour Party women continued to regard the state as the means of improving working-class women's lives. By electing Labour, the state could be adapted to serve workers. Opponents of the war were more suspicious of the state and advocated a combination of direct action and mobilization from below.

In 1913 Emmeline and Christabel Pankhurst had expelled Sylvia Pankhurst, who had continued to be a socialist, from the WSPU. They disliked her sympathy with revolutionary syndicalists and her alliance with labor organizations and with men. Her group, the East London Federation of Suffragettes, continued to work in the East End for a range of causes including equal pay. During the war she campaigned against the harassment of single working-class women in the street by the police and defended the rights of unsupported mothers in her paper *The Workers' Dreadnought*.

She adapted ideas of self-help from Jane Addams' Hull House. A cooperative toy factory was started to provide work and a creche set up based on theories of education through play. The "Gunmakers Arms" was converted into "The Mothers Arms," a health clinic for mothers and babies.

Rents and prices soared in the war and Sylvia Pankhurst supported direct action by encouraging families to occupy empty houses. In 1917, she greeted the Russian Revolution and tried to work out how the direct democracy of workers' councils (soviets) could apply to community life as well.

Housing was also an important question in Glasgow, where the Women's Housing Association led by ILP feminists Agnes Dollan and Helen Crawfurd, influenced by both the Wobblies and the WSPU, organized a mass strike of tenants that coincided with the threat of industrial action and forced the government to peg rents.

The movement for the vote thus stimulated a whole series of campaigns and demands that were partly about women's relations to men but also about women's position more generally in society. Gender was seen as interconnecting with class and women's needs were recognized as arising from a web of oppressive social relationships.

In contrast, by 1913, Christabel Pankhurst was arguing not only for women to unite against men in the struggle for the vote, but was becoming convinced that all aspects of women's relation to men were destructive. Because men saw women only as sexual beings and the bearers of children women were forced to submit to "sex slavery."[3] Venereal disease, incest, child abuse, and prostitution were the result. Women's struggle for the suffrage was the solution. Women again enter as redeemers.

It is the realisation that the moral purity and physical health of the race depend upon votes for women.[4]

Moreover male opposition to the suffrage was, at root, a defence of "sexual vice."[5] Men were afraid that

if women are to become politically free they will become spiritually strong
and economically independent, and thus they will not any longer give or
sell themselves to be the playthings of men.[6]

Male critics of the suffrage movement certainly argued that it made
women "masculine" (characteristics they also naively connected to
lesbianism.) They were not, however, alone in this assumption. When
Rebecca West was selling the WSPU paper, *Votes for Women* in Harro-
gate, a spa in Yorkshire, she and her sisters offered a copy

> to a dear old lady in rustling black silk and widow's bonnet. With superb
> vigour she raised her umbrella and brought it down on my sister's head,
> remarking: "Thank God I am a womanly woman."[7]

Rebecca West objected to the view that women were simply passive victims of male sexuality. She thought Christabel Pankhurst had
forced people to face up to venereal disease but did not see its spread
as being only the responsibility of men. She argued that the social
purity line,

> blamed the impurity of men for a state of affairs to which the impurity
> of woman and the social system were contributing causes.[8]

Rebecca West gravitated to the rebellious group around *The Free
Woman,* a journal asserting women's diverse sexual needs which published articles on psychology, communal living, free love, and art. It
sought to widen feminist debate beyond the vote. West made fun of
feminist puritanism and detested the view that women were to cleanse
the world of sin whether it came from separatists or socialists like the
Labour woman Ethl Snowden. She said '*The Free Woman*',

> smashed the romantic pretence that women had as a birth-right the gift of
> perfect adaption; that they were in a bland state of desireless contentment
> which, when they were beautiful, reminded the onlooker of goddesses,
> and when they were plain were more apt to remind them of cabbage.[9]

Among the rank and file of the suffrage movement, there was a personal culture that rebelled against conventions of all kinds in the search for autonomy. Moral purity was just one manifestation of a feminist life-style. In Derby WSPU members were interested in spiritualism, health food, and syndicalism, for example. They cut their hair short, had abortions, and believed in sexual freedom. The "collection *Dear Girl*[10] preserves the diaries and letters of two lower middle-class Methodists and members of the Women's Freedom League, in Manor Park and Walthamstow, London, Ruth Slate and Eva Slawson; they contain debates on birth control, the "sex question," Syndicalism, Christianity, and pacifism. Eva formed a passionate friendship with Minna, who she met at Walthamstow Chapel. It was not sexual, nor was it an ordinary friendship. They felt they had to create a new language for their feelings.

The suffrage movement had a profound impact on women's aspirations and relationships. The bonds of support that developed through personal networks contributed to an opposing culture in which it seemed women were finding new ways of being.

In other countries militancy was never as extensively adopted as in Britain. Though in the United States Harriet Stanton Blatch's Equality League of Self Supporting Women and Alice Paul's National Women's Party broke with the cautious tactics of the National American Woman Suffrage Association with demonstrations and direct action. In France, Madeleine Pelletier ceremoniously smashed a window and was arrested. However, in Germany, lack of civil rights meant that even peaceful demonstrations by women in the socialist SPD on International Women's Day between 1911 and 1914 were extremely daring and frequently were broken up by the police.

In 1907 Clara Zetkin and the German socialists led the demand for women's suffrage at the Socialist Women's International in Stuttgart. The Belgians, Austrians, and French had agreed to hold back until adult male suffrage was won. An indignant Zetkin was able to win the vote for universal suffrage at the conference but could never ensure it would be put into practice by the Social Democrats internationally.

The Stuttgart conference's directive not to work with bourgeois feminists was also problematic. In the United States, as the feminist movement became more militant and radical, socialist women increasingly gravitated to the suffrage groups—among them was Florence Kelley who had worked at Hull House.

The argument about whether women had unified interests as a group or whether class divided women arose in many differing political contexts. In the United States Kate Richards O'Hare, a prominent socialist writer and speaker, took the position that equal suffrage was not only a "Sex Right"[11] but a "Class Right".[12] In Australia, where by 1903 white women could vote in national elections but not in all states, a conflict arose in Victoria about whether women should support a program that was aimed exclusively at women or vote for parties. Lilian Locke, a Labour Party woman, thought class issues came first; after Labour was elected women's position would improve.

The relation of class and gender was not the only dilemma that troubled the unity of sisterhood. In 1913, when a huge suffrage march was planned in Washington, white suffragists told Ida Wells-Barnett and the Alpha Suffrage Club that they had to march at the back so they would not offend the southern women. Ida Wells-Barnett took personal direct action. When the march was due to start she could not be found; once it had begun she reappeared and slipped into place alongside two white women.

As the suffrage movement gained strength, the National Association of Colored Women became increasingly concerned that black women in the south would be excluded. Alice Paul's refusal to take up the issue of race confirmed the suspicion of black women suffrage campaigners of the white women's movement.

Alice Paul was a resolved supporter of equal rights and rejected arguments for special protection. She did not agree with women such as Florence Kelley in the Consumers' League and also with the Women's Trade Union League who argued for protective legislation for women.

In the United States Crystal Eastman combined this commitment to equality with socialism, which she believed would secure women's independence. She rejected, as did Alice Paul, the need for special protection. She expressed a new optimism that women could live life to the full through work, public commitment, sexual enjoyment, and a motherhood that was shared with men and supported by society. Egalitarianism could, however, coexist with a conviction that women were different in some respects from men. Crystal Eastman believed women put a more intimate value on humanity.

Arguments about equality and difference and the relation between sexual liberation and politics were becoming increasingly divisive issues among feminists. An influential Swedish writer, Ellen Key, argued that the role of women as mothers was eugenically necessary for the race and that the state should acknowledge women as mothers. Consequently, it was not equality but difference that should be stressed by feminists.

The faith that all political problems could be resolved if only women's values shaped society was expressed in Charlotte Perkins Gilman's *The Man Made World* in 1911. A eugenic breed of New Mothers would declare,

> We are tired of men's wars—We are tired of men's quarrels—We are tired of men's competition—We are tired of men's crimes and vices and the diseases they bring upon us.[13]

Olive Schreiner in *Woman and Labour* in the same year maintained that women had a particular horror of war because they bore children.

The problems with this approach, which Rebecca West called the "so simple"[14] view of feminism, became evident when the suffrage movement was to split over World War I. Milicent Fawcett and Emmeline and Christabel were among the patriots; Isabella Ford, Sylvia Pankhurst, and Helena Swanwick opposed the war. The disarray was international. When war broke out the question was whether feminists had a national or international loyalty. Antiwar groups found themselves isolated; the others were swept into the war effort.

The argument that it was a man's war was rather difficult to sustain when women—including feminists—were supporting their respective governments. Emmeline Pankhurst led a "Women's Right to Serve" march urging women into munitions factories and claiming that work and high wages were to emancipate women. But this patriotic feminism ignored the long hours and danger of war work.

Supporters of women's values and equal rights alike, used their particular brands of feminism to justify both nationalism and internationalism. Charlotte Perkins Gilman's eugenicism became increasingly racist, and when America joined the war she sided with anti–German patriotism. German feminists meanwhile insisted that mothers had a special commitment to defending their young and that service to the war effort enabled women to express and fulfill their essential female qualities. On the equal rights front, Milicent Fawcett saw the war as a chance for women to prove they were worthy of citizenship.

Opponents of the war mustered a range of positions. In the "difference" camp feminists observed that women suffered most from wars or that mothers were inherently pacific as guardians of the race. Ellen Kay opposed war because it uneugenically eliminated the fit. Equal rights feminists maintained women's progress was based on reason not force. Ethical socialists denounced militarism and left–wing socialists such as Clara Zetkin and Sylvia Pankhurst opposed the war as being in the interests of capital.

In Germany and France it was very difficult to oppose conscription, but in Britain feminists who were antiwar became involved in both propaganda and defense of conscientious objectors, transferring skills and tactics from the suffrage movement. In Glasgow, the Women's Peace Campaign held kitchen meetings and out-door agitation. It included Agnes Dollan and Helen Crawfurd. Feminists helped conscientious objectors in prison and internment camps. Some broke the law and sheltered men on the run. Police spies followed even the mild and moderate Helena Swanwick. They broke up Sylvia Pankhurst's antiwar meetings and an agent provocateur persuaded a Derby socialist feminist to obtain poison; Alice Wheeldon claimed it was for guard dogs in the internment camps but she was imprisoned in 1917 on the charge of conspiring to kill Lloyd George.

Women organized against the war internationally. Rosika Schwimmer took the initiative in calling a peace conference in The Hague in 1915. Women traveled from many countries and Jane Addams presided. The French feminists, however, rejected the invitation. Their loyalty was with France. Madelline Pelletier, Hélène Brion, and Louise Saumoneau were a tiny antiwar minority among both feminists and socialists and in 1915 managed to call an international conference of socialist women at Bern. Louise Saumoneau managed to go to Bern but was imprisoned for distributing the party manifesto. The forces of nationalism were overwhelming and the advocates of internationalism remained an embattled minority.

After World War I, many feminists worked for the League of Nations and the Women's International League for Peace and Freedom, hoping to rebuild international links.

The demand for the vote was raised in many countries in the early twentieth century. Ideas traveled internationally. In the Phillipines, Concepción Felix and Pura Villanueva Kalaw campaigned for women's suffrage in the 1900s. Filipino feminists had links with American women suffrage campaigns. Agnes de Silva was in touch with British feminists and became the foremost Sri Lankan activist for female suffrage, which was implemented in 1931. In Japan, Ichikawa Fusae was in contact with Alice Paul and led a campaign for women's suffrage in the 1920s. Ichikawa Fusae was, however, opposed by women in left-wing parties when she tried to mobilize for women's suffrage in 1928. They criticized her for ignoring the economic aspects of the women's issue. She said,

> Their reasons were based on their belief that the cause of women's low social status was capitalism which protects personal property. They also believed that if a communist society was established, women's status would rise simultaneously. For them to aid or support our suffrage movement meant the acceptance of a capitalist society.[15]

In China, in contrast, the Communist Party, from its inception in 1921, advocated female suffrage. However, Xiang Jingyu, an early Communist Party organizer in the Shanghai silk and cigarette factories, was critical of the suffragists in the early 1920s. Political rights had no meaning without social change. She believed a national revolutionary movement was a prerequisite to the movement for the suffrage.

There were to be continuing tensions about whether social and economic change took priority over political rights in popular movements in third world countries.

In Peru in 1919 feminists, anarchists, and women workers combined in a movement to lower prices, which went on to assert women's rights. But disagreement between feminists and anarchists over the importance of the suffrage broke the alliance. Anarchists said women workers' economic struggles were the key to the emancipation of women.

The connection between nationalist movements and women's suffrage persisted in the twentieth century. It was to take several forms. In India, women's suffrage was raised by the Women's Indian Association in 1917, and ignored by the British. The nationalist movement gave its support to the demand, partly because of the agitation of nationalist women, but also because any extension of the franchise to Indians benefitted the movement. After independence from the British in 1947, Congress introduced universal adult suffrage.

There have, however, been other models. Nationalist movements, in seeking to modernize, have sometimes enfranchised women, or some groups of women, while creating state-sponsored women's organizations. Post-World War II examples include the General Federation of Iraqi Women's links to the Ba'th Party, Iran under Reza Shah, and Egypt in 1956, where Nasser granted women the vote and outlawed feminist organizations.

Although Latin American women have a long tradition of popular militancy, here too political enfranchisement was often the result of top-down state policy. Women thus got the vote in Ecuador in 1929, in Brazil, Uruguay, and Cuba in the early 1930s, and in Argentina, Chile, Peru, Mexico, and Colombia in the 1940s and 1950s. The hope was that they would vote for the right.

Rather different was the case of Argentina, which, under Peron, granted women's suffrage in 1951. Eva Peron justified women's franchise on the grounds of women's vital role in the family and their influence on children. She also pointed to the mobilization on the streets for the Peronist movement, claiming they had proved their right to be equal citizens. She urged women to use the vote by struggling alongside men to build a great Argentina.

Women's suffrage, ostensibly a basic liberal demand, has proved to be an extremely long struggle. In the United States women in

Wyoming were the first to get the vote in 1869. In New Zealand women's suffrage was won in 1892. Norway, Finland, and Australia followed in the early 1900s. British women gained the vote on the same terms as men in 1928. However, French women had to wait until 1945. Even to this day some women are still waiting; for example, there is no right to vote for women in Kuwait and Saudi Arabia.

The case for enfranchisement has been made on the grounds that women are citizens and mothers, equal to and different from men. It has been presented as a means of including women in humanity and as the claim of a superior sex for power. It has been a revolutionary demand and sometimes a means of stabilizing society. It has had roots both in assertions of national sovereignty and in liberal and socialist aspirations for internationalization.

19

WOMEN AND REVOLUTION IN RUSSIA

The Moscow branch of the feminist Union for Women's Equality issued a statement in 1906 in which they pointed out that they were responsible before the law for their actions and felt with bitter intensity their lack of rights:

> we . . . demand—not request—recognition of civil and political rights equal to yours.[1]

In 1905 when there was insurrection in Russia the Union, which was composed of privileged women, had been open to the various opposition currents. They had begun to reach women in the country-side and some factory women were demanding the right to vote. A socialist tendency had appeared in the Union arguing for a broadly based movement; the Finns after all had won universal suffrage. Russian feminists were cautious and wary of militancy but they never made the explicitly antidemocratic statements of Carrie Chapman Catt or Cady Stanton. They were, however, tiny; the Women's Union at its peak in 1905 had a membership of eight thousand, whereas The National American Woman Suffrage Association grew from seventeen thousand in 1905 to one hundred thousand in 1915. Even a small country such as Denmark had eighty thousand members in its National Women's Council as early as 1899.

The Union for Women's Equality faced opposition not only from the autocratic conservatism of the Tsar, but from the various socialist groups in the left who were extremely hostile to autonomous feminist organization. Though the Women's Union in 1905 had certain resemblances to the Finnish suffrage struggle, its fate was quite different, partly because of contemporary events and partly because of Russia's dramatic radical heritage. The peculiar character of Russian society— where serfdom only ended in 1851 and the power of the Tsars was absolute—left little space for liberal campaigns. Freedom of any kind seemed to require revolution.

Vera Zasulich unintentionally was to initiate a terrorist phase when she impulsively tried to assassinate the cruel governor of St. Petersburg in 1878.

> Even before I had revolutionary dreams, even before I was placed in boarding school, I made elaborate plans to escape becoming a governess. It would have been far easier of course had I been a boy: then I could have done almost anything. . . . And then, the distant spectre of revolution appeared, making me equal to a boy; I, too, could dream of "action", of "exploits", and of the "great struggle". . . . I, too, could join "those who perished for the great cause of love."[2]

Aspirations for a wider destiny, which, in Britain or the United States, might have led to the suffrage groups or settlement work, were to lead some young women to revolutionary activity.

During the 1860s the ideas of the utopian socialists, along with Jenny d'Héricourt, George Sand, Mill, and Bakunin influenced the intelligentsia. Writers and thinkers such as Mikhailov and Chernychevsky argued for women's rights and sexual emancipation. Some young women defied their parents to live a personally defiant life, cutting their hair, wearing black, and living in communes; they were called nihilists.

The cause of women's education attracted women from the upper classes, who campaigned for women's right to enter the university and take degrees. They also were involved in rescue work, which was influenced by Josephine Butler's campaigns. They tried to reclaim prostitutes and set up hostels for homeless women.

Nadezhda Stasova, like many other members of the intelligentsia, was inspired by romanticism, Byron, Heine, and George Sand. She believed she should serve "the universal family."[3] Her meeting with Mariya Vasilevna Trubnikova led her to focus her philanthropic work toward reforms for women. Sunday schools were started by philanthropists, which included workers. To Stasova, workers were children in "the universal family" but younger, more radical women, such as Elisaveta Garshina linked their own frustration with those of women workers. The theme of dedicated service to a transcendent cause persisted, transferred from charity to public action.

> I have children and I love them more than my own life. But there is something else, even higher than one's own children. Now I am not a mother, or a wife or a sister. I am a sister of my country, and I should be happy above all earthly happiness if I could give my small mite to the common cause.[4]

Citizenship and participation in the public sphere were regarded as more important than the personal relations of mothering. The questioning of gender relations within neutral universal categories such as citizenship do not seem to have been part of Russian radicalism. Denial of the personal claims of kin, however, had been a powerful theme in nihilism, and subordination of personal experience and rejection of familial bonds persisted in later groups that had rejected nihilism.

From the early 1870s, young women who were dissatisfied with the government's reluctant concession of allowing women to take nondegree courses defiantly went off to study for degrees in Switzerland.

In Zurich, Russian women students formed a women's-only study circle, which soon shifted from the wrongs of women to the wrongs of society. Among the students, Vera Figner came across the ideas of anarchists like Bakunin and wondered if her dream of qualifying for a degree could be justified amid suffering and exploitation. She and her friends debated these ideas in their lodgings and took the name of their landlady Frau Fritsche. Most of the Fritsche group decided it was their duty to return to Russia and rouse the people. Vera Figner lingered, to return to find her friends had been tried and imprisoned for many years for the propaganda work that they had undertaken with a group of young men.

During the 1870s Russian populists sought to fully emancipate the serfs by agrarian revolution. The populists believed it was wrong to separate women's emancipation from the general movement. Mikhailovsky, a leader of Russian populism, argued that women's emancipation would follow from the reconstruction of Russia. Women's rights in the 1870s were no longer a central theme of debate, though the courage and dedication of women such as Vera Zasulich, Vera Figner, Olga Lyubatovich and Sophia Perovskaya were extraordinary.

In desperation, as repression was intensified, some populists decided terror was the only way to stir the people, who seemed too slow to assert their rights. Vera Zasulich did not agree with this approach but Figner, Lyubatovich, and Perovskaya supported the use of terror.

Perovskaya was to be the first woman to be hanged in Russia. She gave the signal for the assassination of Tsar Alexander the Second—a man whose reign had seen the execution of two thousand people. Figner was incarcerated in a small cell for 20 years in 1883, and somehow kept her sanity. Interestingly, the exiled emotions renounced in service to their cause surfaced in the memories of survivors in intense expressions of love for other women in the struggle. Both Perovskaya and Figner had been troubled by the implications of terror as a strategy, but both were completely resolute once they were convinced there was no alternative.

The costs were high. The circumstances of clandestine organization inevitably suppressed hopes of democracy and loving fellowship. They were not to live like other women. They risked their lives in absolute equality with a dedication and discipline that denied all personal ties.

Olga Lyubatovich had to leave her baby in an attempt to free her companion. The child died in a meningitis epidemic. She reflected grimly,

> Yes, it's a sin for revolutionaries to have a family. Men and women both must stand alone, live like soldiers under a hail of bullets. But in your youth, you somehow forget that revolutionaries' lives are measured not in years, but in days and hours.[5]

Influenced by Marx, the Social Democrats began to organize in Russia in the 1890s they were critical of some of the populists' ideas. They argued that the focus should be on factory workers, not the peasantry, and were opposed to the idea that terror would arouse the people. But Lenin, their leader, retained the concept of the professional revolutionary apart from society, for whom dedication to the party was more important than personal bonds or moral issues.

Social Democrats also were to be imprisoned. Lenin was sent to Siberia in 1896. Nadezhda Krupskaya followed and they were married in Shuskenskoe where they spent their exile helping one another with their writing. Lenin's *The Development of Capitalism in Russia* was a large work; Krupskaya's was a short booklet, *The Woman Worker,* which described the oppression of overworked peasant and factory women. Men and women workers were to unite and in securing their own liberation bring a new society. The little book broke a long silence.

Although Vera Zasulich had been one of the founders of Russian Marxism, there was no special attention given to women's situation. Like the populists, they saw it as part of the general problem of transformation and Marx's impatience with all special forms of oppression was in accord with the Russian radicals' theoretical inclination;

"the people," "humanity," or "the proletariat" universally encompassed all differences. To be distinguished according to one's particularity was demeaning. The young Inessa Armand, who was to become a close friend of Lenin and Krupskaya, was appalled when she read in Tolstoy's *War and Peace* that Natasha Rostova became "a female of the species"[6] on marrying. She resolved in contrast that she would become a "human being."[7]

Lenin was in support of civil and political rights for women but hostile to feminism. The aim of gender neutrality, however, had to be qualified by the actual inequality of women workers. Although Krupskaya's book had brought out the issue of inequality within the working class, Alexandra Kollontai's *The Social Basis of the Woman Question* in 1909 was a much longer study influenced by Bebel and Engels. She was concerned to challenge the feminist Women's Union. "Bourgeois" feminists were criticized for having demands that were too narrow when they struggled for access to education and rights. But she regarded with even more hostility the feminist women who sought to reach women workers through social work. She was also critical of Ellen Key and a member of the German Motherhood League, Ruth Bray, who emphasized motherhood. She said that as a result of their efforts "the bourgeois ideal that recognizes woman as a female rather than as a person has acquired a special halo of progressiveness."[8] Kollontai insisted that class cuts across women's interests and only the Social Democrats could provide women workers with the solution.

There were some snags. One she admits; a deep confusion existed among Marxists about what form the family would take in socialism. Would the family unit be strengthened on the model of the proletarian family in an egalitarian form or wither away as society took over many of its activities? Marx, Bebel, and Engels had left contradictory messages.

Another problem was that Kollontai's own effort to develop confidence among women workers by forming socialist clubs in 1906 was regarded as separatist by some Bolsheviks, as Lenin's grouping among the Social Democrats was called, even though it drew women into the Party. This hostility to recognizing that working class women might have any differing needs and interests forced her to close the clubs.

But she did not give up easily. In 1908 Kollontai was dodging the police and urging women workers to contest the middle-class feminists at a forthcoming conference, the All-Russian Women's Conference. Theoretical opposition to separate organization again provoked criticism. However, Kollontai's success forced a practical recognition of women's special concerns. In 1913 the Bolsheviks started a paper called *Rabotnitsa* (Working Woman). Until the Tsar became involved in the 1914 war and closed it down, it covered maternity insurance and women's working conditions, demanded child-care centers and electoral rights, and printed discussion of family problems and information on hygiene. Yet women were presented always as backward members of the working class. In their concern for unity, conflicts between men and women over skill, wages, housework, and sexuality tended to be disregarded by the Bolsheviks.

Ironically these "backward" women were to start the Russian revolution in an uprising on March 8, 1917 (February 23 in the Russian calendar), International Women's Day. Women textile workers in Petrograd, who worked in unskilled jobs on 11 to 12 hour shifts and then went home to do housework, went on strike. They used neighborhood networks formed in markets and bread queues to bring in other factory women and women from the artisan class. Men joined them in a collective working class rebellion around consumption. During the war the prices of food, particularly the staples of flour and bread, had risen. Merchants speculated in grain, meat, and fuel. Rents and unemployment rose.

The women stopped Cossack soldiers firing on them and their uprising resulted in an army mutiny against the Tsar. A liberal government led by Kerensky ruled until October when the Bolsheviks' revolution created the Soviet Union.

The women's action is usually rapidly passed over. In fact, it is best comprehended as part of a wider pattern of working class protest. Economic pressure on the poor revived crowd action around consumption with women playing a prominent part. A similar rebellion occurred in Turin in Italy in August 1917 when women protested because bakers said they were "out of bread,"[19] but still made expensive sweet raisin rolls for the rich. Again there was a connection between community and work place and Fiat workers supported them. There was a history of such confrontations before in Italy; in Genoa in 1900 dockers and women confronted the police during a strike. In Turin and Florence in 1902 and Rome in 1903 there were other collective strikes in which the women faced the soldiers and police because it was felt they would not be shot. In Malaga, Spain in 1918, however, when women seized fish and potatoes and headed toward the governors' office the soldiers did fire. The men came from the South. They did not understand the Turin dialect when women shouted "We are your sisters we are your daughters."[10]

Sylvia Pankhurst's work in East London along with the movement against high rents in Glasgow and elsewhere in Britain were milder versions of a similar form of class action in which the interconnection of consumption and production is asserted. Also during World War I in France working women in clothing or munitions, desperate as housewives and workers, demanded a shorter working week and struck against sexual harassment. The immediate postwar years were stormy internationally. In Jamaica, war veterans protested with men and women workers in 1918–1919. Again in 1923, in Veracruz, Mexico, women rebelled against rents and demanded the recognition of the Tenants' Union. Dockers and sailors went on strike. In Malaga the women had sent away men and children for fear of danger. But in Veracruz they marched together with portraits of Marx, Lenin, Trotsky, and Bakunin. Rent boards were established and the Tenants' Union was recognized, but women were excluded.

These communal strikes were far from ideas of women's rights in a feminist sense. In the tradition of women's collective action and in the French revolution and Chartism they marked out the area of consumption as being as significant as production. They suggested a wider concept of class in which struggle in the workplace interacts with the circumstances and relations of daily life.

Not only resistance, but the transformation of relations in the community and the household briefly appeared on the international socialist agenda in the early 1920's. The need to establish communal forms before socialism, for which Lily Braun, a German social democrat, had argued, had been initially dismissed by Clara Zetkin on the left as utopian. But the Russian revolution inspired hope that it was possible to change many aspects of living. Some left Communist women, such as Henrietta Roland Holst from Holland, argued against the effects of private household labor on women's consciousness during the 1920s. Kollontai also was becoming increasingly aware of the problems of trying to establish a new culture after seizing state power. It became evident to her that postrevolutionary societies are partly formed by prerevolutionary circumstances.

Proposals for liberating women did not face immediately congenial conditions. Even after the Bolsheviks withdrew from World War I, they had to fight the "Whites," supporters of the old regime who were supported by their allies, Britain and the United States. Kollontai switched from peace propaganda to urging women to defend the revolution. In fact, women fought on both sides and also worked as nurses. The Whites treated captured women nurses without mercy; Some were frozen alive. Women, as well as men, on the Bolshevik side were ruthless fighters too—the basis for the Western stereotype that caricatured "the revolutionary woman."

The war caused terrible poverty, social disruption, even starvation, in which epidemics took their toll. Amid economic and administrative chaos, a woman who belonged to the Socialist Revolutionary Party, which still believed in terror, tried to assassinate Lenin. The numbers of opponents to the regime from both right and left who were imprisoned mounted. The revolution, moreover, remained isolated; workers in the rest of Europe were either quelled or dormant.

The Bolsheviks and their supporters faced a tragic choice. All their analyses had told them socialism was impossible in one country where an illiterate peasantry predominated. But to relinquish power to the Whites seemed unthinkable after so much effort. How to produce enough to survive and recover from the war became the overriding concern. Freedom and democracy appeared secondary. The Party and Lenin seemed the only way of holding chaos together.

Emma Goldman was an early critic; as an anarchist she was appalled by the Communist Party's rule through the state and by the denial of liberty. Some socialists too decided it was a doomed project. Angelica Balabanova, who had worked with Zetkin in international women's organizing, left the Soviet Union in 1921 and became involved in the Italian socialist movement. She thought the "deformation"[11] of the October Revolution arose because the Party and the cult of individual leadership replaced "the masses."

The substitution, which was made at the onset in good faith, was bound to degenerate in time.[12]

Others, however, thought it inconceivable that they should abandon the Soviet Union simply because circumstances were adverse. Alexandra Kollontai took a leading part in a movement for greater working class democracy in 1921. After the defeat of this "Workers Opposition" she was marginalized, and removed from events in the Soviet Union by being sent abroad as a foreign diplomat.

Kollontai had been Minister of Social Welfare in 1917; in 1920 she took over the leadership of the Zhenotdel (Women's Organization), which had been formed as a result of Party women's protests. It had initially been headed by Inessa Armand, who had died of cholera in 1920. She and Kollontai, though not personally friendly, had been most active in asserting the specific problems of women.

The Zhenotdel, Kollontai told Emma Goldman, existed to raise women's consciousness as 'mothers and citizens.'[13] Kollontai realized that the reforms in marriage and maternity protection for working women that she had initiated were inadequate without the active participation of women. The Zhenotdel brought peasant women and workers together from vast distances, where they listened to speakers such as Inessa Armand and Kollontai and cheered Lenin, who, despite his dislike of feminism, supported women's mobilization. Women had to face male opposition in the family to go to local women's meetings. This was particularly severe in Muslim areas where women were even murdered. Tearing off the veil became a symbol of freedom from religious and male authority.

Kollontai's stress on human agency and the will to change was shared by many leftist communists in the early twentieth century and by anarcho-syndicalists. In 1904 she had opposed the ideas of Nietzsche. "Our slogan is not the triumph of individualism, but the victory of sociality (obshchestvennost)."[14] However, the vitalism in his and Bergson's writing was pervasive. It was transposed into ideas of human collective action by socialists and anarchists' impatient with the evolutionary socialism of Bebel and the parliamentary road of Bernstein and the Fabians.

Many left communists focused on production and saw the workers' councils or factory soviets as the most democratic force in society, which appeared to make formal representative democracy superfluous. An obvious problem in Russia was that workers composed a tiny proportion of the population—a point Lenin made in attacking "The Workers Opposition." Another difficulty—which Sylvia Pankhurst tried to overcome—was that women who often worked at home were excluded. Kollontai, like Pankhurst and Roland Holst, became convinced that a conscious effort to change daily life was necessary.

It is possible to find in Lenin and in Trotsky's writing recognition that cultural transformation had to occur as part of the revolution. But Kollontai put much greater emphasis upon cultural change. Her criticism of both lack of party democracy and denial of workers' needs also contributed to her view that struggle to change personal relations could not be conflated with the Party's power or with production.

When the drive to increase production was being emphasized in the 1920s Kollontai revealed the gap between rhetoric and reality. Communist men still sought personal control over women while unemployment forced women into prostitution. She tried to understand personal relations and relate them to the creation of a new "society." Communism would make a new kind of sexual love possible. She thought this would not be merely physical lust in which she believed male power meant women were unable to assert their sexual desires. Nor would it be the free union in which she considered women lost autonomy. Struggling to recognize the force of both passion and freedom, she looked back on her own life and wrote,

the man would only see in me the feminine element, which he tried to mould into a willing sounding-board to his ego. . . . Repeatedly the moment arrived when I had to shake off the chains of our relationship. Then with an aching heart but with a sovereign uninfluenced will, I would once more be alone. And yet the greater the demands life made of me, the more important the work waiting to be tackled, the greater grew my longing to be enveloped by love, warmth and understanding—And so all the easier began once more the old story of disappointment in love.[15]

Kollontai believed sexual relations were emotionally serious affairs but argued it should not be assumed they would be for life. In 1919 her essay on the German psychoanalytic writer Grete Meisel-Hess was published in Russian. She noted Meisel-Hess' wry comment "Marriage is like a flat: you become aware of its dark corners only when you've lived in it a while."[16]

Her interest in sexuality and her dream of individual love merging with new forms of communalism increasingly diverged from the ethos of Soviet society. Production as a means of emancipating women became the orthodox approach; human beings' potential for loving as the basis for communism appeared heretical.

Kollontai's attempt to acknowledge the complex intertwining of personal relations with social transformation was suppressed. However, the obstacles were not just political but cultural. The ideas of communal housekeeping that she and Inessa Armand advocated, and that Lenin called the "social economy"[17] in 1918 were not what most peasant and working women actually wanted. The idea of individual rights that was behind the easier divorce laws introduced by the Bolsheviks was at variance with the peasants' view of marriage as an economic arrangement vital for communal survival. The internal struggle between the assertion of an autonomous sovereign will and receptivity in relation to a man; the pull between public action and the desire for immersion in intimacy, were experienced still only by a minority of women.

Any attempt to find a new balance between personal desires and Kollontai's "sociality" had to confront familial and social crises. The revolution and civil war had left orphans wandering the streets, many parents had died or become separated, single mothers struggled to survive. Abortion was made legal but was performed often under bad conditions. The Bolsheviks, including Kollontai, retained the anti-Malthusian suspicion of birth control—much to the exasperation of foreign socialist women such as Antoinette Konikow. The Communist

Party emphasized better conditions for mothers and child-care so women could have babies but ideals conflicted with scarcity.

Although Kollontai insisted on the personal nature of sexual relations, she saw motherhood not as an individual affair but as a social relation. She tended, like many of her contemporaries, to use state and society interchangeably. The relationship was reciprocal. The mother had duties toward the state/society from which she could claim collective resources for her welfare.

This view of motherhood was not peculiar to communism. It was shared by many reformist socialists and by social liberals, who also were inclined in welfare policy to subordinate the individual to the state. Because the pregnant woman carried a future member of society, they did not think her body could be seen as belonging only to her self. However, the equation of this concept of community with existing states assumed there were no conflicting interests—not simply between individuals and society but between society and the state.

In the early years of the Soviet revolution, the Bolshevik tradition was firm on equality, but was suspicious of strands in both socialism and feminism that sought to give value to the existing activities of women. This avoided sentimental idealization, but dismissed areas of experience that were important to many women. Such an approach had strategic consequences. The vision of socialized housework and motherhood assumed it was inherently oppressive to cook and care for children. There is little sense that women in the household gained any social fulfillment or understanding. Kollontai and other women socialists envisaged an enlightened future in which technology and professional experts would take over housework and child-care. Women who protested were simply regarded as backward.

As increased production became synonymous with socialism the reorganization of housework was advocated for its efficiency—a theme already present in Owen and Bebel's ideas. One enthusiast for industrialization in the five-year plan exclaimed,

> Down with the kitchen. We shall destroy this little penitentiary! We shall free millions of women from house-keeping. They want to work like the rest of us. In a factory-kitchen one person can prepare from fifty to one

hundred dinners a day. We shall force machines to peel potatoes, wash the dishes, cut the bread, stir the soup, make ice cream.[18]

None of these proposals was inherently socialist. American capitalism applied technology to housework in the 1920s and 1930s through private consumption whereas European countries began to change marriage laws and introduce welfare through state policies.

Under Stalin, women suffered like men in forced collectivization, imprisonment, and military terror. The Zhenotdel was abolished in 1930 and laws stressing parental responsibilities introduced in the face of the disintegration of the family in the frantic process of industrialization. In 1936 divorce was made more difficult, nonpayment of alimony became a more serious offence, and abortion was prohibited.

The rhetorical assertion that socialism allowed women to be liberated accompanied a state policy that oscillated between emphasizing women as producers or reproducers. The main result was more work because distribution was inefficient, men did little housework, and social services were inadequate. Women's own needs or feelings were not the starting points for policies. Lack of democratic rights of all kinds made it impossible to challenge either the heritage of the "Woman's Question" or its reinterpretation to fit the requirements of the Soviet State.

Communist women in the Cominterm in 1920 had dismissed the suffrage for its limitations as a "fig-leaf."[19] But even a "fig-leaf" would have provided some means of curbing the Communist Party's power to define women's needs and to assert their complexity, variety, and changing aspect democratically.

Opposition to the autonomous organization of women and the dismissal of feminism contributed to the imperviousness of the orthodox Communist regime; even after the fall of Stalin, little social space existed for groups to organize outside Party control. There was consequently no means of challenging the body of ideas on "the Woman Question," which fossilized over time.

Women have played an important part in the public sphere of Soviet society as workers and as political administrators, but their varying needs have not shaped political priorities. The power relations between men and women were submerged in rhetoric about socialism emancipating women. The universal categories concealed differences, which in turn involved inequalities. For women to question these hidden inequalities and suppressed grievances democratic freedom was vital.

This questioning, however, has wider implications. It is an argument partly about the relations and organization of daily life, who does housework and how housing is designed and partly about the macro planning process. Who decides investment policy? Who combines the market and social planning? How can macro planning respond flexibly to varied and changing human needs? Behind these economic questions there are moral issues of social aims. How can everyone be equally considered in a socialist society? And what balance can be created between individual freedom and security in society? These questions were bequeathed to the future because not only did the exigencies of the Soviet Union distort the form that socialism took there, but the Soviet model was imposed on communists in many other countries.

20

INDIAN WOMEN AND
SELF-RULE

Countries that have been subjected to imperialism, either through direct colonization or indirect economic pressures, were, by the early twentieth century, developing movements of resistance. Examples include Ireland, Egypt, Turkey, India, China, the Caribbean countries, and later Algeria and the new African countries, which gained independence after World War II. Struggles for national liberation were to take various forms in the course of this century; some aimed to set up Western liberal economies, whereas others were inspired by aspects of the Russian revolution.

Although every country has its own history, and there are many strands in nationalism, which has been in some cases a top-down reorganization of the state and in others a popular grass roots mobilization, in which national liberation has linked with socialism and communism, women have been important in several ways.

First, nationalist movements have questioned how gender is seen. They have brought new ideas of how a man should be, how a woman should be, and how they should relate. There has been a particular interest in defining new ways of seeing women as mothers.

Of course these ideas have been mainly thought out by men who have sought to impose them on women. But it would be wrong to see women as entirely passive recipients. Women have been crucial communicators of these new images to other women and to their children. They have also shaped them to fit their own purposes in the process. Moreover, there has been an active intellectual minority creatively and theoretically connecting the emancipation of women to nationalism. Two examples from the 1930s in the Caribbean are Una Marson, the poet, and Amy Bailey, who theorized domestic labor.

Second, women have played a significant part in nationalist and antiimperialist struggles in many countries—even though the men have not always wanted them to become involved initially. In the 1950s, for example, in Algeria women were able to act as intermediaries in the resistance to the French because the soldiers did not suspect them.

Third, these movements have reached and affected the lives of millions of women who faced very different problems than Western women, both workers and peasants. In the 1930s in Trinidad, Elma Françoise was active in both the workers' movement and in nationalism. The Vietnamese National Liberation Front in the 1960s mobilized thousands of peasant women.

There was considerable interaction between Western feminists and women in nationalist movements from the late nineteenth century into the 1930s. The extent of this is only just emerging in historical accounts. However, it was not just a matter of borrowing concepts from Western liberal feminism, for these were not always appropriate. Some Western feminists too assumed they would be the teachers without understanding that in countries such as India there was already a tradition of women's resistance. Nor did they often understand the social impact of changes.

From the 1920s communists were involved in nationalist movements and raised questions of women's emancipation. One example was Iraq in the 1920s.

Both nationalism and communism effected extraordinary changes for women in mapping out the new public sphere that women entered. These changes occurred within an overall social context that was culturally oppressive and in some cases amidst extremes of economic hardship. This contradictory and often painful process of economic modernization and social transformation contributed to a new set of problems for women who sought emancipation.

Difficulties emerged most clearly when there were conflicts of power between men and women. Nationalism and communism were uneasy about the autonomous organization of women. Both movements needed unity, but men had the power on the whole to define how unity was best achieved. They remained predominant both within gender relations and within the wider relations of society. Though accusations of Western ideology could as well have been made against nationalism and communism themselves, the conflict repeatedly occurred over 'the Woman Question.'

The actual interconnections however were always infinitely more complex than the political stereotypes implied, nor were they all one way. If Indian and Chinese women took up Western feminist's ideas, Western women were influenced by movements in the East which struggled for social change and an autonomous national identity.

India and China present two important examples of countries that developed along differing courses. India won independence from the British in 1947 after the partition in which Pakistan became a separate country. India modeled itself on Western democracies, while the communists took power after a long war in China in 1949.

In both India and China the problems that had become evident in the Soviet Union appeared as nationalists and communists sought to mobilize women. There was not only a gulf between the educated daughters of intellectuals, professionals, officials, or merchants and those of trading, artisan or factory workers' families. There were peasant women in small villages whose lives were so linked with communal economic and kinship ties that the imperialistic impact of individualism, without social transformation to secure alternative forms of well-being, had resulted in worse conditions, by threatening the customary structures in which they survived. Class was not the only hierarchy in which women's lives were enmeshed. In India there was the caste system and in China women were still sold as concubines. Not simply the father or husband's authority oppressed women; in the family young brides, in China especially, could be treated virtually as if they were in bondage by their mothers-in-law.

India and China are vast countries and no single system of social organization existed; thus the lives of peasant women varied from place to place. But even so the meeting between ideas of individual rights and personal autonomy and the patterns of peasant life was complex in its effects. Its consequences were confronted head on by the Chinese communists in their long march to power and remain unresolved in the two societies despite the political, social, and economic differences between them.

Such large events were remote from the life of Rassundari Devi, a housewife in Bengal who wrote the first autobiography in Bengali, *Amar Jiban* (My Life) in 1876. She was not one of the privileged women who had attended Indian or European schools, but had taught herself to read by secretly scratching the letters of the alphabet onto the blackened kitchen wall. She wrote about the domesticity that over-whelmed her. Some days she was so busy looking after the household and attending to her children, her husband, and guests that she never ate.

Yet amid outward conformity she had a most passionate sense of her individuality and of the wrongs of women. "I was like a caged bird"[2] she wrote. In *Amar Jiban* she questioned the custom of sending young girls away to be married, leaving their mothers so young, without education. "Shut up like a thief, even trying to learn was considered an offense."[3]

She thought it was wrong that widows should have a completely restricted life and low status and foolish that women's clothes had been so restricted in her youth. Rassundari Devi did not see her situation just as a personal question. "Actually the man who was my master happened to be a likable person. But it is difficult to ignore or reject accepted customs and practices."[4]

Pandita Ramabai, the daughter of a learned Brahmin social reformer, was the author of a systematic critique of women's oppression, *The High Caste Hindu Woman* in 1886. She had been taught Sanskrit by her mother in a house in a remote forest. Lakshmibai, her mother, had been educated by Ramabai's unconventional father, who believed that women had equal rights to education. As a result of his resolve to teach his child bride, the family had become outcasts; Pandita Ramabai was born in a forest and traveled all over India with her parents. Her knowledge of the history of Hinduism made her sceptical of the Golden Age invoked by some nationalists, but she also criticized the assumption of Western liberals that the British had unequivocally improved women's conditions in India, pointing to the economic consequences of colonialism. Pandita Ramabai was one of the 10 women delegates to the Indian National Congress in 1889. Like many Indian women she was widowed while still young; she then defied convention by leading an active life.

She started women's organizations, campaigned for education and medical training, and set up several charitable projects, girls schools, orphanages, and widows' homes. She was friendly with the English feminist Dorothea Beale and traveled and lectured in the United States. Although committed to nationalism she converted to Christianity, which angered some Hindu nationalists.

Nationalist men in India might believe women should change but tended to think they should determine how. Nationalism was imaginatively making a new woman, in the late nineteenth century male novelists had conceived ideal women characters who were sacrificial and self-affirming, gentle and strong, symbols of a ravaged society and the mythical agents of its revenge.

The men themselves were under pressure from actual "customs and practices."[5] They might criticize early marriages and believe widows should remarry, claiming in defiance of their fathers' wishes that they would marry widows. But in practice they often yielded to family pressure and in fact did not marry a widow. Ramabai Ranade, who was married to a nationalist and reformer while young, describes in her autobiography how her husband, one of those who had compromised, presented his young bride with his reforming ideas in a sternly, authoritarian way. These new ideas and demands could be confusing and contradictory but nonetheless they could open up a certain space for women, even if it was not entirely of their own choosing.

In various ways women devised their particular mix of duty and independence. For instance, Ramabai Ranade worked with her husband in one of Pandita Ramabai's widows' homes. She did charitable work, including famine relief in 1913. After her husband died she became part of the more militant nationalist movement, which created new images of Indian womanhood. Sarala Devi was a living symbol of this militant nationalism. A rebellious young woman from the privileged Tagore family in Bengal, she exhorted young men to resist the humiliation of British rule. In 1903 she was organizing training sessions in sword and lathi (wooden stick) play where pledges were taken to sacrifice life for independence. Sarala Devi devised her own festivals celebrating a heroic version of Hindu history.

Her mother, Swarnakumari Devi, the sister of the poet Rabindranath Tagore, had been attracted to theosophy. This was a European antimaterialist movement that took a comparative approach to religions in which Hindu spirituality was emphasized. The aim was to develop Indian culture that could be enriched but not dominated by the West. In 1882 Swarnakumari Devi had started the Ladies' Theosophical Society for women of all religions, and in 1889 was among the first group of women at the Indian National Congress. She sought, like many nationalist women of her generation, a mixture of reforms and traditional values.

Several foreign women were attracted to theosophy and became supporters of Indian nationalism. Annie Besant, who after being involved in the socialist and birth control movement in Britain, had come to India in 1893, was a leading figure in the Theosophical Society. Aware of Irish nationalist debates she formed the Home Rule League in India and was the first woman president of the Indian National Congress in 1917. Margaret Cousins, an Irish feminist who arrived in 1915, was a theosophist, as was Dorothy Jinarajadasa, who formed the Women's Indian Association in 1917 with Besant and Cousins. Margaret Noble, an Irish Nationalist was inspired by another spiritual movement led by the Hindu monk, Swami Vivekananda which stressed the power of the goddess Kali; 'the Mother'. These religious variants to orthodox Hinduism provided an arena in which both Western and Indian women could be active in public affairs within an ethos of spiritual service.

It took longer for Muslim women to mobilize but by the early twentieth century members of prominent families had formed local women's associations in several towns and in 1916 the Begum of Bhopal formed the All-India Muslim Women's Conference. Muslim women were concerned with promoting education. They also started charitable centers and there was protest against polygamy.

Rokeya Sakhawat Hossain wrote a utopian fantasy in 1905 called *Sultana's Dream*. She was from a Muslim family in what is now Bangladesh and her husband encouraged her education. In her story the men are all confined to their quarters in the household while the women take over the affairs of the country. This situation arose because of the men's inability to withstand invasion. The women had marched off and defeated the enemy by applying the science of solar heat they had developed in cooking to warfare. Now everything was well ordered and peaceful. There was no crime and sin so neither police nor magistrates were required. The men busied themselves in the kitchen. Rokeya's husband described her fantasy proudly as "a terrible revenge on men."[6]

In the early twentieth century nationalism entered a militant phase. This was known as "swadeshi," the demand for self-rule and indigenous culture. The partition of Bengal in 1905 had precipitated a political crisis; amid widespread unrest and strikes, women helped to boycott foreign goods. Pressure continued for women's rights. In 1917 a deputation of Indian women, accompanied by Margaret Cousins, went to see the Viceroy and demanded votes for women. Women from the Home Rule League visited Britain in 1919 to lobby for reforms and political rights.

The Indian National Congress supported votes for women in 1918. By this time women's journals in Bombay, Madras, Calcutta,

Ahmedabad, Mysore, and Pune were debating women's education, health, the problems of widows, opposing purdah, and the forced marriage of young women to old husbands as well as political rights.

Hukma Devi, the headmistress of a girls' school in Dehradun, called on women in an article, "Women: Man's Equal Partner or an Old Shoe?" in 1918.

> Sisters! You have slumbered long enough awake! . . . When the whole world sings of freedom then is it right that Indian women should lie inert.[7]

Writers in the journals ridiculed men who thought women should not play an active role in public affairs. In 1917, Hridayamohini turned the English Victorian ideal of the "angel by the hearth" around in a Bengali women's magazine called *Stree Darpan*. If men would be content with staying like "gods at home"[8] the women would "set you up as idols on the shelf and worship you," thus sparing the "lats"[10]—the British rulers—"much anxiety and tribulation."[11]

Uma Nehru, who was more closely connected to European feminism, criticized nationalist ideals of womanhood that looked backward. Attempts to valorize an historical myth of a nobler tradition of womanhood ignored that changes in the status of women were part of the European economic and political systems, which the middle-class nationalist men sought to emulate.

She wrote in *Stree Darpan* in March 1918

> Our Hamlet-like young Indian male finds himself grappling not with the question "To be or not to be" but with the more intractable question. Whether to lift the veil or not to lift the veil, and if lifted then how far it must be lifted?[12]

After 1917 the nationalist movement widened the scope of its protests, including workers on plantations and in textile mills where wives of male workers, widows, and deserted women were among the female work force. Peasants' resentment against the taxes they had to pay to the British was another issue. Prices were high and in 1918 the two million demobilized Indian soldiers returning added to social disruption. Meetings of protest were held all over India. In 1919 British troops fired at an unarmed crowd that included women and children and many people died in what became known as the Jallianwala Bagh massacre.

Mahatma Gandhi was concerned to develop a popular base for the nationalist struggle and stressed women's self-realization through commitment to the cause of independence. He was critical of men's assumption of superiority both personally and through institutional legal power.

Gandhi's political approach was based on tolerance of all religions, cooperation, and mutual service. He said that he had developed the strategy of nonviolent resistance against the British from black South African women, whose courage in protests and strikes he admired, and from his wife Kasturba, who was extremely persistent. He argued that women's capacity to give themselves meant they were nobler than men. This ability to serve should be an individual choice and not imposed by one sex on the other through male supremacy.

He expected India to develop differently from the West. So he did not stress the economic independence of women and going out to work. He articulated a concept of emancipation that was based on women's difference. Education should equip men for the external sphere and women for domestic life and the upbringing of children. The tactics of nonviolence were presented as inherently suited to women's disposition to self-sacrifice.

Although Gandhi rejected those strands of Western feminism that stressed women's individual autonomy or equality of opportunity his views are not dissimilar from feminist currents that emphasized women's difference, "female" values of service and cooperation. And the vision of handicrafts and the cooperative division of labor in the household had echoes of Ruskin as well as some socialist and anarchist alternatives to capitalism. It was to be an ambiguous legacy.

Gandhi's thought inspired many Indian women. A women's journal *Stri Dharma* in 1930 described nonviolent resistance as "feminine rather than masculine"[13] and characterized the struggle for Indian independence as "the women's war"[14] because of the nonviolent tactics Gandhi adopted.

A poet, Sarojini Naidu, was involved in the Gandhian wing of the movement. Naidu supported women's right to vote while urging unity and harmony in gender relations. Like many nationalists she believed there had been an earlier golden age in which Indian women had not been oppressed. When in 1926 Naidu was made president of the Congress, she saw this as reverting to a lost tradition of women's power.

Jawaharlal Nehru brought a more sceptical, secular approach to nationalist politics. Wary of historically dubious invocations of the past, he believed Indian society, including the family, had to be refashioned and modernized. He rejected the idea of a fixed sphere for women that reinforced difference between men and women as perpetuating inequality; women should have access to the same education as men and economic independence.

In the early 1920's ideas of emancipation were also emerging which emphasized not so much sacrifice and service as self-rule, strength and fulfillment as an individual in relation to nationalist struggle. The women who joined the nationalist cause anticipated wider equality. Amiya Devi, for instance, said this kind of self-rule and fulfillment could not be given by "well-wishing men"[15] but had to be taken by force.

Reflecting on the interaction between feminism and nationalism, Radha Kumar, in *The History of Doing; An Illustrated History of the Women's Movement*, observes of the women in this period:

> Not only did they link women's rights with nationalism, they used nationalist arguments to defend demands for women's rights to equality with men.[16]

She notes that two differing rationalizations for women's resistance coexisted. Women's rights were being presented in terms of various ideals of the role of the mother and also because women had the *same* needs, desires, and capacities as men.

By the early twentieth century loyalist women's organizations in India, which worked with English feminists such as Margaret Balfour and Eleanor Rathbone, had begun to emphasize the protection of motherhood. The nationalists too were to take up practical welfare reforms in the 1920s. Nationalist women in this period encouraged self-help associations among poor women such as learning embroidery skills.

By the early 1930s nationalist women were participating in nonviolent demonstrations in which they were arrested and beaten by the police. The movement was also being drawn away from its upper class origins; peasant women, influenced by Gandhi, joined nonviolent resistance and went to jail; there was also growing awareness of the need to organize women workers. But it seems that less emphasis was being placed on the individual fulfillment of women as participants in the nationalist cause than in the early 1920s.

Not all Indian women were to accept nonviolence as the best tactic. A militant revolutionary nationalism emerged, which led to armed rebellion, and a few women helped to produce bombs and took part in raids and in assassinations. In Calcutta in 1928 a group of women students trained in armed struggle. Some women from this revolutionary wing of nationalism joined the Communist Party.

Though nationalism had a formative influence on the Communist Party in India, there were disagreements about the relationship of the two movements among communists. Inspired by the Russian revolution, an Indian delegation went to the Soviet Union in 1921. But rival groups emerged. Virendraneth Chattopadhyaya and his American companion the socialist feminist Agnes Smedley advocated working with other nationalist currents. M.N. Roy thought the Communist Party should be apart and lead its own struggle.

Suspicion of the west was from the beginning a current in Indian communism. M.N. Roy, for example, accused Agnes Smedley of being a British spy. But communists also brought internationalism to the nationalist struggle. For example, a Cambridge graduate and active communist, Renu Chakravartty told women students in 1940 of the inspiring Spanish Civil War leader Dolores Ibarruri, La Pasionaria. The pull toward India and an international perspective were both present.

Not only were communists working among students, they turned to workers, peasants, and the urban poor. In the late 1920s and early 1930s there were strikes involving women in the textile mills and among bidi (cigarette) workers helped by communist women organizers. Left-wing women organized a hunger march of 5,000 Hindu and Muslim women during the 1942–1944 famine in Bengal, demanding price control and economic intervention. Communists sought to overcome class, caste, and religious difference.

Their universal ideal of equality inspired women of very different social backgrounds. For example, Bani Dasgupta joined the Communist Party of India Students Federation in 1939. Her family were landlords and punished her by locking her in her room, beating her, and eventually driving her from home. The Communist Party provided her with refuge in an egalitarian communal house in Calcutta.

A mass movement of peasant resistance against a feudal ruler in Hyderabad involved three million people in the period between 1945 and 1951. Organized by the communists, the Telengana uprising included many women, who were tortured and killed. Some women joined the guerrillas in the forests. Dayani Priyamvada, the 15-year-old daughter of a village policeman, slipped away from her home to join the rebels. Years later she explained why women risked so much.

> When we left home and stepped out braving all this we did so in the faith that there was a good future, a fine society coming, in which all of us would live really well. We dreamt that in families there would be no such thing as women bending before men. We dreamt that we would live so freely and happily. But repression came so soon that we never had time to question whether that equality was there in the Party itself.[17]

The communists imbued women with a vision of a future society based on equality and well-being. Their ideas of universal equality, however, failed to address actual gender differences, which had social and cultural consequences for women. The Communist Party tended to blame women for infidelities, wavered about girls leaving their families, and assumed child-care was the women's responsibility.

Independence from the British in 1947 was followed by splits in the Communist Party between the Soviet Union and China. The Communists abandoned armed struggle and the women of Telengana were left stranded.

The unresolved issue of gender equality was not just the local problem of the women in Telengana. Membership in the Communist Party meant chosen marriages for women, sometimes with a secular rather than a religious ceremony, though women remained responsible for the household and children. It was a relative and problematic freedom that was to prove precarious, for these breaks with custom also intensified the separation of the Communist Party from the rest of society—a contradiction that continued to trouble the Indian left.

Indian independence secured representative democracy and political and civil liberties. It also brought with it a considerable body of social legislation, protecting women at work, for example. There was controversy about reforming Hindu personal law on marriage and inheritance. Opponents of reform argued that women who wanted these changed were westernized and untypical of Indian women. Supporters of reform said individual equal rights and sexual equality in a secular state were not foreign concepts but integral elements of the nationalist movement. Nehru's support for reform was crucial at the time, but the argument continued to simmer.

Emancipatory laws are excellent in principle. They do not, however, automatically work in practice. India, like China, has tremendous cultural, regional, and religious diversity. There are, moreover, in India extremes of social inequality and divisions among various communities. The economy has faced the constraints suffered by all third world countries in competition with Western capital in an unequal global division of labor. All these general social questions affect women's lives.

These were some of the problems the Indian women's liberation movement expressed when it emerged in the 1970s. Clearly women had difficulties in relation to men—but these were by no means the only oppressions to be dealt with.

In retrospect now it is possible to see that there was to be neither an easy egalitarian utopia nor benign automatic capitalist progress. In India, for example, as in many third world countries the pressures on poor women have intensified amid global crisis. The existence, however, of formal democratic rights has made it possible to articulate alternative ideas and also to organize and mobilize women, both in the towns and in the countryside against both gender and wider social subordination.

Less tangibly Indian feminists face complex problems about how the boundaries between public and personal domains that have such crucial consequences for women are to be recast by women.

The novelist Ashapurna Devi glimpsed this imaginatively in a light-hearted short story in 1964, "Ja Noy Tai," which means in Bengali literally "Not what it seems" and more freely translated "On with the show." Gayatri stands before her mirror reflecting on her husband's obsessive jealousy. Old friends have asked her to take part in a charity show. How can she say to them her husband does not approve? Anyway to reveal his jealousy would be to expose him to derision. Risking his anger, possibly violence, she was resolved not to "throw open to public view the ugly scenes of her home life to outsiders."[18] 'A woman who was unable to put her husband in her pocket might be an object of pity, never of respect.

So what else to do but pretend a bulge in that empty pocket and put on a big show for the whole world to see.[19]

21

THE LONG MARCH OF CHINESE WOMEN

China faced persistent attempts from Britain, the United States, and Japan in the nineteenth and early twentieth century to open it up for economic trade and investment. Foreign traders arrived with narcotics and cheap textiles. They established banks and controlled certain ports. Foreign manufacturers established factories in which Chinese women worked in the production of silk. They brought with them a challenge to oppressive customs, for example, Christian missionaries established schools and opposed the foot binding that hobbled Chinese women. But the foreigners also regarded the Chinese with contempt. In Shanghai they put up a notice in the parks "Dogs and Chinese not allowed."[1]

Even in the nineteenth century, Chinese women had taken part in rebellions against foreign imperialism. In the early twentieth century resistance erupted against the decaying Manchu dynasty, which was unable to prevent both the domination of local warlords and the penetration of foreign capital. Many young women, often from leading families, became involved in this republican movement.

Their rebellion was extreme, overtaking the ideas of western missionary teachers and of the western feminism that young girls encountered at schools. After studying in Japan, Chinese women returned, excited by ideas about enlightenment and emancipation, opposed to male authority, and committed to the revival of China as a nation. Women's meetings were held and journals formed.

A few women joined revolutionary groups that sought to overthrow the Manchu regime. Sophia Chang, a schoolteacher who admired the Russian revolutionary Sophia Perovskaya, and Jiu Jin, a poet who sometimes dressed as a man in Western clothes with a jaunty cap, were members of Sun Yat-sen's "Revolutionary Alliance."

Jiu Jin had started the *Chinese Woman's Journal* in 1906 and became principal of Tatung College of Physical Culture. She took the name "Qinxiong," which means "compete with men"[2] and believed man's desire to enslave women must "be torn up by the roots."[3] In 1906 she wrote,

> slowly, slowly, a thread of light is piercing the black darkness of your women's realm.[4]

She compared women to "lamps in dark chambers."[5] Enlightenment and emancipation were inextricably linked to creating a new China. "I cannot sit by and watch the maps change colour, I cannot sit by and let our country turn to ashes."[6] Jiu Jin not only wrote and spoke she learned riding, fencing, and sword play and like other young women carried and manufactured explosives for the revolutionary cause. She was executed and honored as a martyr to the cause of the new woman and antiimperialism not only in China but far away in South India where a radical Tamil poet Subramaniya Bharathi translated one of her speeches and an article about her life.

Observers were amazed by women's part in the uprising against the Manchu dynasty in 1911. One Japanese journalist described women in Canton "as veritable walking arsenals."[7] He remarked that compared to the "modern Chinese woman the militant London suffragette is nothing."[8]

After the revolution of 1911 a constitution was introduced and women began to press for the vote. The Chinese Suffragette Society was modeled on the Pankhurst's Women's Social and Political Union. It demanded education, the abolition of foot binding, prohibition of concubinage, child marriages, and prostitution, the provision of social services for women in industry, improved status, and rights in marriage and the family, along with political rights. They believed that winning the suffrage was the means to achieve these reforms and used militant tactics. Young women broke windows and marched on the National Assembly and on local Assemblies.

A revolutionary warlord took power in 1913 and harshly repressed all protest, but on his death in 1916 a radical cultural renaissance emerged among the intelligentsia influencing, among others, Mao Zedong (Mao Tse-Tung). Personal freedom and rejection of every form of authority and domination were the themes of this movement. The young Mao founded the New People's Study Society in autumn 1917, in which all members vowed never to marry because of their hatred of traditional arranged marriages. Mao of course did get married but he continued to be concerned about women's emancipation.

Every institution and belief, including Confucianism with its stress on authority, was questioned. Both Marx and Kropotkin were being read along with Nietzsche and Ibsen, though Chinese "Noras" were keen to escape from the traditional family rather than from "The Dolls House" of the nuclear family. Visits from John Dewey, Bertrand Russell, Rabindranath Tagore, Ellen Key, and Margaret Sanger contributed to the ferment of ideas.

Birth control groups were formed. Free marriage, celibacy, and divorce were debated. The new woman adopted distinct styles, bobbing their hair, wearing fashionable pill box hats or Western clothes, and sometimes dressing as men.

China had no effective government between 1916 and 1927 and its sovereignty was threatened repeatedly. Women took part in the student movement against Japanese imperialism (May Fourth movement) in 1919. Not only college but school children were involved. In Hunan school girls formed discussion, investigation, and communication groups. Discussion groups of four or five girls went to public places, where they talked to women and girls about Japanese imperialism and explained that they should boycott foreign goods. Investigation groups toured the shops, watching what women were buying and telling them to buy Chinese goods. The communication groups distributed posters and leaflets.

Socialist and Marxist ideas about the emancipation of women were discussed and linked to the emancipation of workers. Chinese left-wing intellectuals followed debates in the Soviet Union. One worker, Tai Chi-t'ao, argued the revolution for social equality between men and women would precede 'the workers' revolution.

Women began to demand not only political rights but economic equality. Women factory workers had a history from the 1890s of militant strike action against appalling economic conditions in which anarchists had been involved. Strikes and walkouts began to occur among women in Japanese owned factories. When the Communist Party was formed in 1921 their journal *Women's Voice* carried articles about working women. Song Meiling, later the wife of the Nationalist leader Chiang Kai-Shek, was secretary of a joint committee of American, Chinese, and British women's clubs established in 1921 to study factory conditions. The investigators found women and little girls working in intolerable heat and steam in the silk factories for 12 to 18 hours while babies rolled around on filthy floors.

Some women set up small model projects to train young girls; others such as Xiang Jingyu were to join the new Communist Party. Xiang Jingyu was from a merchant family and had studied in France. She had founded and taught in a coeducational school and campaigned against foot binding, but decided that feminism alone was not sufficient. As head of the Communist Party Women's Department she stressed the exploitation of women workers, struggling valiantly against the patriarchal attitudes held by many male workers. Communists, like Nationalists, were dismissive of the suffrage as a means of solving women's economic and social oppression. However, Xiang Jingyu stressed that women had to be agents of their own emancipation in the revolutionary process and urged intellectual women to ally with women workers.

In her own life Xiang Jingyu asserted her personal freedom. She ended her marriage with a high ranking party official and had an affair with another. The Communist Party broke radically with some of the sexual restraints that had been a feature of Chinese society. In the previous decade women in China could be executed for adultery. However, as an unattached woman, Xiang Jingyu's power was diminished in the Party and she lost her position.

Nonetheless the new Communist Party put great emphasis on working with women and when they formed the Nationalist Alliance in 1923 with Sun Yat-Sen's Guomindang Party, both women's organizations demanded social and economic equality; along with changes in marriage, the family, and employment they also called for day nurseries and orphanages for children. Though there was less stress on the cultural process of self-emancipation than there had been a few years earlier in the May Fourth movement.

In 1924, on International Women's Day, the Guomindang organized a demonstration in Canton. A small band of women workers and students shouted "Down with imperialism," "Down with warlords," "Same work, same pay," "Prohibit the buying of slave girls," "Abolish polygamy," and "Equal education,"[9] to the towns people.

The unionization of women workers and propaganda work among peasant women were taken up enthusiastically. In 1926, young women with bobbed hair, trousers, and caps accompanied Chiang Kai-Shek's army against the warlords, forming Women's Unions. They were often welcomed by city women but rural women were much harder to reach. One of the campaigners said, "Those of us who advocate women's rights are like a voice crying to the clouds."[10]

The Women's Union's rescued prostitutes and slave girls, granted women divorces, and encouraged them to stand up against their husbands. But all this aroused hostility. In the Yangtse Valley when a woman was granted a divorce from a man who belonged to the peasant union, the men began to send their wives home to their families in a strike against the Women's Union.

There were also cases of spontaneous acts of excessive zeal in which members of the women's union forcibly cut women's hair and compelled them to unbind their feet. Nor surprisingly, these provoked acrimony among the peasants.

One of the most enthusiastic organizers was the daughter of a peasant, Wang Suzhen, in Hunan, who had been educated at an American mission school. She became a model for young women, with her necklace, with a watch and a fountain pen on it, and her assertion of a woman's right to choose her marriage partner freely. But other people hated her confidence and defiance of custom.

By 1927 the tiny band of demonstrators on International Women's Day in Canton had swollen to 25,000. However, in that year the alliance between the Communists and Nationalists broke apart after a workers' rising in Shanghai. Without warning, Chiang Kai-Shek began his attack on the Communists and left-wingers in the alliance. The Women's Union was disbanded.

As civil war broke out there was an anti-Red reaction in which over a thousand of the young women activists, easily identifiable by their bobbed hair, were killed. Some were bound in cotton blankets and burned alive. Wang Suzhen's neighbors led the soldiers to her and they cut her to pieces with knives and bayonets. Xiang Jingyu decided to stay in Wuhan when other Communists fled; it was an act tantamount to suicide. She was executed on May 1, 1928.

The Chinese Communist movement was deeply scarred by the horrors of these years. Many years later, the dissident Communist Wang Shih-wei was walking by a river and saw someone wearing "old-style padded cotton shoes"[11] like those worn by "my dearest and very first friend,"[12] Li Fen, who had studied at Peking University and joined the Communist Party in the mid-1920s. Wang Shih-wei described in an article, "Wild Lily" in 1942, how her own uncle had forced her to the soldiers.

Before going to her death, she put on all her three sets of underclothes and sewed them tightly together at the top and at the bottom. This was because the troops in Pao'ch'ing often incited riff-raff to debauch the corpses of young girl Communists they shot."[13]

When Wang Shih-wei heard of her death he said he was "consumed with feelings of deep love and hatred."[14]

The Nationalists told the peasants that communism meant moral and sexual chaos. Ignoring the fate of the women who were killed, Nationalist women set about disassociating feminism from communism. Feminism was redefined to mean a complementary role for women. As the philosopher and writer Lin Yutang put it, the new ideal was a wife "with new knowledge but old character."[15]

Song Meiling encouraged philanthropy. Professional women's clubs set up orphanages and settlements for beggars. They ran literacy classes and gave guidance to mothers and housewives. Social uplift rather than gender relations was the emphasis.

In contrast Mao stressed the specific oppression of women, which he saw, more than any other Communist leader, as of crucial strategic significance for transforming society. He wrote, in 1927, that although men were dominated by political, clan and religious systems of authority, women were also bound by the authority of men. These he called "the four thick ropes binding the Chinese people, particularly the peasants."[16] He believed that among poor peasants the dependence on women's productive role meant husbands had less power and saw signs that this was being further undermined by economic crisis in rural areas. He regarded the organization of peasant women as particularly important, if the peasants were to be roused.

Investigating the conditions of the peasants in the area where the Communists had established a base, the Jiangxi (Kiangsi) province, Mao observed that whereas all the landlords and rich peasants had wives and some had concubines many of the poor peasants and hired laborers could never afford to pay money for a bride. He decided sexual emancipation was not simply an aspect of the liberation of women, it was also part of class emancipation.

In 1931 the Communists announced there should be freedom of marriage and divorce for everyone in the Jianaxi Soviet. They also tried to reduce the stigma against illegitimate children by recognizing cohabitation as a legitimate union. Considerable confusion ensued; some marriages were exceedingly brief; also VD appeared. The communists were embarrassed by mysterious "Societies for research into love,"[17] which secretly formed. Free love had a chaotic impact on the archaic structure of Chinese peasant society and it victimized many women, arousing opposition among women cadres.

By 1934 Mao had backtracked and decided political and economic freedom had to precede sexual emancipation.

Surrounded by the Nationalist forces, the Red Army eventually had to break out of its base and begin the Long March—an incredible 6,000 to 8,000 mile trek on foot through almost inaccessible mountains and marshes, under constant attack from their foes. Only 50 women made the journey, the peasant women among them proving the most resilient.

As they marched the women approached the peasants to talk about equality. They found peasant women would listen only when they donned peasant clothing, helped with housework, and looked after the children. Gradually the women began to form groups in which they discovered common grievances by "speaking bitterness" and "exchanging experiences"—a form of organizing that was to influence the early women's liberation consciousness-raising groups in the United States of the 1960s.

Eventually they arrived at the natural fortress of Yan'an, a rocky basin about one hundred miles north of the Great Wall. The irrepressible Agnes Smedley, who had fallen out with her friend Emma Goldman because of her support for the Chinese communists, managed to slip through the Nationalists' blockade and arrived in Yenan (Yan'an) with a writer and actress Ding Ling (Ting Ling) and her translator who was in Ding Ling's drama troupe, Wu Guangwei, or Lily Wu, as Smedley called her. She established herself with Lily Wu in a cave. All three were divorced and strong-minded, independent women. Lily Wu was also extremely beautiful.

Mao visited to take tea and discuss romantic love with Agnes Smedley. He had been reading Shelley, Byron, and Keats. Lily Wu translated. Mao wrote poems with Lily Wu. Agnes Smedley enthusiastically taught the Communists square dancing. The Red Army men came along and so did some students, but the women members of the Long March disapproved. They thought it was immoral and suggestive. Agnes Smedley had plans to teach Mao the foxtrot but these were cut short when his wife He Zizhen became very jealous of his visits to Lily Wu. Calling Lily Wu a "Dance hall bitch"[18] she attacked her and Agnes Smedley. Smedley defended her translator and herself by knocking He Zizhen to the ground.

Yenan was buzzing with talk of romantic love and Mao's inability to control his wife. Lily Wu was sent off to Ding Ling's theatrical troupe weeping and tearing up Mao's poems. Mao and He Zizhen were divorced and Smedley left. The square dancing, however, continued and the tune of "She'll Be Coming Round the Mountain" echoed down the roads of Yenan. American Square dancing was to merge with traditional peasant dances, to be called Yanko, "popular dancing"; as it passed from the villages to the cities of northern China.

The conflict marked divergent views among women about emancipation. The Yenan communist women believed monogamous marriage was a cultural advance to be protected. They were determined there would be no return to the free-love system of the Jiangxi Soviet. The Chinese women from the city knew little about the countryside. Agnes Smedley was a sexually radical rebel formed by American anarchism, socialism, and feminism, who believed marriage was an oppressive institution for women. Ding Ling, like Smedley, admired Alexandra Kollontai and struggled to reconcile sexual independence with the circumstances of Chinese society.

Ding Ling's 1942 'Thoughts on 8 March (Women's Day)' explain He Zizhen's bitterness and the suspicion the women participants of the Long March felt toward Smedley and Lily Wu. Amid outward conformity to women's emancipation, there was material and psychological inequality in the power relations between men and women in Yenan. Ding Ling wrote that women got married,

partly due to physiological necessity and partly in response to sweet talk about "mutual help". There upon they are forced to toil away and become "Noras returned home". Afraid of being thought "backward" those who are a bit more daring rush around begging nurseries to take their children. They ask for abortions and risk punishment and even death by secretly swallowing potions to produce abortions.[19]

They would be reprimanded for seeking to advance themselves and not wanting to look after their children. They were reminded that after all they had chosen marriage freely.

Under those conditions it is impossible for women to escape their destiny of "backwardness",[20]

observed Ding Ling.

Their skin is beginning to wrinkle, their hair is growing thin and fatigue is robbing them of their last traces of attractiveness.[21]

In the old China their predicament would have been seen as unfortunate but now "their tragedy is seen as something self-inflicted, as their just deserts."[22] Communist morality concealed the actual inequality between men and women and was bolstered by an element of male hypocrisy.

Her criticism of gender relations in the party touched a raw nerve. The Communists wanted to maintain unity, not open up grievances and bitterness between men and women. Ding Ling, attacked for "feminism," admitted her attitudes were outdated and harmful to the cause. However, her unrepentant fellow critic Wang Shih-wei, was sent to work in a match box factory and killed by security forces during the evacuation of Yenan in 1947. The Central Committee was apparently not responsible for his death, but the combination of popular participation and egalitarianism with the suppression of dissent was to be a feature of the Communists' rule when they finally took power in 1949.

China was a very poor country that had suffered from the civil war and war with Japan. The problem was how to develop the economy and also emancipate women. The focus was on land reform to improve peasants' conditions and make sure women got their share in the land, accompanied by laws to end forced marriage, concubinage, child-betrothal, and interference with the remarriage of widows. The effort to make these laws take effect involved an enormous effort of popular mobilization. Social welfare measures, improving education, for many women were illiterate, and imaginative approaches to popular health were started in the 1950s and 1960s.

Economic scarcity and the theoretical emphasis on production in Marxism meant that there were strong pressures to equate women's emancipation with production, rather than seeing it as one element in a wider cultural process. However, Mao's own emphasis and the extraordinary place of women's struggle for liberation in the Chinese revolutionary tradition meant that the specific social problems of women and to some degree—given the lack of democratic power at the centre—the autonomous organization of women was not completely subsumed.

It was not clear though how women's subordination was to be tackled. Were women's needs socially different from men or was the aim to integrate women in the public, political sphere. "Anything men can do, women can do"[23] chanted young women in the Cultural Revolution of the 1960s. The snags came with child-bearing and the solution of separating parents and children, not only like Owen within one community, but sometimes sending quite young children far away, was often upsetting to both parents and children. More generally, the attempt to break with all earlier outward patterns had both egalitarian and authoritarian aspects. The effort to demolish social differentiation of all kinds was democratic in its aim, but the reality was frequently bullying even in the name of the consensus. Women did become more visible in local public leadership positions, but the intrusion of politics into personal life was coercive. Ironically their personal experiences of sexual oppression could become harder to voice. In rebellion against this, women, by the mid-1970s, were again stressing their specific needs as women, for example, trying to get more flexible working hours, so they could be with their children. Nor did popular participation at the base solve the issue of democracy higher up the power structure for women—or for men in fact.

The opening up of Chinese society and the economy was accompanied by a greater degree of intellectual freedom. By the 1980s again, women in student circles and the intelligentsia were able to focus on individual needs and personal forms of expression that had been subordinated in China's tortured saga of transformation. These ranged from interest in feminist scholarship to glamour and style. Market pressures, however, reduced some of the social measures that had enabled women with children to work. In the countryside old customs proved resilient.

When, in the late 1980s, a new idealistic movement emerged for democracy among young people, horrified older Communists watched as their children were imprisoned or killed, in the name of the ideas they had spent their lives defending. To pessimists it seemed as if all had been in vain. More optimistic critics simply said that it was evident that change took much, much longer than anyone had envisaged. The Chinese effort to alter the lives of poor women in the countryside as well as the town was economically and socially ambitious and has had an international impact. But this had been done at a high cost; by silencing dissent and denying formal civil liberties. This has made it much harder to challenge the effects of policies and renew a rigidified power structure.

V

IDENTITY AND DIFFERENCE

THEMES FOR DISCUSSION

* ★ The implications of ideas about nature for women's sexuality.
* ★ The creation of a lesbian identity.
* ★ The strategic consequences of a case for emancipation based on the assumption that women's needs differ from men's and that women require protection from the state.
* ★ The connection between production and reproduction.
* ★ Are women really the peaceful sex?

22

SEXUAL POLITICS

An Australian woman confined to a Sydney asylum for 16 years wrote to her husband, who had seduced her when she was 17,

> *you* were not *pleased,* you said conception was a *d----d* nuisance for you and you could not get at your victim in your old *pleasant satisfactory* "ways" . . . you monster you!¹

We are only able to glimpse her rage against the oppression of this coercive intimacy because the asylum authorities never let the letter out.

Open expression of sexual unhappiness rarely surfaces in the political movements of the nineteenth century. It appears fleetingly in utopian socialism, less often in later socialist writing. It was the undercurrent in the social purity strands of feminism and was to contribute to the interest in psychology pioneered by writers such as Krafft-Ebing and Ellis.

Its more traditional expression had been the confessional. An anonymous priest in Poland in 1910 recorded the troubled reflections of peasant women in Galicia. Women's organizations seeking to reform and modernize their lives were setting up welfare and education projects in an emerging wave of nationalism. But the Church kept its hold over their personal world. Along with anti-semitism, their confessions contained complaints about sexual relations with their husbands and descriptions of masturbation and lesbian sexual experience. The priest is their only guide on "sexual questions."[2]

An alternative counsellor was the doctor. An American doctor at the Psychopathic Hospital in Boston kept notes on a working-class patient of 23 in 1912–1913. "I am not contented,"[3] she told him. She was tortured by anxiety about her masochism and her sexual feelings toward another woman. The doctor's disapproval did not subdue her desire, even though she regarded him with reverence.

Mary Austin, born in 1868 and brought up in an American family of abolitionists and temperance supporters, had been active in the suffrage movement. Looking back on her experience of feminist politics in the liberal journal *The Nation* in 1927 she reflected on how difficult it had been for her generation of American women in the suffrage movement to articulate a positive assertion of female sexual pleasure.

Not only did the current phrases of birth control and contraceptives not come into use until the women of the pioneer suffrage generations were past being interested in them, but nobody, positively *nobody* had yet suggested that women are passionately endowed even as men are; not good women.[4]

She said they "lacked even a vocabulary by which measures of escape could be intelligently discussed."[5]

The silence had not been as total as she imagined. But she did express a shift in the way in which women's sexuality could be expressed. The new "vocabulary,"[6] she noted, marked a move from a personal discourse into a public arena. With this went a rejection of the "measures of escape,"[7] which had been formulated by those feminists who had advocated social purity or argued that a spiritual transcendence of physicality was what women wanted. Instead there was a resolve to recognize desire as a physical need and find a new balance between mind and body. Rather than seeing sexuality as a threat to women's autonomy, it was being redefined as an aspect of emancipation.

This move into the public gaze with its assertion of the body and desire was materialist and rationalist. It was based on the assumption that by applying reason it would be possible to get to the root of much unnecessary bitterness and unhappiness. Rephrasing that enlightenment optimism, which had envisaged the transformation of all aspects of human relations, it used ideas of "the natural" and assumed progress. Its supporters self-consciously identified with "the modern" and rejected late nineteenth-century feminist arguments that women represented a higher spirituality than men. The new mood emerged in opposition to older organized feminist groupings. Freedom to express one's sexuality and the capacity to understand it were both seen as vital for women in developing a new personality. Rejection of the view that the emphasis on the body and sexuality inevitably threatened the development of women's autonomous being had consequences on approaches to both heterosexual and lesbian desire.

It involved delight in the female body and an affirmation of pleasure. Crystal Eastman, a feminist and pacifist, remembered in *The Nation* in 1927, her father "startled and embarrassed to see his only daughter in a man's bathing suit with bare brown legs for all the world to see. I think it shocked him to his dying day."[8]

This was not the passive, still nude of the portrait but an active exposure, self-definition in movement, personified by the controversial dancing of Isadora Duncan. Irritated by complaints in Boston in 1922 that she had "mismanaged"[9] her "garments,"[10] she retorted "concealment is vulgar."[11] She believed her dancing symbolized women's emancipation.

Dora Russell, a feminist, socialist, and advocate of birth control summed up the new spirit that had been emerging for independence and emotional fulfillment in a book entitled *The Right to be Happy* published in 1927. She argued that sex was an instinct and refuted asceticism. Social and economic changes should be based on enabling present needs to find "new, free and varied expression."[12]

She was critical of the behaviorist psychology of John J. Watson, which saw human beings as machines programmed to respond to stimuli and which influenced advertising theories, industrial relations and child rearing particularly in the United States. Dora Russell noted a similarity between Watson's behaviorism and Bolshevism. She thought both believed that human beings and society could "be re-made like a machine to suit a definite plan in their minds . . . the *criteria* by which he—or the Bolsheviks—would judge completed individuals are reminiscent of industrial organization: efficiency in action and quantity in output."[13]

Instead of denying biology, Dora Russell sought a wider concept of material existence that could include sexual desire, control over fertility, and better conditions for mothers. She was by no means an isolated voice.

Crystal Eastman wrote in *The Birth Control Review* in 1918,

> Feminists are not nuns. That should be established. We want to love and to be loved, and most of us want children, one or two at least. But we want our love to be joyous and free—not clouded with ignorance and fear. And we want our children to be deliberately, eagerly called into being, when we are at our best, not crowded upon us in times of poverty and weakness. We want this precious sex knowledge not just for ourselves, the conscious feminists; we want it for all the millions of unconscious feminists that swarm the earth,—we want it for all women.[14]

It was to be the practical struggles around reproductive rights that made visible this resolve to connect emancipation with the body, pleasure, and emotional fulfillment.

The movements for birth control or "neo–Malthusianism" had differing strands. One reduced women's emancipation to the demand for control over fertility. This was one reason for French feminists' opposition to the anarchist Paul Robin's arguments for contraception.

Another source for antagonism arose because the feminist mainstream was socially and politically conservative. A minority, however, argued that freely chosen motherhood was a vital aspect of women's emancipation, even though it was not the only social change needed by women. A young journalist and mother of two children, Nelly Roussel, wrote and lectured extensively in Europe in support of contraceptive information before her early death in 1922 from tuberculosis. In 1904 she evoked the "birth strike," a slogan that had been around in late nineteenth-century debates on "voluntary motherhood." Roussel said mothers were "the worst paid of all workers"[15] and no strike could be more legitimate than theirs.

The link between reproduction and production, mothers and workers persisted. It brought together radical concepts of ownership of one's person and control over nature. These found a new connection in the syndicalist emphasis on workers' control. Margaret Sanger's "birth control" gave it a name.

Sanger's campaign for birth control had an important international dimension. Not only was her work known in Europe and in China, but also in Japan, for example, where women's political and economic emancipation, and the personal freedoms of the "new women," were all being debated in the early twentieth century, along with labor organization and socialism. Birth control was advocated by Ishimoto Shizue, after World War I, on returning from visiting Sanger in New York. When the Tokyo police prevented Margaret Sanger from lecturing in 1922, this stimulated more interest in her writings, which were translated into Japanese.

In Britain, a young Canadian socialist feminist Stella Browne, who was in contact with Sanger, was campaigning in this period, first in the Communist Party and then in the Labour Party, for birth control. She expressed a dual concept of control and self-determination in relation to production and reproduction in a Communist Party Journal in 1922.

birth control for women is no less essential than workshop control and determination of the conditions of labour for men. Birth control is woman's crucial effort at self-determination and at control of her own person and her own environment.[16]

She saw birth control as part of a wider struggle, "the work of liberation and human happiness implied by 'creative revolution.' "[17]

Stella Browne, who, like Kollontai, sought to interconnect "the increasing joint operation of psychical influences"[18] with economic forces, insisted that reproduction was as significant as the workplace which Marxists stressed. She also sought to engender the element in Marxist theory which presents human beings as agents of their own destiny. But she did this ironically by reinforcing the division between the personal sphere of women—procreation and a public male sphere of work. In this dualistic view men appeared not to be sexual persons and women in the workforce vanish.

The Communists' suspicion that birth control would necessarily be presented as an alternative to the redistribution of wealth began to shift in the 1920s. But the orthodox approach was to present birth control as a reform, which would help working class women, rather than a principle of women's self-determination and active control over their fertility and sexuality.

The Labour Party leadership, concerned to establish a respectable electoral image, was not enthusiastic when Stella Browne, Dora Russell, and other socialist feminists campaigned for women's right to birth control advice in the maternity welfare centers that were just being set up by Labour local authorities. But their agitation throughout the 1920s revealed considerable interest in birth control among working-class women in the Labour movement. Birth control clinics fitting the diaphragm, pioneered by Dutch socialists and feminists and known popularly as "the Dutch cap," were established.

In 1924 the Labour Party women's conference passed a resolution by 1000 votes to 8 in favor of birth control and the Workers' Birth Control group was formed. In 1926 the Labour Party conference voted for birth control but the Party Executive ignored them. Not only their voting image, but their Catholic working-class supporters, made it an awkward issue.

Dora Russell echoed Nelly Roussel and Stella Browne in equating reproduction and production:

> It did not occur to us that a party claiming to stand for sex equality, and for scientific organisation of workers according to their job, would take so short-sighted and unenlightened an attitude on the job of the mother. We mothers are claiming, like every worker today, simply the right to decide our working conditions, hours, wages, capacity to have and rear so many children.[19]

Invoking the argument of the nineteenth-century free thinkers such as Annie Besant, she said working class women had a right to know about birth control; it was a "class issue."[20]

The Workers' Birth Control Group deliberately disassociated itself from "Malthusianism," population control as an alternative to socialism, and eugenic ideas of selective breeding. Eugenic desires to prevent the "unfit" from reproducing, which were an element in Marie Stopes' arguments, were criticized by Stella Browne for their "class bias and sex bias."[21]

However, eugenic arguments permeate the debate on sexuality in this period and were not only used by the right wing to demand sterilization of the "unfit," who they invariably defined as working class, immigrants, black people, or the colonized. They were also part of left-wing and feminist visions of "scientifically" planned societies. Stella Browne, for example, assumed Communists and feminists were the "fit." Opponents of birth control and abortion also used eugenic concepts to demand improvements for mothers.

Before World War I a social panic about the supposed decline of the white stock had militarist and imperialist implications while after 1918 a pronatalist climate emerged in which abortion laws actually became harsher in several countries. A political discussion of women's reproductive rights was thus being raised in a context when war and imperialism made motherhood a matter of state policy. The public assertion of women's sexual and reproductive feelings and conditions is partly expressed in a language of individual rights, control, and self-determination and partly in terms of the citizen-mother's relation to the state. The latter was part of both the right-wing and left-wing discourse.

Marxist distrust of Malthusianism could be dismissive of individual choice whereas advocates of sexual self-determination could restrict reproductive rights through a class, race, or ethnicity bias. As late as 1909, Clara Zetkin and Rosa Luxemburg opposed Social Democratic women who argued for a "birth strike" on anti-Malthusian grounds; the socialist movement needed children. On the other hand, Madeleine Pelletier, an opponent of pronatalism in France, espoused eugenic ideas of a hierarchy of races before World War I, a view she repudiated in the 1930s when fascism brought home the political implications of eugenics in an horrific manner.

The black nationalist leader Marcus Garvey in the United States rejected the birth control policies of whites because he thought they would lead to the racial extinction of black people. W.E.B. Du Bois took a less absolute position in 1919 when he said he believed the black woman had the right to "knowledge . . . and . . . motherhood at her own discretion."[22]

Afro-American women did not regard birth control as the cure-all for all women's problems, which was increasingly the approach taken by Margaret Sanger as she shed her socialism. Nonetheless there was an interest in birth control in the context of wide ranging reforms. For example, in 1918 the Women's Political Association of Harlem, which called on black women "to assume the reins of leadership in the political, social and economic life of their people,"[23] included birth control in its lecture series. There was also pressure for birth control clinics.

Black women's writing in the period from World War I to the early 1930s in the United States depicted women who refused to have children in a racist world and also argued that smaller families would help the black struggle to advance. Women who faced unwanted pregnancies because of the lack of birth control were a common theme in fictional work. A woman in Jessie Fauset's 1931 novel *The Chinaberry Tree* is in conflict with a man over the right to birth control.

A character in a serial in *The Courier* called the "Bad Girl" in the same year says,

> The hospitals are wide open to the woman who wants to have a baby, but to the woman who doesn't want one—that's a different thing. High prices, fresh doctors. It's a man's world, Doc. The woman who wants to keep her body from pain and her mind from worry is an object of contempt.[24]

The novelist Zora Neale Hurston discusses domestic and sexual violence in *Their Eyes Were Watching God,* a problem that troubled black women social reformers. But this is in the context of a wider sense of identity, autonomy, love, and expression of inner feelings. Poetic language is better able to convey being desirous and the longing to be desired than the public discourse of rights, control, and self-determination. An example is Helene Johnson's, "Gee, brown boy/I loves you all over" and "Take my hand and I will read you poetry,/ Chromatic words,/Seraphic symphonies,/Fill up your throat with laughter and your heart with song."[25]

The social purity strands in mainstream white feminism simply bypassed the question of how women were to assert sexual desire. Sexual radicals' effort to make this part of feminist politics tended to lose the nuances possible in more personal communication. Bessie Smith's apt metaphors in song voice silences around pleasure that could not be expressed in the public discourse, which could assert women's autonomy but had difficulty with ecstasy and sensuous union. Stella Browne and Alexandra Kollontai's attempts to find a more expressive style appear somewhat flowery in contrast.

If birth control embarrassed the feminist organizations, abortion was even less respectable. Abortion as a demand was raised by small groups of dissident feminists close to the anarchist-syndicalist left in the United States, but was never taken up by any feminist organization until the 1960s. In Germany it emerged in the Motherhood League in the early 1900s. The League, which had irritated Alexandra Kollontai by its maternalist feminism, campaigned for better conditions for mothers and opposed male sexual control over law and culture. Conflict over eugenic ideas caused it to split before World War I.

In France, Madeleine Pelletier, an early advocate of abortion, was in almost continual opposition to both the anti-Malthusian socialists and conservative feminists. She regarded birth control and abortion as part of a sexual politics. As a working-class woman she had a tremendous struggle to qualify as a doctor and was interested in psychoanalysis. Like other French feminists she saw language as gendered and in 1908 argued that gender was constructed through psychological processes. However, like Dora Russell she believed the sexual act was a physiological instinct. She regarded sex as a subject for scientific enquiry and believed that psychoanalysis would contribute to socialist and feminist transformation of society. In 1939 when France veered to the right Pelletier was charged with performing illegal abortions and confined in an asylum where she was to die.

The USSR passed a law in 1920 that made abortion legal. The Soviet example and particularly Alexandra Kollontai's efforts to fuse psychology and Marxism inspired both Pelletier and Stella Browne, who was almost a lone proabortion voice in Britain during the 1920s.

However, by the mid 1930s the official silence on the consequences of backstreet abortions that resulted in the deaths of many women was broken in Britain. The terrible personal misery of poor women who could not bribe doctors became a public cause when the Abortion Law Reform Association (ALRA) was founded in 1936. It included Browne and Russell, along with Janet Chance, Alice Jenkins, and Frida Laski. ALRA argued for abortion as "the right of every woman . . . to decide what should happen to her body."[26]

In Stella Browne's words, "abortion must be the key to a new world for women . . . For our bodies are our own."[27] Stalin reversed the Soviet abortion law in 1936, leading Janet Chance and Alice Jenkins to distinguish critically between the state's use of women's reproductive capacity and women's sexual self-determination. However, the sex reformer Alec Craig saw ALRA's commitment in terms of "racial betterment"[28] not woman's right to choose.

The relationship between the state and fertility was an explosive issue in the context of fascism during the 1930s. Postwar pronatalist pressure in the 1920s had led to a harsher law in Germany and in February 1931 two doctors, Friedrich Wolf, a Communist, and Else Kienle, a feminist, were arrested and charged with performing abortions. A women's coalition was formed in their defense, growing to include a wide range of liberal and left-wing people, including Albert Einstein and the artist Käthe Kollwitz. Three thousand women demonstrated on International Women's Day, despite a ban on outdoor marches, and there were numerous local meetings, where women took the floor to "speak bitterness"[29]; the personal suffering of many working-class women became a matter of public political contestation.

The Communists in Germany regarded abortion as an aspect of wider forms of class inequality. There were demonstrations throughout 1931 in which working-class women protested against unemployment, rising prices and taxes, lack of housing, and cuts in social services. They demanded equal pay and social protection for women and children. The Communists recognized that class inequality was gendered. Working-class women were bearing the cost of the crisis disproportionately, as they were likely to be unemployed or low paid and dependent as mothers on social services. The criminalization of abortion intensified the pressure on women's lives.

They also presented abortion rights as necessary for the well-being of the working class family and ridiculed the hypocrisy of bourgeois morality. Rich women went abroad or paid a doctor to issue a medical certificate. Poor women died from illegal abortions.

Kienle however saw abortion as a specifically women's struggle. In her prison journal she wrote,

As a woman, I stand against the man; as a woman I must defend women's cause against the law, against the court of men.[30]

She questioned the use of "suffrage to woman if she is still to remain a helpless baby machine."[31] She went on hunger strike, nearly dying before her release. Her approach to abortion was in the tradition of the feminism of the Motherhood League, which linked the demand for abortion to a challenge to male domination in the whole culture. At a non-Communist rally, Thea von Harbou, defending Kienle, said,

We need a new sexual code because the old was created by men and no man is in a position to understand the agony of a woman who is carrying a child that she knows she cannot feed.[32]

The Communists' advocacy of abortion gained them support from professional middle-class women as well as working-class women. And they were themselves influenced by the emotional campaign. Some Communist Party women were responsive to Kienle's arguments and the slogan "Your Body Belongs to You"[33] was raised.

The mainstream feminist organization in Germany did not support abortion. In 1931 they urged a retreat into the home, because the struggle for jobs was resulting in the "spiritual impoverishment of women."[34] There was a rejection of political struggle as unwomanly.

In this period 1928–1932 the Nazis were gaining women's votes, though proportionally more men still supported the Nazis. In their efforts to attract women from religious groups the Nazis emphasized social purity and the sanctity of the family. It was, of course, a selective sanctity, for they enforced the sterilization of minority women even before the genocide of the concentration camps. The approach, even to German women, was not consistent. Their eugenic obsessions undermined the family's separation from the state and their concern for the birth rate led to efforts to improve the status of unmarried mothers, while they were also trying to persuade women to marry. But their opposition to the "New Woman" and her quest for autonomy was seen by some Nazi women as an affirmation of a collective social world, apart from male politics that asserted essentially "womanly" values of welfare and care. They rejected "the political front"[35] to build their "racial community."[36] This safeguarding of the female sphere by a strong state was a myth that involved the mass annihilation of millions.

In Italy, fascism stressed the subordination of women to men in the family, devotion to Mussolini was expressed by women in terms of an expansive male vigor that diminished other males. Mussolini told them to bear more children. He gave the vote to rich, educated women in 1925 but it was little use even to them as all political rights were revoked shortly afterward.

In contrast anarchist women in Spain (Mujures Libres) from the mid-1930s supported contraception, abortion, self-help health projects, and parental care and child-care centers, though the male anarchists gave this emphasis on reproductive autonomy and social welfare a low priority. The fascist victory in 1939 suppressed the emancipatory visions of Mujeres Libres and of the other antifascist women in the Spanish Civil War.

In Germany, Italy, and France and in countries occupied by the Nazis, women also took part in the resistance to fascism, but it was difficult to develop ideas about controlling reproduction, sexual autonomy, and the assertion of desire amid fascism's authoritarian redefinitions of a woman's place.

The optimism of 1915, when Stella Browne had asserted the "variety and variability of the sexual impulse among women,"[37] had become difficult to sustain as an element of political and social transformation by 1938, when she gave evidence before a committee investigating maternal morality. Yet still indefatigably rebellious, when questioned on the effects of abortion, she publicly referred to her personal experience of abortion. Not until the 1960s and early 1970s was this barrier of subjectivity to be broken by women campaigners.

Nonetheless significant boundaries had been ruptured by both debate and by collective action. Sexual oppression had partially found new vocabularies. However, the focus on birth control and abortion won space for the expression of women's *heterosexual* pleasure. This had been mainly based on the premise that sex was a natural instinct and that repression of nature was damaging. The application of these assumptions to lesbianism (which was called "inversion" or "homosexuality among women" within the discourse of sex psychology) was to be exceedingly problematic.

Following Havelock Ellis, Stella Browne believed in 1915 that some women were naturally lesbian. "I repudiate the wish to slight or depreciate the love-life of the real homosexual."[38] However, she saw "artificial or substitute homosexuality"[39] among women as a result of "repression of normal gratification." She did not think it was "advisable to force the growth of that habit in heterosexual people."[40]

In 1923 she returned to the theme. The lesbian's problems arise from a repressive society. Again she distinguishes between an "innate" attraction to women and what she sees negatively as an enforced social choice. The strong passion of the former should be recognized as part of a general assertion of physical "impulse"[41] in love.

> Every strong passion, every deep affection, has its own endless possibilities, of pain, change, loss, incompatibility, satiety, jealousy, incompleteness: why add wholly extraneous difficulties and burdens?[42]

In taking a terrain in which passionate desire among women can be publicly asserted, she was opposing strands in feminism that saw heterosexuality as an invasion of women's autonomy. Lesbian relations existed within the suffrage movement, but they could not be part of the public political platform. They were nonetheless part of feminist culture. They also appear to have been seen by feminists as a means of retaining one's autonomy from men. Browne contests an implicit assumption that "more or less erotic relations with other women"[43] are preferable to those with men. She is conscious of "a huge, persistent, indirect pressure"[44] on women toward lesbianism and has to emphasize that it "*is not in any way superior* to the normal."[45] The notion of "the normal" that she invokes, however, is not an established fact but an attempt still in the process of becoming. It is a space to be won. Browne maintains that a woman who rejects marriage and prostitution, but is not content "to limit her sexual life to auto-erotic manifestations"[46] will be forced into the political arena. "She has to struggle against the whole social order for what is nevertheless her most precious personal right."[47]

Browne describes this quest, which was her own, in tragic heroic terms. This is, to quote Mary Austin, "the measure of escape"[48] that fires her. In contrast, she is low-key in her attitude toward lesbian desire. She never acknowledges that sexual relations between women might be a *preferred* means of developing an emotional and physical sense of self and thus about expression not repression. She and Dora Russell were involved in a political battle against older feminists who held social purity attitudes; the mark of infighting is apparent.

I am sure that much of the towering spiritual arrogance which is found, e.g., in many high places in the Suffrage movement, and among the unco'guid generally, is really unconscious inversion.[49]

The question of lesbian desire and feminist politics in this period is complicated because the shift into the public sphere was much more problematic. There is no "movement" in the sense of marches and meetings. Nor are there social and political definitions that compare to post-1970 contemporary assumptions. Several images of lesbianism coexisted in the early twentieth century. In the nineteenth century literature lesbians are portrayed in romantic novels and poems as passionate, sexual, if unstable, "femme fatales." Emotional affection between women of a spiritual kind was acceptable within general assumptions of female nature in the second half of the nineteenth century in Britain and North America. This presented an alternative though erotically subdued space. The sex psychology that emerges in the late nineteenth century brings ideas of a congenital "masculine" tendency in some women. Psychologists such as Havelock Ellis imposed their interpretations but in complex ways women entered and redefined these predominantly male definitions.

In Greenwich Village, New York, the Heterodoxy Club, which, in the early twentieth century, included Elizabeth Gurley Flynn and Crystal Eastman, explored women's intellectual and psychological repression as well as supporting political and economic equality. There was both a strong stress on sisterhood and a nascent lesbian subculture. Tensions were appearing in the 1920s. The reasons were possibly partly because of a cultural emphasis on a "normal" sexuality but probably also because as the feminist movement fragmented "sisterhood" wore thin.

By 1927, when the series of autobiographies of feminists were dissected by "experts" in *The Nation,* psychology and psychoanalysis had become current. Not all were saying the same thing about women. Feminists such as Pelletier, for example, used Freud and thought psychoanalysis could help to explain women's resistance to emancipation. However, particularly in the United States, there was a strong tendency to produce "scientific" dismissals of feminist commitment. The more conservative forces within this modern, "scientific" approach were busy telling women what they ought to need rather than seeking to remove the social and psychological barriers to women defining their own sexual desires in new social relationships. These conservative psychological dogmas prevailed and it was to be immensely difficult to form a "vocabulary" to articulate an alternative.

"More or less erotic relations"[50] between women can be observed, if the women came into the limelight of celebrity. Singers such as Ma Rainey and Bessie Smith, literary figures such as Virginia Woolf and Vita Sackville West, and political figures such as Jane Addams, Lilian Wald, Winifred Holtby, and Vera Brittain lived in very different social worlds, but erotic or emotional involvement with women was a vital force in their lives. The writer Gertrude Stein began to live with Alice B. Toklas in 1910. Her opaque literary style constructed an elaborate persona through which clarity flashes. "I like loving."[51]

More self-consciously there were middle-class friendship circles and artistic salons, such as Natalie Barney's in Paris, where Vita Sackville West, Colette, or Ezra Pound might appear. Some women claimed like Mary Casal, author of *The Stone Wall,* in 1930, that they enjoyed the "highest type of human love."[52] Others such as Natalie Barney connected heterosexuality with a cultural submission to men. She liked men's company but desired women and this did not always imply love. But in her autobiography Barney takes her stand on the ground of innate inclination not political choice.

> I consider myself without shame: albinos aren't reproached for having pink eyes and whitish hair, why should they hold it against me for being a lesbian? It's a question of nature: my queerness isn't a vice, isn't "deliberate", and harms no one.[53]

The ideological basis of the claim for lesbian desire in a culture defined by heterosexual assumptions appears to shift during the 1920s in Europe and the United States. When Radclyffe Hall wrote her famous novel *The Well of Loneliness* in 1928 she had come to accept the ideas of the nineteenth-century sex psychologist Krafft-Ebing;

lesbianism was congenital. Her earlier writing, in contrast, had examined psychological and cultural rejection of a male-dominated society.

The novel created a scandal, which did force lesbianism into the public arena of politics. Not all lesbian women liked the book and not all thought it was helpful to make lesbian sexuality a public cause. Vera Brittain had a rather different objection. It was written with "a humourless sincerity worthy of a conscientious Sunday-school teacher."[54] She opposed, however, the censorship imposed in Britain and America in her sardonic feminist fantasy *Halcyon or the Future of Monogamy* in 1929. Knowledge of "homosexual tendencies among women"[55] should be communicated freely along with sex psychology and the birth control books of writers such as Marie Stopes.

Lesbianism thus appeared rather uneasily and solemnly in the public gaze and was admitted into the radical claim of the right to knowledge. But it was encircled by a definition of its distinct congenital "nature."

In translating personal erotic desire into the public sphere, meanings became less nuanced. For instance, the lesbian's visible symbol was the masculine clothing worn by Radclyffe Hall during the 1920s. However, Madeleine Pelletier had adopted male styles before World War I. She saw them not as a statement of sexual preference but an expression of her autonomy as a woman and her rejection of the subordination she associated with femininity.

The process of sexual self-definition, apparent among women in the early part of the twentieth century, was to be stranded, as feminism as a political movement splintered in the United States and Europe. The cultural assertion of women's potential sexual variability, spanning both lesbian and heterosexual desires, was to remain unfulfilled. Indeed the personal and the political grew more apart.

Gertrude Stein was Jewish, but by the 1940s she had concentrated so determinedly on the personal that she perceived the Nazi occupation of France and the war as "unreality."[56] As a student at Radcliffe she had pondered the infinite complexity in probing the "natures" of men and women. Later lecturing in the United States she said the cinema provided a new language.

By a continuously moving picture of anyone there is no memory of any other thing and there is that thing existing.[57]

Though the need to subvert gendered language had been a theme in feminism, especially in France in the late nineteenth century, the concept of self-definition as constantly in flux questioned all fixed structures. How this was to become politics is another matter; but the linking of personal life with politics did resurface during the 1950's.

Lorraine Hansberry, the black American author of *Raisin in the Sun,* wrote to a New York lesbian periodical *The Ladder* anonymously in 1957. She welcomed its existence and argued it was necessary to challenge a male culture that had never admitted women's equality in relation to "marriage . . . sexual practices. . . . and the rearing of children."[58] She reflected prophetically,

In this kind of work there may be women to emerge who will be able to formulate a new and possible concept that homosexual persecution and condemnation has at its root not only social ignorance, but a philosophically active anti-feminist dogma.[59]

A few years later there they were, trying again for that most elusive "right to be happy," and tussling over how women, regardless of sexual preference, were to say "I like loving."[60]

23

BATTLES AROUND BOUNDARIES: CONFLICTING STRATEGIES AFTER WORLD WAR I

"Now we can begin,"[1] wrote Crystal Eastman in the American socialist journal *The Liberator*, in December 1920. Gaining the suffrage was regarded by many women in the United States and Britain in the 1920s as the first step toward a wider social and economic program of emancipation. There was agreement among both liberal and socialist feminists that political rights were not sufficient, and an awareness was growing among many women of the need to tackle the wider forms of oppression that affected women. The problem was how? Should the emphasis be placed on equality with men, or on acknowledging and improving the differing circumstances of women as mothers? This was not a new argument, of course, but it arose in the changed context of women's democratic political rights. Although still limited, these meant that in theory women had the power to change laws and policies.

It became evident, very soon, that many of the changes women needed were not easily summed up as equality with men. Not only the issues of biology, psychology, and sexual culture raised in the struggles for birth control and abortion and the discussion of lesbianism, but the problems of mothers, particularly working-class mothers, raised questions of sexual and social difference. The differing needs of women were sometimes seen as arising biologically and sometimes socially. 'Difference' also became an issue between women. Class, race and imperialism meant that the idea of all women's needs being the same was questioned.

In her introduction to a collection of life histories by members of the Women's Cooperative Guild, *Life as We Have Known It,* Virginia Woolf wondered how middle-class women's preoccupations related to their lives.

> It was hard enough for middle class women with some amount of money and some degree of education behind them. But how could women whose hands were full of work, whose kitchens were thick with steam, who had neither education nor encouragement nor leisure, remodel the world according to the ideas of working women?[2]

Arguments about strategies that would best emancipate working class women, as workers and as mothers, became increasingly divisive in the 1920s and 1930s. There was disagreement about whether to insist on equality, or to take account of women's biological difference and position in the family and back protective legislation. There were also contrary views on whether women should concentrate their efforts on women-only movements or become involved in other struggles for social change. Argument arose over *where* to focus: was the main problem economic dependence or psychological bondage; should the strategis emphasis be on state welfare or organizing at work?

Debate about equality was occurring also in this period among Afro-Americans. Were they seeking to be like white people or developing an alternative identity and culture? For black women there was a further problem—what was their position to be in this affirmation of a distinct culture?

After World War I, the militant leadership of the National Association for the Advancement of Colored People (NAACP) in the struggle against lynching was male. But the antilynching campaign seemed to many black women to have priority over arguments about male–female relationships. Moreover, the claims of sisterhood were dubious. Not only was there the memory of white women's failure to support Ida B. Wells in opposing lynching, the white suffrage movement had again not been prepared to challenge southern white resistance to black women voting.

Exclusive insistence on equality with men was missing the point argued Elise Johnson McDougald in 1925. Instead she called it "The Double Task" of "Race and Sex Emancipation." Black women's "feminist efforts are directed chiefly toward the realization of the equality of the races, the sex struggle assuming a subordinate place."[3]

During the 1930s the rise of fascism presented all women struggling for emancipation with a dilemma. Fascism explicitly opposed feminism; on the other hand, in joining united movements with men, women frequently reverted to a secondary role.

The issue of equality or difference and the relationship of gender to class and race involved complicated political choices between the wars. Consequently positions shifted on egalitarianism or difference, autonomy or alliance. Nor was it clear where to concentrate, for women's oppression at work and at home and in the economy and in the culture was so interconnected.

Crystal Eastman believed in 1920 that economics were the key to "women's freedom." She defined the crucial problem confronting the feminist movement as

how to arrange the world so that women can be human beings, with a chance to exercise their infinitely varied gifts in infinitely varied ways, instead of being destined by the accident of their sex to one field of activity—housework and child-raising. And second, if and when they choose housework and child-raising to have that occupation recognized by the world as work, requiring a definite economic reward and not merely entitling the performer to be dependent on some man.[4]

This economic independence required an extensive rearrangement of society—even though Crystal Eastman saw it as only a beginning. She always acknowledged the necessity of changing in an "inner sense."[5] But feminists should concentrate on creating "conditions of outward freedom in which a free woman's soul can be born and grow."[6]

The first condition was "breaking down all remaining barriers, actual as well as legal"[7] in employment. This had to be accompanied by transformation in the upbringing and culture of men and women.

It must be womanly as well as manly to earn your own living, to stand on your own feet. And it must be manly as well as womanly to know how to cook and sew and darn and take care of yourself in the ordinary exigencies of life.[8]

Although many women, working class as well as middle class, were earning money, "these bread-winning wives have not yet developed home-making husbands."[9]

She thought "co-operative schemes and electrical devices"[10] were important, but they could not substitute for housekeeping, which should be shared. She supported birth control but stressed the need to tackle mothers' economic dependence.

If the feminist program goes to pieces with the arrival of the first baby, it is false and useless.[11]

Eastman thought the problem of women's economic independence could best be served by motherhood endowment "at least in a capitalist society."[12] It should be recognized "that the occupation of raising children is peculiarly and directly a service to society."[13] Hence the government should provide all mothers with "an adequate economical reward."[14]

Though she was a socialist and believed that capitalism had to be overthrown, she argued that "the true feminist, no matter how far to the left she may be in the revolutionary movement, sees the woman's battle as distinct in its objects and different in its methods from the workers' battle for industrial freedom."[15]

Women's oppression was not simply about "the profit system"[16] and "complete emancipation[17] was not assured by the downfall of capitalism."[18] She broke with the Marxist perspective on the "woman question" by insisting on the need for an autonomous feminist struggle, though the question of how or why there should be a connection between the two apart from the economic exploitation of the working class woman was left unresolved. Crystal Eastman was unusual in advocating an egalitarian feminist strategy in combination with much wider social changes. The emphasis of most equal rights feminists was on reform within the existing society.

After the vote was won in the United States discrimination against women persisted in laws over property, the guardianship of children and divorce. The National Women's Party introduced the Equal Rights Amendment in 1923. This would enforce legal equality throughout the states. Florence Kelley, who had been one of the leaders of the campaign for protective legislation, was alarmed that the Equal Rights Amendment (ERA) would invalidate the special protection of women at work and also threaten widows' pensions and the maintenance of deserted wives. When not only the Consumers League, but the Women's Trade Union League, the League of Women Voters, and the Women's Bureau opposed the ERA, the Women's Party was isolated.

In Britain, the Women's Co-operative Guild and the labor movement were for protective legislation at work. The National Union of Societies for Equal Citizenship (NUSEC), which had been formed in 1919 out of the National Union of Women's Suffrage Societies and the Women's Freedom League, supported equal legal rights and equal pay, but was in disagreement on protective legislation. In 1926 the Open Door Council aimed at complete equality without any barriers and NUSEC split on the issue.

Socialist feminists Crystal Eastman and Rebecca West, who were rather isolated egalitarians, worked with the Open Door Council and Lady Rhondda's Six Point Group. Eastman was employed by Lady

Rhondda's feminist weekly *Time and Tide* during the 1920s when she lived in Britain. But most socialists and trade union women believed that protective legislation should be defended, some arguing that it should be extended to men.

Eleanor Rathbone and Maude Royden, a Christian feminist, were convinced that "a new feminism" was needed based not on equality but on women's needs. Eleanor Rathbone had become convinced that women with children should not have to work, either at home for very low pay or leave their children. There should be a state payment for mothers and equal pay for women who were in paid employment. Eleanor Rathbone called the egalitarians "Me Too?"[19] feminists and said women should not measure themselves in male terms.

> It is after all a poor kind of equality which Mr. Fox accorded to Mrs. Stork when he invited her to partake in equal terms of refreshment served in a flat saucer specially adapted to the elastic contours of his own flexible tongue. And feminists awake to the fact that from some aspects our whole social fabric, man-made through generation to suit masculine interests and glorify masculine standards, was in the nature of that incommodious saucer to which Mr. Fox accorded Mrs. Stork equal access.[20]

Working-class socialist women were divided on family allowances because of the fear that state benefits would mean lower wages. Selina Cooper, for example, agreed with mothers getting an allowance of their own. Ada Nield Chew disagreed; she thought nurseries were the solution. In the mid-1920s women in the Independent Labour Party were discussing a range of measures that would benefit working-class mothers. Margaret McMillan, who had been involved in the settlements and in the suffrage movement and campaigned for free school dinners, set up nursery schools. There was support for birth control and family allowances.

Dora Russell, with two small children, "Bertie" Russell away on lecture tours, and the birth control agitation

> began to wonder if the feminists had not been running away from the central issue of women's emancipation. Would women ever be truly free and equal with men until we had liberated mothers?[21]

The Women's Co-operative Guild campaigned for equality for working class women at work *and* for social resources to help them at home and at work. They argued for communal services to be funded by local authorities, maternity welfare centers, and laundries (to the fury of the owners of private laundries). Their demands were based on the grass roots problems of their members; there was an emphasis on democracy and on developing confidence among the women in the Guild. The aim was to allow women a choice between work and motherhood.

Unemployment and poverty, however, were widespread and infant morality rates high. One Labour MP, Ellen Wilkinson, said in 1929, "Marriage should be scheduled as a dangerous trade, since there are more deaths from childbirth than from dangerous diseases."[22] In these circumstances many women reformers put the stress on reproduction rather than production.

Demands for improved housing and health care, unadulterated food and fresh milk, better education, free milk and school dinners for children, as well as clothing and shoes ("Boots for Bairns") became part of the struggle to improve the conditions of working-class women and children.

These aimed not at making working-class women equal to men. They were directed at the inequality that working-class women experienced in society as a whole. Women campaigning in these organizations laid the basis for policies that were introduced nationally during World War II, and then brought together by William Beveridge's welfare state. These welfare campaigners did not tend to call themselves feminists because they regarded feminists as women who denied the needs of working-class mothers and workers by demanding equality for professional women.

Similarly the network of women who worked with Eleanor Roosevelt in the American New Deal during the 1930s called themselves social reformers and rejected the feminism of the National Women's Party. They believed the biological and social difference of women required special protection from the state both as producers and reproducers. They have been labeled "social feminists" by historians, however, because they concentrated on women's welfare. The Social Security Act of 1935 provided federal money for programs in maternal paediatric care and the Fair Labour Standards Act of 1938 fixed a maximum hour-minimum wage standard for workers in interstate commerce.

The gains for working class women were important if limited by the circumstances of the economy. The public identification of Eleanor Roosevelt with workers and black people moreover meant that women reformers were able to affect policy. A President's wife who had stood on a picket line with women box makers, had represented the Women's Trade Union League, and worked closely with the black woman leader, Mary McLeod Bethune, was a new phenomenon. "Through dreams many things have come true,"[23] Mary McLeod Bethune told the founding meeting of the National Council of Negro Women in 1935. Dreams can be sustained by the treasury too; at least black housing project was saved by Bethune getting Roosevelt to intervene.

Change at the top encouraged hope at the grass roots; although self-help community organizing had had a long history among Afro-Americans before the New Deal. Bake sales, rummage sales, and church dinners had funded kindergartens, nurseries, schools, old people's homes, and community centres. These self-help projects were innovatory responses to needs. Black women retained this self-help tradition; for example, a black women's sorority, Alpha Kappa Alpha, created the first mobile health van when Mississippi landlords refused to rent space to open a preventative health-care clinic for share croppers. Every summer from 1935 to 1942

> they turned their cars into mobile health vans, immunizing over 15,000 children and providing services such as dentistry and treatment for malaria and VD for 2500 to 4000 people each summer.[24]

In both Britain and America, it was very difficult to organize at work when unemployment was mounting, though Communist Party women tried to organize women workers for improved pay and the right to unionize in the garment industry. There were also women on the unemployed marches in the 1920s and 1930s, but it became harder for women workers to assert their distinct interests when these conflicted with men's. They also tended to be concentrated in unorganized sectors. Many women had been forced to return to domestic service after World War I.

Yet amid the devastation of the depression, a new method of organizing production, based on the assembly line, was appearing in both the United States and Britain. These new mass consumption industries were to lay the basis for changes in employment and domestic life. Many of the new semiskilled workers were women, though Afro-American women employed in manufacturing tended to get the low-paid jobs such as cleaning.

In the 1930s an important kind of women's struggle in the United States were the "Ladies Auxiliaries." Wives of strikers continued traditions established in textiles and mining and adapted them to the auto industry.

Members of women's auxiliaries acted from a position as wives, although their involvement in dramatic and sometimes violent strikes broke down conventional ideas of a female role and in some cases resulted in a more personal rebellion. These class-based forms of women's action differed from egalitarian feminism and from social reformers who emphasized public legislation. Instead of claims based on the autonomy of the individual, the legitimation is the relationship of the women to their family. The interconnecting fortunes of wives, husbands, and children provides the starting point for resistance. But women in the auxiliaries were not simply acting on behalf of others. It was rather that the material and social reality of their lives was enmeshed with others. Their husband's wage rate affected their livelihood. This was not the autonomous, independent woman of egalitarian feminism, or the downtrodden woman who needed protection, but a new kind of working-class wife who wanted her husband to be well paid and not claim any hand-outs from the state.

Forced on to the defensive, the question Virginia Woolf had posed about how working-class women themselves were to remodel the world had to be shelved, along with Crystal Eastman's confidence that feminists could at last get on with the necessary social arrangements for women to fulfill themselves as human beings.

Women's struggle to make ends meet in the home made the defense of the basic conditions of reproduction vitally important throughout the depression. In the 1920s and 1930s women were seeking to gain greater access to resources. The argument that the state had a responsibility for the health and welfare of workers was one way of transferring resources to the family. Another was to adopt the auxiliary tactic of insisting that a man should earn enough to keep a family. This approach came up against the problem that as familial bonds were not necessarily egalitarian, the male wage earner had economic and social power. However it posed a challenge to the feminist emphasis upon the woman's individual autonomy. Working class women's mobilization within their communities was often based on their connection to their families and neighbors rather than their own rights to equality or even their own welfare needs.

During World War II, the wartime state could never decide whether it wanted Rosie to be a riveter or a mum. In this context it was possible to make some gains in terms of extending communal services such as restaurants and nurseries while women's access to jobs and pay improved. When the war ended, in Britain and other European countries, the welfare state was to establish, albeit from on top and in a modified form, many of the demands made by the new feminists and women social reformers.

The gains people can make are, however, affected by factors they cannot control. Welfare partly involved an extension of democracy into social existence, which was the result of grass roots pressure for public resources. It was also a means of reorganizing reproduction to further increase productivity and produce a labor force fitted to a modern capitalist state and a household geared to domestic consumption. Ironically state policy thus institutionalized differences in male and female spheres. These contradictory implications of state intervention in personal life have been the source of great strategic confusion. Women's need of resources controlled by the state has not meant that they had the power to define the terms of the state's regulation of their reproductive and productive activities. From the early twentieth century assumptions and methods that had been pioneered by new methods of mass production were applied to housework and even to child-care. In countries that were developing their economies and keen to catch up with Western capitalism, state regulation in the sphere of reproduction was presented as progress. In Mexico, for example, after the revolution in 1917, there was a sustained effort by the state to develop habits of order and efficiency in the household. Catholic ideas of motherhood were translated into a secular sphere, reconstructed, and modernized. Anarchist women's critique of this policy in the 1920s was marginalized. In Japan in the same period the relation of the family to the state was controversial. Feminists in the 1920s disagreed about how to free women from the traditional family. Hiratsuka Raicho supported state aid for maternal and child welfare but Yosana Akiko argued that state allowances would only perpetuate women's subordination in the family.

Colonialism and imperialism have affected the contours of the state's intervention in reproduction with agitation for policy reform interacting with a selective expediency. For example, Australia pioneered much social legislation and family allowances were introduced in New South Wales in 1927. Five shillings were to be given for every child subject to a means test. However, Anne Summers in *Damned Whores and God's Police. The Colonization of Women in Australia* notes that "Excluded from eligibility were most illegitimate children . . . also children with fathers who were aliens, Asiatics or aboriginal natives of Africa, the Pacific islands or New Zealand unless born in Australia."[25] In Jamaica social purity groups and philanthropists tried to control prostitution and argued that mothers should not work after World War I. In the 1920s a few projects to improve maternal health were backed. In India during the early 1920s the stress of western feminists such as Eleanor Rathbone on mothers' welfare was twisted into a convenient argument for retrenchment in recession. In the late 1920s and 1930s the British used ideas of the family wage to argue against women in India working, even though many women factory workers were without husbands.

Policy links thus existed between reproduction and production, but were defined in the interests of the imperial state not of colonized women. As a consequence the imposition of "modern" Western ideas has been resisted by women when it has seemed to endanger their livelihood. Legitimation of resistance against an invasive imperial state could invoke a past in which tradition was reshaped to fit new purposes. For instance, women's involvement in agricultural production in many parts of Africa meant that they retained a degree of economic independence. Encroachment of this relative autonomy by the state could mean that women's position was made worse rather than better. In Nigeria in 1929 in response to a rumor that the British were going to tax women as well as men to pay for improvements in the "Native Administration," an Igbo woman, Nwanyeruwa, refused to count her goats and sheep. She retorted angrily to the tax collector "Was your mother counted?"[26] and they seized each other by the throat. Inspired by her defiance, women rose up against the chief who was responsible to the British for collecting taxes and "sat on" him. They applied a form of "women's war" that was used against men who mistreated their wives or violated women's market rules or persistently let his cows eat their crops. To "sit on" a man involved dancing, singing songs that questioned his manhood, banging on his hut, and even pulling the roof off it. In this case they got the chief imprisoned for "spreading news likely to cause harm."[27]

By the 1920's not only individual equal rights strands in feminism were being questioned, there were also signs of unease about clear cut assumptions of progress and development. In fact, underlying assumptions about the inherent superiority of the West were being subjected to a cultural critique between the wars. Ambiguities in the modernizing impulse within both socialism and feminism were noted by the feminist pioneers in anthropology Margaret Mead and Ruth Benedict. Their starting point in the 1920s was the assumption that all races were equal, and that human cultures had relative values and could be compared. They believed that if women were to develop their potentials the differences between men and women had to be more fully understood across cultures. Ruth Benedict's concern in the early 1920s was moreover with inward processes of change or "the soul," which Crystal Eastman had believed could grow *after* changing the externals.

In *Three Guineas* in 1938 Virginia Woolf asserted the significance of women's experience of the personal. She is ostensibly addressing a man who asks her to help stop war. Her nephew Julian Bell died in the Spanish Civil War while she was writing the essay. It originated in a talk she gave with her friend Ethel Smyth, veteran suffragette and lesbian. Woolf writes,

> A common interest unites us; it's one world, one life. How essential it is that we should realize that unity the dead bodies, the ruined houses prove. For such will be our ruin if you, in the immensity of your public abstractions forget the private figure, or if we in the intensity of our private emotions forget the public world. Both houses will be ruined, the public and the private, the material and the spiritual.[28]

Virginia Woolf, who rejected female difference in literature as a trap, and strangles that creature of male power and fascism, 'the Angel in the House', believed also that women, the excluded outsiders, needed a new language and form of politics. They could not join the men's society without abandoning vital personal experiences. In a footnote though she quotes Coleridge, Rousseau, and Whitman as allies in the supposedly female perspective. She also quotes George Sand who said that woman as an individual realizes herself in relation to others. The subversive footnote suggests that it is not male politics simply but a particular form of male antifascist politics in the 1930s left that is being rejected.

Her complex struggle to rework difference and equality, personal and public, appeared at a time when many women saw the world as so polarized that the contemplation of ambiguities seemed impossible. While Virginia Woolf was writing her tortured feminist response to fascism, a young Jewish Communist office worker, Vera Leff, who had been part of the movement against fascism in Spain, returned from her honeymoon to find that she and her husband were the target of black shirt abuse. Swastikas were daubed on their front gate.

> Events seemed to be telescoped and speeded up like one of the early films. We were living so intensely . . . We felt that time was not on our side.[29]

Instructed by the Communist Party to join the Women's Co-operative Guild, her heart sank. Like many young left wing women in the 1930s, she wanted to be in a mixed political group. She ended up by becoming deeply involved in the Guild and part of the tendency within it that opposed the pacifism that had persisted as an element in women's politics since World War I.

In occupied France, Simone de Beauvoir and Sartre were forced to abandon their existentialist concern with the individual making freely chosen acts. Choice was denied by fascism. So too were their assumptions of equal freedoms. Jews were arrested around them. Yet in 1949, when Simone de Beauvoir wrote *The Second Sex,* she begins with a remark that Vera Leff would have understood before she obediently entered the Women's Co-operative Guild.

> For a long time I have hesitated to write a book about women. The subject is irritating, especially to women; and it is not new. Enough ink has been spilled in the quarrelling over feminism, now practically over, and perhaps we should say no more about it.[30]

Ironically of course *The Second Sex* helped to bring a new generation back to reconsider the past she swept away.

She broke away from what seemed like a clutter of confusion around difference and equality. Woman as "the other" is what man is not. She is the repository of no fixed female values yet she is in a distinct predicament. She is not just a human being who happens to be described as a woman. De Beauvoir examined biology as contributing towards, but not determining women's experiences. She rejected ideas of there being fixed instincts. Instead of essentially different character traits between men and women, de Beauvoir declared,

> One is not born, but rather one becomes, a woman; no biological, psychological or economic fate determines the figure that the human female presents in society.[31]

She cut through a great swathe of stuff here, feminist, psychoanalytic, and Marxist. She is intellectually like a musketeer, extraordinarily invigorating, and the lingering effect of existentialism breaks through to assert the possibility of women's transcendence. Her analysis was abstract; it disregarded material life and indeed history. De Beauvoir did not present a strategy; it was unclear how women's emancipation would occur. Nonetheless, she restored subjective action, examining why women collude within the relationships and forms of representation, where they are only what men are not.

The Second Sex is structured around the premise of freedom as autonomy. This was its most serious snag. Pregnant women were somewhat out of it. Mothers too have poor prospects.

> There is one feminine function that is actually almost impossible to perform in complete liberty. It is maternity . . . having a child is enough to paralyse a woman's activity entirely; she can go on working only if she abandons it to relatives, friends, or servants.[32]

Given that so much of the feminist ink spilled had been about overcoming mothers' exclusion from the franchise of humanity, this is a glaring weakness. Another is her conscious superiority and distancing from other women who were not part of an intellectual milieu. Later she was to reject these weaknesses in her earlier work and also criticized her lack of attention to the material problems women faced.

Nonetheless, for young women in the 1950s and early 1960s Simone de Beauvoir's life, her mix of intellectual rigor and individual audacity, represented an escape route from the suburbs. We seized autonomy and ran with it into the unknown.

VI

THEMES FOR DISCUSSION

* The relation between women's subordination by men and other forms of social oppression.
* The problems in assuming that women are a unified group.
* The strength and weaknesses in the slogan "the personal is political."
* What kind of society is suggested by contemporary movements among women?
* Is feminism enough?

24

'BORNINGS' AND BEGINNINGS: ORIGINS OF WOMEN'S LIBERATION IN MANY COUNTRIES

In August 1968 a group of young women protested against the Miss America beauty contest by crowning a sheep and depositing girdles, curlers, and issues of the *Ladies' Home Journal* into a trashcan. This rebellion of a radicalized student generation against a manufactured and commercialized ideal of female beauty, in a land that specialized in making dreams into images on a mass scale, received a glare of publicity. Less newsworthy was the "Poor People's March," organized by the movement for National Welfare Rights in the same year. But it included many poor women, white and black, demanding access to resources in a rich country, where it seemed as if organized labor had become increasingly part of the system.

The beginnings of movements are elusive. Origins and visibility are often worlds apart. Currents of dissatisfaction had been contributing to new forms of politics in the United States throughout the 1950s and 1960s. These influenced "women's liberation" profoundly. Not only was the growth of what students called the "knowledge industry" reshaping young women's future world. There was that suburban unease among housewives described by Betty Friedan in *The Feminine Mystique* in 1963 as "the problem that has no name,"[1] along with a growing impatience among working women about inequalities. Most important, the Civil Rights movement had created the basis for the renewal of a left that broke from both Communism and Social Democracy and struggled to express aspirations for change that were not only about the conditions of labor.

Civil Rights was not only ideologically, in Bernice Reagon's words, "the centring borning essence"[2] of subsequent social movements, it was crucial in different ways for black and white women. Jo Ann Gibson Robinson, a professor of English at the Alabama State College, Montgomery, had organized hopelessly for years in the Women's Political Council against the abuse that black passengers using the transport system received from whites. When Rosa Parks was arrested in 1955 for contesting segregation on the buses, she produced a leaflet calling for a bus boycott and Montgomery's black community stayed at home.

The use of nonviolence, the conviction that the means of struggle influenced the ends, the stress on self-emancipation as well as on rights, the claims on space and the demand to be part of the shaping of American society were all to be formative characteristics of a prolonged struggle to make a new politics. Women's liberation as a movement was to owe much to the Civil Rights and black movements.

Ironically "sex" was tagged onto the Civil Rights Bill to try and stop it going through. When it passed in 1964, Betty Friedan formed the National Organization of Women (NOW) to make sure that the equal employment implications would be realized.

In the mid-1960s young white women from the north went down

to the south and worked with the Student Non-Violent Co-ordinating Committee (SNCC). It was an experience that for many changed their lives and challenged their understanding of the nature of American society. It was also an encounter between "Americas" who had hardly known each other, between whom there were histories of death, distrust, and betrayal. It was psychologically explosive, complicated by personal tensions and culture incomprehension. Not only racism and sexual jealousies but a profound gulf in experience of politics and organization existed.

For example, one of the leading black organizers, Fannie Lou Hamer, was already 46 in 1964. She had lived all her life in Mississippi without knowing black people could vote until SNCC workers arrived in 1962. Though people were being killed, she resolved to register. She was beaten with leather straps when they arrested her. In such a context it is not surprising that black women, on the whole, felt race was the most crucial issue.

A few black men and women nonetheless listened sympathetically when Casey Hayden and Mary King produced a discussion paper for a SNCC conference in 1964 stating,

> the assumption of male superiority was as widespread and deep-rooted and every much as crippling to the woman as the assumptions of white superiority are to the Negro.[3]

But many thought the assertion was ridiculous. Some saw it as an insulting comparison between relative privilege and a blatant and ruthless discrimination. Men in the white student left were also dismissive and hostile when New Left women wanted to talk about their own feelings of oppression. Nonetheless small "rap" groups started and Kathy "Sarachild" coined the phrase "consciousness raising."[4]

Rosalyn Fraad Baxandall explains that consciousness raising was a way of understanding "the roots of women's problems in society and with men."[5] She says that

> many of us came from the civil rights movement and the New Left, and our aim was to build a mass movement to end the barriers of segregation and discrimination based on sex.[6]

Some of these initial groups described themselves as "radical feminists." Early radical feminists organized autonomously, but they were not separatist. They wanted to confront and change men and believed that women's shared situation of oppression in relation to "male supremacy" required a revolutionary solution. They also believed that movements should create the relations desired in the future. "Sisterhood" was part of a wider vision of more equal democratic relationships, though lesbian women were soon to point out that they were excluded by heterosexual definitions.

The idea of "supremacy" and the emphasis on organizing on the basis of one's own oppression were borrowed from the black movement, which was shifting from demanding Civil Rights to black power. Though a few black women were part of early women's liberation groups the relation of feminists with the organized black movement was often tense.

Women in the Black Panthers, who had their own battles with the men in the Party, did not see women's problems only in terms of male supremacy in 1970:

> As women, we recognize that our struggle is against a racist, capitalist system that oppresses all minority peoples.[7]

The differing emphases were to lead to many arguments, not only in the United States but internationally.

In practice early groups did take up other social issues that were not only about women's oppression by men but about society as a whole. In Baltimore they organized with welfare rights mothers, in New York they set up self-help cooperative child-care, in Boston they were involved in community organizing, and in Seattle they were involved with working women. But the idea that got through was of women's oppression in relation to men—a single structure of domination.

One of the early New York Radical Feminists, Ellen Willis, says in retrospect that this presented an "unsoluble contradiction"[8] because

> To build a women's liberation movement we had to take male supremacy out of the context of social domination in general. Yet from the very

beginning we ran into problems of theory and strategy which could only be resolved within a larger context.[9]

"Women's liberation" was to resonate in many other countries. A new consciousness among young women in a student milieu emerged in France out of the uprising among students and young workers of May 1968. In Françoise Picq's words,

It shared May '68's overwhelming desire to change the world, to liberate speech; it shared in the massive political awareness that was developing outside traditional political structures.[10]

Like their American counterparts they noted the gap between word and deed, "the anti-hierarchy discourse of the men was contradicted by their political practice."[11]

"Lesbians," "strip" shouted the men in a meeting at the University of Vincennes. Resolved not "to waste our energy and our strength in struggle against male-chauvinism"[12] Monique Wittig, Gille Wittig, Marcia Rothenburg, and Margaret Stephenson declared, "You can't liberate another, they have to liberate themselves."[13] When the women demanded that men should leave, they noted that "the first among them" to go were "the blacks in the audience."[14]

Autonomous organization was not assumed everywhere; for example, in Britain and Holland early groups included men. Groups became "women only" partly in retaliation to male hostility and partly through a desire for space to develop ideas among other women.

No existing theories fitted the feelings of young radical women who were often the first generation to enter higher education, who had both a tremendous sense of new possibilities, and an upbringing in which a particular form of passive femininity was pervasive in the media.

We were prepared to challenge every sexual convention, yet woefully ignorant often of contraception, abortion, and our own bodies. We faced contradictory attitudes toward female sexuality and we were part of a ferment in which received theories and authority of every kind was contested. Every aspect of life was political.

In France students organized "creches sauvages" in July 1969 by occupying a room in the Sorbonne and declaring it to be open for the use of local working-class families. When police tried to storm the building, parents and infants confronted the state. Anarchical defiance of society and an "outlaw" image was transmitted to the early French women's movement.

The German student movement was determined to eradicate authoritarian relations in the family, which they regarded as contributing to fascism. They squatted empty shops and formed "kinderladen." While the parents discussed Marx and Freud the children should play unrestrained.

Women began to put forward *their* ideas about the democratic relationships, which they thought should "prefigure" the future society. Helke Sander argued at a student conference in 1968 that

> Women can only find their identity if the problems previously hidden in the private sphere are articulated and made into the focus for women's political solidarity and struggle.[15]

Sexuality was a political matter. "Why do you talk about class struggle here and difficulties of orgasm at home?"[16]

Not only were apparently personal aspects of life to become part of the public sphere, Sander noted that women's demands were regarded by the men as "frontiers trespasses."[17]

In Holland, the "Dolle Minas" formed during an occupation of the University of Amsterdam in May 1969. They took their name, which meant "Crazy Mina," from an earlier Dutch feminist, Wilhelmina Drucker. They were playful rebels, influenced by anarchism and the situationists' idea that the "spectacle" was a site of power. They burned a black corset by Wilhelmina's statute, fenced off a children's play space, tied ribbons round a men's urinal to protest the lack of women's toilets, carried enormous paper flowers to the unmarried mothers' homes on Mothers' Day, and invaded a gynecologists' conference with proabortion slogans printed on their bellies.

The Danish "Red Stockings" believed not only that "the personal is political" but also that there would be "No Women's Struggle

Without Class Struggle, No Class Struggle Without Women's Struggle."[18] They demonstrated for abortion on demand and equal pay. They did a bus sit-in, demanding that women travel for 80% of the fare because their wages were 80% of the men's. They opposed the World Bank Congress with street theatre about Third World women. A defiance of conventional femininity meant they busied themselves being ugly. Young women assumed a deviant marginal role; they were cultural guerrillas and permanent rebels, defiant outsiders.

In Britain in 1969 women set off into the underground with stickers. One declaring "This Exploits Women" went on the provocative swimwear adverts. We opposed being consumer sex objects. The others demanded Equal Pay. A demonstration at the Ideal Home Exhibition protested against domesticity. At the Miss World Contest feminists disrupted the event in 1969 and again in 1970, chanting "We're not beautiful, we're angry."[19]

Several strands existed in the British movement. The first women's rights group formed in Hull in 1968 in support of Lil Bilocca's campaign in the fishing community against unsafe trawlers, which earned her hostility from the owners and some fishermen. A class led by Juliet Mitchell for mothers with young children turned into a consciousness raising group; another was set up in North London by North American women involved in the opposition to the Vietnam War. Several were mothers of young children and alternative forms of collective childcare involving men was important in their approach to women's liberation. These groups surfaced in 1969, linking with the political challenge to male leaders among left-wing students.

In the trade union movement a campaign for equal rights started in 1968. Women in the trade union movement, influenced by the black movement in South Africa and in the United States, were talking in terms of job "segregation" and the internalization of oppression by the late 1960s.

In Northern Ireland, the Civil Rights demonstrations in 1968 sparked off a wider rebellion. In the South women took the train to Belfast to buy the pill in a blaze of publicity over lack of legal contraception. When a Dublin group went out to a working class area, Ballymun, they were "expecting the 'bra burners' image to have stuck"[20]; instead women came forward to speak in public for the first time about their marriages, children, husbands, priests, and lack of birth control.

International and national currents interacted in the emergence of the early movement in Ireland as well as elsewhere. There were also echoes of the past. The American connection was evident in Nell McCafferty's use of the slogan "Bread and Roses"—which had been readopted by women's liberation in Boston in memory of Elizabeth Gurley Flynn and the Lawrence strike led by the IWW. The defense of feminist autonomy written in 1913 by James Connolly had been republished by radical feminists in New York. Consciously identifying with women's part in Connolly's rising against the British in 1916, a group at Cork University in 1970 called itself the Markiewicz Women's Movement after Countess Markiewicz, who, when elected to the House of Commons, could not take her seat because she was in prison after the Easter Rising.

Irish women in the North faced a continuing pull in the pressure between the movement against British troops' presence and the women's liberation movement. In Israel too there were conflicting perspectives about the Palestinian question in the women's groups that appeared in the mid-1970s. Elsewhere "antiimperialism" coexisted with "feminism," but there were contrary emphases that were eventually to produce splits in some countries.

The initial impetus was internationalist. The Vietnamese struggle against the American government had an inspirational influence and women's liberation journals carried many articles about Vietnamese women. There was also support for Palestinian women, for instance, in Canada, a "Leila Khaled Collective" formed in solidarity.

However, when the New Feminists in Canada in 1971 claimed "our revolution is the most important revolution in the history of human beings,"[21] it is conceivable that Arab women in Jerusalem demonstrating over the confiscation of land in 1968 might have disagreed.

When socialist feminist groups emerged in Toronto and elsewhere they tried to bridge the gulf between an emphasis on women's oppression alone and antiimperialism and other social demands. As well as

solidarity in support of Third World women they supported cooperative child-care and formed links with the trade unions, which in Canada
were to be continuing.

American feminism influenced Italian New Left women in several
cities. In Turin the first women's group formed in 1971. However,
local labor movement traditions had a strong influence for they "believed firmly in the leading role of the working class and the centrality
of the struggle in the factory."[22] Soon the feminist collective was torn
apart by arguments about whether to emphasize external activities or
to give priority to consciousness raising, which the Italians called "self-
knowledge." It was not so easy to combine the personal and the
political, self-emancipation and social emancipation.

Nonetheless the interaction between international influences and
the radicalization of young mainly educated middle-class women con
tinued. Efforts to go beyond the initial social base depended very much
on the local political circumstances. Approaches also varied regionally
and between cities and smaller towns. Anne Summers describes
women from the Australian countryside being "puzzled by the anti-
organization, anti-leadership slogans being parried at them"[23] from the
big cities at the Women's Electoral Lobby Conference in Canberra
in 1973. Debates moved over boundaries, campaigns were started,
magazines passed from hand to hand, histories were rediscovered,
splits shattered the rosy glow of sisterhood, and, incredibly, the wom-
en's movement *went on* beginning.

By the late 1970s autonomous women's movements had appeared
in Greece and Spain, both countries that had recently had right-wing
regimes. In Spain there was both a feminist upsurge after Franco and
militant organization among women in working-class neighborhoods
around housing and other social needs.

In Turkey women's groups were to form from contacts made
among women who were resisting the right-wing regime in the mid
1980s. They began talking actually in the prison visitors' queues. The
necessity for an autonomous group was strongly contested by men on
the left.

The Indian movement had been having the same arguments for a
decade. The first groups had been started by maoists influenced by

China in 1975. Shortly afterward, during the state of emergency, women's liberation started in big cities. They organized autonomously but tended to be socialist feminist in orientation and saw women's oppression in relation to wider subordination.

Similarly in Sri Lanka, Hema Goonatilake, a lecturer at Kelaniya University, described the position of "Voice of Women," which emerged in 1978:

> Our struggle cannot be fulfilled only by men and women achieving equality in an unequal society. We are struggling for a radical change of such a society, and for the principle of participation in it and the self-reliance of poor women.[24]

"Voice of Women" have been involved with the problems of women workers in rural villages, on plantations, and in the Free Trade Zones. They have also taken up the cause of migrant women working in the Middle East, struggled against violence against women, and contested images of women in the media. By the late 1980s mounting conflict in Sri Lanka made their work increasingly difficult and dangerous.

In Pakistan, "The Women's Action Forum" was formed in 1981. When three hundred women demonstrated in Lahore the following year against the Islamization policy, under which women accused of adultery were being publicly whipped, more than 20 women were wounded and 31 were arrested. This was the first demonstration since the military regime had taken power in 1977. The women's action was important as part of a general movement for democracy.

Subsequently women's groups elsewhere have conflicted with Islamic fundamentalism, for example, in Algeria. Approaches differ between those who take a secular strand and those who contest fundamentalist readings of Islamic religious teaching.

Asian feminists were forming international links through the 1970's and 1980s. Yayori Matsui, a Japanese journalist, encountered "the women's lib movement that was . . . spreading like wildfire"[25] in the United States in 1970–1971. It made her question the sexism in Japanese society and seek to "analyze . . . its root causes."[26] Aware of environmental and economic problems and recognizing that Japan was becoming one of the colonial rulers in Asia, the group she formed in 1974 with some friends "The Asian Women's Association," focused on "sex tourism, Japan-South Korea relations, war responsibility, Japanese multi-nationals, exploitation of women for cheap labour along with discrimination and sexism."[27] Yayori Matsui concludes,

> We Japanese women play a double role: we are discriminated against in Japanese society and at the same time, we benefit from the exploitation of other Asian women. Just as do the women of the United States. We are both victims and oppressors.[28]

In both Taiwan and the Philippines the initial attempts to start women's groups were crushed. Lu Hsui-Lien returned from Harvard in 1972 and started a "telephone to protect you"[29] service to help poor women and victims of violence along with an abortion campaign. But her arrest, for taking part in a demonstration by the Taiwan Independence and Democracy movement, resulted in a 12-year prison sentence.

Lorena Barros, leader of "MAKIBAKU," the first women's liberation group to be formed out of the Filipino student movement in the late 1960s, was forced underground and shot by government troops in 1976.

In 1984 a coalition of 70 women's groups, workers, and rural women as well as middle class created 'GABRIELA.' They argue Asian women are oppressed as Third World people through foreign dominance, as the working class by their own ruling elite and as women by male domination. Filipino women were being confronted not only by economic and political oppression but by prostitution, sex, tourism, rape, and sexual abuse, as well as the migration of women as mail-order brides or as domestics who have no rights.

Latin American women's movements came out of situations in which it was almost impossible to disassociate themselves from the overall political contexts of popular movements. The groups for "self-reflection" were formed by mainly educated middle-class women, but closely involved with women in the slums and with trade unions. In Peru and Nicaragua as well, rural women were to mobilize.

The boundaries between public and private, the significance of a space for feminist concepts and demands, and how to transform society democratically have been continuing debates. Restructuring political images and language has involved arguments with the left. Internally problematic are the differing concerns of women of various classes, the questions of race or caste and of lesbianism.

There is no single Third World approach to feminism. Also emphases change. An organizer from the Bolivian mining area Domitila Barrios de la Chungara decided in 1975 at the United Nations International Women's Conference in Mexico that there was the feminism that thinks "women will only be free when they equal men in all their vices"[30] and the liberation, "which consists of women being respected as human beings."[31] In Palestine women's groups have stressed commitment to the overall struggle rather than their specific oppression as women. In India, in very different circumstances, *Manushi,* the feminist journal, covers health hazards at work, drought, rape, and the revival of sati (widow immolation). In South Korea "Women for Equality and Peace," which started in 1983, argues,

> Unless women are liberated, human liberation is impossible. Unless a society where women can live as human beings is realized, women's liberation will remain only an illusion.[32]

In Peru feminists, such as the organizer and writer Virginia Vargas at the "Flora Tristan Centre," are convinced of the need for autonomy for the women's movement while recognizing that gender relations are shaped by other social relations such as slavery and class.

International feminist ideas and women's movements have influenced Third World countries. As Kamla Bhasin from India and Nighat Said Khan from Pakistan observe in a pamphlet called *Some Questions on Feminism and Its Relevance in South Asia,* "an idea cannot be confined within national or geographic boundaries."[33]

Equally though groups were formed by the circumstances and experiences of women in many differing countries. Socialism and movements for national liberation have both been important catalysts as well as movements for democracy more generally.

Also in some Third World countries there has been a longer history. The authors of *Some Questions on Feminism and Its Relevance in South Asia* note,

> while the *term* feminism may be foreign, the concept stands for a transformational process, a process which started in South Asia in the nineteenth century as an organised and articulated stand against women's subordination.34

They also say that although it is middle-class women who become visible through the media, there are many women raising women's issues, equality at work, sexual harassment, wife battering, and antialcohol campaigns along with class and poverty, in a wide range of grass roots movements.

Women's groups are arising in the early 1990s in completely different circumstances in the former Soviet Union, East Germany, and Eastern Europe. They are raising issues such as rape in the Soviet Union, lesbianism in Yugoslavia, defending abortion in Catholic Poland, and forming sections in the Hungarian trade unions. None of these countries had a strong feminist tradition before the Communists took power, apart from Germany, and except for the Yugoslavs they have been largely cut off from the contemporary women's movement.

Ideas did travel nonetheless. One Soviet socialist feminist read about feminism in the British Communist journal, *Marxism Today,* for example. Many of the new groups however do not identify at all with socialism or with feminism because they connect both with the lack of freedom and democracy that existed under the Communist Party. But women in these completely new movements still face many problems because the impact of the market removes some of their social protection and benefits. In Helga Rapusi's words, "As a human being I have gained. But I have lost out as a woman."[35] Theirs is a completely new beginning.

Anastasia Posadskaya, who is head of the Gender Studies Centre in Moscow and a member of the feminist group "Lotos" (Liberation from sexual stereotypes), says the "Marxist concept"[36] of "the women's question"[37] in the past "concealed or misrepresented"[38] legal and social equality, participation in production, and gender relations in the family. But now the problem is that women's groups have little influence on policies that affect their lives. She is convinced "there is no ideal prescription"[39] for creating new organizational structures. Eastern European countries and the former USSR,

> Share the bitter experience of going the same way and making similar mistakes. It wholly depends on people who are building the national machinery whether it will be the dead bureaucratic mechanism or the flexible, developing and responsive to the people's need structure[sic] So the main principle is the principle of creativity.[40]

25

PERSONAL POLITICS: CHANGING DEFINITIONS THROUGH ACTION

"I am a woman giving birth to myself," announced an early American women's liberation slogan. Movements present contradictory ideas, especially when they are as distrustful of leaders and conscious direction as the movement was in the early 1970s. Moreover, although international interactions resulted in theoretical crossovers, every new beginning has assumed differing shapes. It is as if thousands and thousands of women were busy making a gigantic garment, borrowing and creating their own patterns. Despite varying emphases there have been common themes and common problems and over time several attempts to unravel the knitting and make fresh starts.

The take off point was not simply the circumstances of women but a critique of the inadequacies in existing "politics." One of the most remarkable characteristics of modern feminism has been its capacity for continual political innovation. Initially theory was formed in defiance of, but in relation to the body of ideas about how to organize, which was handed down through prevailing traditions of radical protest. The impact of the "new left" was important.

The women's liberation movement focused, like the new left, on the individual and on self-emancipation. The idea behind consciousness raising was to link the self to others. It did not always work in practice, but in theory the individual was situated in relations within society. Thus personal experience could reveal dynamically a social reality. This was a significant break. Older forms of socialism had lost sight both of the individual and of personal daily life.

The assumption was made that organization and action should be based on one's own oppression and that all women were oppressed. This concept was closely related to debates within the black community in the United States. It was quite different from those Marxist views that emphasized class and regarded middle-class women simply as members of a privileged elite who could support the working-class struggle. Nonetheless, although rejecting the subordination of all other forms of oppression to class, in practice early women's liberation politics were concerned not only with the directly experienced grievances of a new strata of educated young women. Awareness of a subjective oppression as a woman could coincide with a wider opposition to socially oppressive relations.

Though in America "NOW" was concerned with gaining reforms within society as it was, most early women's liberation groups were trying to change all relationships in society. Consequently dichotomies that had troubled earlier feminists about whether women should claim equality or back policies based on difference, biological or social, and whether women should be protected from men and capitalism or assert their desires without any restraint, were not seen as particularly troublesome. It was assumed they were to be surpassed in a project of social revolution that was to transcend all previous efforts, which were seen to be inadequate, especially for women. This was rather ambitious and not particularly modest, but this tends to be the way with young movements.

One of the issues that quickly came to the fore was the contribution of unpaid domestic activity to society and the need to change the whole sexual division of labor between men and women. As we have seen these were not completely new ideas. The economics of domestic labor had been raised by American and Canadian Marxist women as well as by Amy Bailey in Jamaica during the 1930s and interestingly in the left in Japan in the early 1960s. By the mid-1960s, in Sweden the policy of sharing child-care and both parents working was established as an aspect of Social Democracy. Nonetheless, the emphasis placed on sharing housework and child-care was to be much greater than in earlier feminism. The position of young middle-class mothers had changed in the postwar world.

The modern women's movement linked inequalities of home and work. It brought into the main political arena housework and sexuality; daily life in the community and the family were seen as sites of struggle and consciousness. Indeed, in contrast to political parties, the women's movement has been concerned more about changing daily life than gaining power through the state. Particularly in the United States, self-help tended to be stressed as the strategy for change combined with direct participatory democracy. Though over two decades the need to relate more to state structures and existing institutions came to be recognized.

The aim of many women's liberation groups was to live the ideal future relations in the present. The effort was made to prefigure an alternative to enable women to gain confidence through trust. *Sisterhood is Powerful* was the title of an early collection of writings. There are echoes of earlier religious communitarianism, and of Mary Wollstonecraft's "Society of beings who can love"[1] through connection to the Civil Rights' vision of community.

These new processes and relationships were originally conceived as making a movement to transform society possible. Practically this resulted in many kinds of service groups—publishers, book shops, women's centers, cafés, cultural projects—all encouraging creativity among women. But as a general strategy it was problematic. Quite soon the means started to become ends in themselves. Already by the early 1970s a shift occurred in the United States and the radical feminist emphasis on external change was being replaced by versions of cultural feminism in which changing oneself became the *aim*. Versions of cultural feminism occurred in many countries. By the mid-1970s in Britain we were wondering whether we were a movement for the liberation of women, or a movement of liberated woman. There was a narrowing of ambition. In her study of radical feminism in the United States, Alice Echols states,

> The radical feminists' declaration, "organise around your own oppression", soon degenerated into the narrower position, "organise around your own interests."[2]

Disputes soon arose about whose interests. Lesbian women disputed whether heterosexual women could reliably express their interests. By 1970 Mary Dana wanted to know where lesbians were in all the new talk of a new sexuality. Afro-Americans felt ambivalent toward a white-dominated feminism. In 1973 the National Black Feminist organization was formed in the United States. In 1972, 67% of black women polled were in sympathy with efforts of women's liberation groups[3] as compared to 35% of white women, but this did not imply great enthusiasm for the Equal Rights Amendment, probably because their most pressing problems were not equality but lack of access to resources. Chicana feminists, Asian American women, and Native American women began to define their specific perspectives as feminists.

There were real dilemmas about who could speak for "women." This was partly a paradox inherited from earlier feminisms. As Rosalind Delmar remarks, "Feminists have not always had the same concept of woman, either at any time or over time."[4] What "concept of woman is being mobilized"[5] and by whom became an explosive issue partly because of the utopian denial of conflicts of power among women. Many of these clashes around identity and power have been destructive and painful; however, important new emphases have been made in modern feminist politics as a result. For example, both lesbianism and race have been much more thought through and debated than previously. Similarly issues of ethnicity and disability have been raised.

A distrust of individual leaders or of groups taking a vanguard role was part of the libertarian heritage of women's liberation. It also grew from awareness that individuals could be accommodated. Mass collective risings could not.

The aim was to *extend* democracy and it has had an extremely creative impact in challenging the idea that an organization should simply concentrate on power rather than linking the process of change to the outcome. It has involved a critique of formal political procedures and representative democracy. The effort was made to allow every woman to participate. Democracy was also seen to be about how we related to others, how we lived, how we expressed sexual desire, dressed, and used language. Ironically though, this urge to break entirely with dominion could breed its own self-righteous authoritarianism and it could deny actual inequalities. Hidden forms of power emerged within the tyranny of structurelessness.

The women's movement has been about politicizing "the personal" and bringing personal issues into politics. "The personal is political" was a slogan taken from the American new left. It made sense to the young women drawn toward women's liberation groups because so many problems they faced were outside existing political definitions. They had the confidence to question not only how politics was defined, but how personal life was constituted, for instance, inequality in sexual relations. Democracy and liberation should apply at home and involve transforming fantasy and desire. It should break down existing demarcations and challenge male-defined exclusions.

The body surfaces as a vital element in this reformulation of politics through the demands of women's liberation from its origins. For example, abortion campaigns in many countries including Catholic Italy made mass movements out of an issue that had been difficult to raise in earlier movements. It was actually the first time organized American feminism had taken up the demand. Abortion involved questioning the whole social context of women's lack of control over fertility and thus challenged not only existing divisions between personal and political, but concepts of control and power that were confined to production. Implicitly women's liberation as a movement questioned the narrowing of material life to work. Quite quickly too it can be seen in practice connecting oppression in society to the state, because of the need for access to resources, demands for better protection, resistance to coercion, the effort to alter laws and policies.

The creation of battered women's centers and rape crisis centers also raised the issue of sexual violence. Marches to "Reclaim the Night" made women's fear in the city visible. In Peru they held symbolic days against violence and in Latin America in general the link was made between domestic violence and state violence.

In India women's groups raised rape by the police, forcing all the major parties to take up the issue. The campaign against dowry deaths was started in Delhi in 1979. It was the first time that they were actually named as murders; before then they had been regarded as suicide. Radha Kumar observes that this was theoretically significant for the Indian feminist movement.

> It was the first time that the private sphere of the family was invaded, and held to be a major site for the oppression of women. The public/private dichotomy was broken by groups of women demonstrating outside the houses and offices of those who were responsible for dowry deaths within their families, and demanding the intervention of both state and civil society.[6]

Power to change legal definitions has been an important area of challenge. But the democratic development of feminist policies has proved much harder than was evident at first. For instance, in the late 1980's a real dilemma was faced in India over the death of a young widow by sati (immolation). How was such an act by a widow to be defined? Feminist pressure resulted in a law that when finally passed defined this as suicide, a problematic compromise that blamed the victim. This difficulty is part of a wider problem. What should be done when feminist perspectives are in conflict with those of other women?

In "Black Sisters Speak Out" Awa Thiam[7] struggles with the difficult issue of genital mutilation. African feminists have confronted here a basic democratic difficulty. Can practices be defined as oppressive when women themselves do not necessarily oppose them. Perspectives on this have varied. One approach has been to try and change consciousness; another has been to link campaigns against traditional sexual practices to wider social needs for better health care.

Attempts to challenge personal life have also come up against conflicting wants among feminists themselves, which have made sexual practices, behavior, and attitudes explosive political areas. Sometimes the challenge to existing social stereotyping became rigid definitions of what kind of sexual relations are "liberated." For a time some feminists viewed heterosexuality as sleeping with the enemy.

There are also conflicting approaches to pornography. The opposition to a male-defined culture led to demands for protection. Some feminists argue pornography should be banned because it degrades women and leads to violence. Other feminists disagree because the evidence of connection to crime is dubious and efforts to ban fantasy are futile. They say it is better not to put more restraint on women's sexuality. The best challenge to male-defined fantasy is not suppression, but the assertion of women's desires and fantasies, which are still taboo.

These arguments have not been confined to Western feminism but erupted in differing demands among Nicaraguan women just before the Sandinistas defeat; some argued sexual imagery should be banned, others who disagreed with censorship produced their own paper with representations of women's sexual desires.

Although the modern movement has made a significant political breakthrough over lesbianism there has been a problem in affirming heterosexual passion. Fears that physical desire is antithetical to freedom have been reasserted among some feminists. Sexuality in general has been once again regarded as a dangerous zone from which women need protecting. Ironically the aim to liberate women's sexuality has sometimes resulted in new forms of prescription.

Politicizing personal relationships has been the most complicated area of feminist politics. Painfully the lesson has been learned that fantasy, desire, sexual love, and relations between parents and children cannot be approached in the same ways as people might negotiate for higher wages. This has led to searches for alternative means of mapping the interior either through psychoanalysis or greater stress on spirituality.

In the process the connection between self-emancipation and social emancipation has sometimes become strained. Does the lack of any neat fit mean there are aspects of personality that politics can never reach? Lynne Segal observes that feminist attempts, influenced by Juliet Mitchell's writing on psychoanalysis, "to connect the divisions and complexities of the psychic with the patriarchal linguistic structures of the social "was always likely to prove" precarious."[8] Janet Sayers has argued that a distinction should be made between psychoanalytic interpretations of consciousness and feminist attempts at changing the world. Although the effort to understand complexity in the personal perceptions of human beings is vital—"such consciousness does not of itself alter the social conditions that produce it."[9]

Some feminists felt that exploration of the personal is itself a sufficient purpose. For example, certain strands of feminist spirituality deny the need for material changes and simply turn inward. However, Ursula King presents a contesting view; although spiritual introspection and mystical vision are vital aspects of women's freedom and self-realization, the aim should be to "find a truly creative balance."[10] She defines the spiritual quest in relation to external commitment in the world. "The problem is how to connect inner and outer freedom, how to integrate spiritual and social power?"[11]

In seeking to raise personal issues around the body, modern feminism has thus also raised psychological and spiritual areas of experience as integral concerns of the movement. Both these connections have been controversial and raise many new ways of thinking about the "self" in relation to the social, which are part of an ongoing process. There are no easy resolutions; but they can provide a context for criticizing the absence of an inward awareness in many forms of radical politics.

The modern feminist movement has challenged the arbitrary theoretical separation of production from reproduction in the process redefining how material and social existence can be conceptualized. The contemporary movement has generated a wide range of practical activities that not only go beyond earlier feminist demands for welfare from the state but suggest that the definitions of rights and needs have to be reexamined and situated in new frameworks. For instance, black feminists have shown the importance of placing the demand for abortion within the wider social context of reproduction rights. Technological innovations now are also raising a new set of ethical and social problems in relation to reproduction. Does biology confer individual rights? How are claims to be assessed between women who bear test tube babies and women and men who want to care for children?

Feminists' exposure to reproductive health hazards from new technology at work has shown that it is not simply a matter of protecting women, but that men too are in danger. It is not only women who have bodies after all. Human bodies and the environment have been aspects of feminist politics that have led to a broader ecological politics. In many countries women have participated in movements against environmental hazards that affect the whole community. In Bombay in 1981 a meeting on "Women Health and Reproduction" extended its definition of health to environmental and ecological concerns, enlarging the concept of health as "well-being."[12] Feminists in India have been active in the struggle of the Bhopal community after the disaster at Union Carbide brought death and illness to many people. Here how "well-being" was seen became a vital political point, because compensation for suffering rather than simply loss of wages has been at issue.

Peace, as well as ecology, has also mobilized feminists in the 1980s, involving not only confrontations with governments, but new challenges about how to combine action in society with political effectiveness. Feminists have played a significant role in linking grassroots social movements with institutional power. For instance, in Germany, a new kind of party, the Greens, became

> The first political organisation to achieve a victory at the national level that expressly gave prominence to the goals of women's liberation in their program.[13]

Autonomous women's movements in many countries provoked stormy debates about who decided policy in more traditional parties throughout the 1970s and 1980s, resulting in a sustained effort to create new forms, which break with existing models of what a political party should be.

During the 1980s feminism of various kinds was increasingly having an impact not only on political parties but on many existing institutions, both religious and educational. For example, Sr Maria, an Irish
Catholic nun, reflected,

> The Church is certainly one of the last bastions of sexism in the world,
> but things are beginning to happen that are good.

She said,

> People ask me how I can be a feminist and a Roman Catholic. While I
> recognise it would appear to be a contradiction, it is not a contradiction
> for me.[14]

Feminists quite consciously went outward in many directions,
taking political ideas of the personal into every kind of established
social organization. Their efforts were often innovative. For example,
Judith Adler Hellman, in *Journeys Among Women*, describes how Italian
feminists emphasis on the link between home and work, leisure and
employment, not only led to increased time off for both men and
women when children were sick, but gained 150 paid hours schooling
for Fiat workers in 1972. By 1977–1978 women workers in Turin,
many from the rural south, were being offered courses in

> health, family relations, women's historical identity, psychoanalysis and
> women's sexuality, body language and women in literature, as well as the
> more predictable theories of "women and union militancy", "women and
> the labour market" and "women and the meaning of work."[15]

Women's adult and trade union education have been also important
to other countries such as Norway and Britain. The effort to reach
working women and make links with the labor movement has occurred in many Third World countries too: India, Sri Lanka, Korea,
the Philippines, Mauritius, Latin America, and South Africa are notable
examples. Feminists have helped to create many grass roots international networks exchanging information and supporting women's or-

ganizing, not only among those employed in factories but in rural areas and among women home workers.

It is of course difficult to disentangle how peoples' consciousness changes. However, ideas brought from a middle-class feminist movement have been adopted when they met their experiences, by both women and men in the trade union movement internationally. In some cases feminist demands for equal pay or a reduced working week without pay cuts have in Heather Jon Maroney's words, "created a class demand supported equally by and understood to be in the interests of women and men."[16] She argues that by the late 1970s in Canada, a distinct working-class feminist current was evident in the women's movement with its "own outlook on what feminism should be."[17]

Because the kind of work women do often differs from men, feminists internationally have questioned male definitions of "a worker," brought issues like childcare and sexual harassment onto agendas, and linked organizing at work to the community. The difficulties have come when men's economic interest and power in the trade unions have been challenged.

Feminists have been able to influence consciousness at the grass roots level, but power in pyramid structures such as union bureaucracies and parties has been another matter. Also existing institutions are much harder to change than it appears to people who develop new demands on them. In the last two decades significant shifts have nonetheless occurred.

Circumstances arose that brought new problems; recession in the North and global economic crises in the South. During the 1980s, the gap widened between the utopian vision of transformation and everyday survival amid growing inequalities, not simply between men and women, but also among women.

These pressures accelerated the move of women into existing institutional frameworks, not only unions, but also the national state or international aid agencies. For pressure on the outside alone was not sufficient to secure resources.

The shift from autonomous feminist organizing and grass roots community groups to working within the state has opened up new areas of feminist activity and debate, locally and regionally in Britain,

Peru, Australia, the United States, Canada, and nationally in Spain, France, Greece, and Scandinavia. In Nicaragua this combined with a revolutionary attempt at social transformation. In other Third World countries it has taken the form of aid funding for voluntary groups (NGOs).

Sue Findley's comments on the Canadian experience during the 1970s indicate the aims of feminists working within the state in many countries.

> to maintain their relations with the women's movement and to use their position to advocate reforms that will affect women's lives rather than reforms that have only symbolic value.[18]

An immediate snag of course is that significant reforms require redistributive policies if they are to affect the circumstances of poor and working-class women. These, of course, meet with opposition from powerful vested interests both within the state and in society, nationally and internationally.

But the question of the link to "the women's movement" also has brought into relief the points where the original formulations of women's liberation fell short. As soon as there are resources and power at stake the unified concept of "women" dissolves into conflicting, competing groups and individuals with claims based on a range of identities of oppression.

The issue of who can marshall the category "women" becomes then not simply theoretical, but part of the customary nitty gritty of political negotiation. The initial assumptions that framed the political thinking of the emergent 1960s feminist movement never took this into account. In dismissing the state and representative democracy in favor of self-emancipation and participation their necessary interconnection tended to be evaded.

Subsequently the contemporary women's movement has had bitter struggles over how to enable groups excluded from power and resources to find a voice and reshape society without trampling one another down in the rush and the crush.

Whereas representative democracy gives some means of deciding between contending points of view and interests, participatory democracy aims at a consensus based on varying aspects of experience. Both have strengths and weaknesses, but the problem of finding the best manner of combining forms to extend the possibility of democracy into society has proved more difficult than feminists envisaged.

Though in some countries "the women's movement" managed to develop autonomously and to combine differing strands, in other places it was becoming acrimonious and divided by the late 1970s. So it was not always possible for women who were working in unions, the state or aid-funded projects, or institutions such as education where women's studies has generated a vast literature challenging many aspects of knowledge, to refer back to a coherent movement.

Fragmentation and diverse areas of activity are not in themselves a weakness. Indeed the ideas of women's liberation actually reached many more women in the 1980s than in the 1970s. However, any systematic consideration and critique of the whole political experience has proved difficult. Awareness of weaknesses in the insistence that the personal is political has thus sometimes led to a total dismissal of the insights it contains.

There have also been doubts and questions about the whole project of regarding personal areas of life like the family as political. Some feminists have criticized the attempt to dissolve all boundaries as invading personal spaces vital for women. Feminists meeting in Latin America in 1987 decided to make a thorough critique of a consensus about a distinct women's political culture. They argued forcefully that the tendency to become complacent about women doing politics in ways that were essentially different from men needed to be completely rejected because it was leading to too many dead ends. It was a myth, for instance, to see women as not pursuing power.

No approach to politics solves all problems or is able to foresee changing realities. It is important to keep on reassessing without throwing the proverbial baby out with the bath water. The perspectives modern feminism has brought to politics have been creative; they have also raised many new political and theoretical problems.

26

KNOTS: THEORETICAL
DEBATES

Hanging onto utopia and getting your kit together for repeated journeys into the unknown, whether these take the form of an exodus,
guerrilla forays, or besieging existing hegemonic citadels of power,
becomes rather a strain as the years go by and the world goes on
without dramatic evidence of the desired transformations. Moreover,
sweeping visions are inclined to overlook nagging details about what
is to be done between "now" and heaven. Many of the tensions in
feminist theory have arisen in relation to the problem of how to live and
what to do in the meantime. These have been compared by feminists in
Latin America, Julietta Kirkwood and Virginia Vargas to "knots."

Knots are not only tangles; they are the circles on tree trunks. They thus indicate points of intimacy and intersections that can be vulnerable. They do not just need cutting or untangling, but provide nodular clues for making new connections and reorientating thinking.

Broadly knots are to be found in three areas: how the situation of women has been perceived and analyzed, how to go about change, and what kind of society is being envisaged. Though every country— probably every town—has its own story, certain tensions have been recurrent.

An early argument was whether tackling simply women's oppression was the way to wider change, which some of the early radical feminists had believed, or whether it was one form of subordination that had to be resisted among others. Socialist feminists argued the latter was the case, opposing both the radical feminist focus on sexual inequality alone and the Marxist assertion of the primacy of class.

Socialist feminists, however, have disagreed among themselves about how to relate the subordination of women to other oppressions, sometimes conceptualizing through structures, "patriarchy," or "the gender system." These approaches were theoretically neat and tidy but individual women in contradictory and interconnected relationships in society vanished from view. Interestingly, an important challenge to this removed slicing up of experience came from black feminists who have expressed exasperation over its denial of the interconnections between race and gender. Their anger forced a rethinking among white feminists. Black feminists showed ones gender awareness is shaped not simply by being a woman or a man but by a much wider history and by other social circumstances.

The isolation of gender is misleading because it obliterates these interconnections. Initially the problem feminists confronted was that gender was being ignored. In seeking to correct this a theoretical shift occurred, even among socialist feminists. Gender started to gobble up all other relations, which drop out of view.

This ellipsis has had wider implications, which Lourdes Benería and Martha Roldán point to in *The Crossroads of Class and Gender*, in 1987. Rather than posing two systems of male domination and class rule, they observe

The specificity of real life does not present itself in a dualistic manner but as an integrated *whole,* where multiple relations of domination/subordination based on race, ethnicity, nationality, sexual preference interact dialectically with class and gender relations.[1]

They also criticize a "tendency to view women as the passive recipients of change and victims of forces they do not generate or control,"[2] in writings on women and development in the Third World. This has been a feature of approaches that emphasize how women are caught within an oppressive dualism of patriarchy and class.

In rebellion against an abstract and determining structuralism, some feminists by the late 1980s were to become preoccupied purely with subjective identities. Himani Bannerji in "But Who Speaks for Us?" argues, instead, that agency and experience have to be reasserted *without* being detached from social and cultural relations. Experience is always interpreted. It is neither "seamless subjectivity [n]or psychological totalization, but rather a subjects' attempt at sense-making."[3] This is an active and reflective process.

The social analysis we need, therefore, must begin from *subjectivity,* which asserts dynamic, contradictory and unresolved dimensions of experience and consequently does not reify itself into a fixed psychological category called *identity* which rigidifies an individuals' relationship with the social environment and history. Subjectivity and experience understood in this way, argue for a coherence of feeling and being without forcing either a homogeneity or a fragmentation of subjectivity, as advocated by postmodernism.[4]

These perspectives provide the means of avoiding the oscillation that has existed within both socialist feminist and radical feminist debates. Women's subjectivity has been presented either as quite external to culture or as totally determined. In cultural feminism, for instance, the individual is seen in some moments as a self-propelled force, acquiring the perfect body, the latest therapeutic insight, or assertiveness training and at other times as completely "conditioned" by external influences. Although some strands of feminism have celebrated everything women do uncritically, others have defined social existence as a series of structures, or indeed a single structure of male supremacy in which human historical agency and individual women have completely vanished.

The separatist feminist view that all culture can be seen as an undifferentiated male–dominated structure and that all existing characteristics of masculinity are inherently evil has led to positions of considerable desperation and gloom. The biological category men it seemed was fatalistically doomed.

In some feminist perspectives women were depicted as completely outside society; in others they were morally exhorted to join the exodus of the saints as rapidly as possible:

Nothing exists that has not been made by man not thought, not language, not words. Even now there is nothing that has not been made by men, not even me; especially not me,[5]

Anne Leclerc bemoaned in France in 1974. She concluded that women had "to invent everything anew,"[6] disregarded all "things made by men,"[7] for those were

not just stupid, deceitful and oppressive . . . they are sad, sad enough to kill us with boredom and despair.[8]

Three years earlier Mary Daly had symbolically led women out of Harvard Memorial Church after preaching the need for an "exodus community"[9] apart from male culture: "We have to go out from the land of our fathers into an unknown place."[10]

Both perspectives were to be influential on feminism, particularly in western capitalist countries from the late 1970s. They are best regarded as imaginative ways of approaching women's cultural representation and the need to find a place apart in order to gather oneself together. But this is a temporary device to gain "self-affirmation, strength and spiritual power"[11] in Ursula King's words, not a general strategy. Both deny women's historical action, which partially shapes culture despite continuing relations of subordination and the real circumstances of women, which, like men, are within society, individual women being in social relations that both differ from and are shared with men. As Bernice Reagon said in 1981,

> There is no hiding place. . . . In that little barred room where you check everybody at the door, you act out community. You pretend that your room is a world.[12]

Although the emphasis on conditioning presented women as victims or dupes, the effort to hew out a separate place, either outside culture or among the elect, allowed space for women's "difference" to be celebrated. Women could inhabit a playful subversive zone as marginal outcasts from a stuffy patriarchy or they could be presented as the lynch pins of civilization in a morally superior woman-centered culture. These both had attractions. The first promised fun; the second promised self-righteousness. Moreover, they focused on the individual who got lost in the structuralism pervasive in theoretical socialist feminism. The outcast stance made it possible to discuss delight, which had become increasingly difficult under the weight of attempts to "politicize" sexual desire. The woman-centered morality offered a higher spiritual fulfillment in separatist feminist communities even though reality did not always live up to the sisterly ethic.

Recognition of women's difference also revealed snags in egalitarian strategies that had come to the fore as hope for utopian transformation of social relationships as a whole diminished. American liberal feminists' pursuit of equal rights between autonomous individual units was to influence some socialist feminists in Europe, from the late 1970s. "Disaggregation" and equal opportunities presented a strategy for the meantime, as the hope of fundamentally changing personal relations and the existing divisions of labor and culture grew dim. Although "difference" feminists and some radical feminists stressed a vision of a limited communalism, the new hard-headed socialist feminism mixed an abstracted individualism with state oriented policies.

Both these kinds of liberal and socialist feminism missed the significance of dependence and interdependence that has positive as well as negative features and can be seen by women as more pleasurable and reliable than atomistic autonomy, the state, or impoverished sisterhood.

"Difference" in its radical feminist cultural expression, in contrast, could offer an alternative way of being for some women. Cultural feminism consequently retained aspects of both self-emancipation and a social celebration of a nurturing culture that was still a communitarian project.

Even goddesses have their "Achilles heels," however, for power politics is by no means gender bound. The creation of alternative cultural spaces is fraught with difficulty. They can exclude and ostracize and the ideal of sisterhood can turn very sour indeed. What about the women who do not recognize themselves within the existing definition of woman centred values? Joan Nestle observes of lesbian feminist politics in New York,

> I learned that class played a role but wasn't to be talked about and certain sexual practices were taboo. . . . Now I was living another double life in feminism.[13]

Claiming an "identity" could be a liberating means of realizing new aspects of oneself in relation to others, or it could be a means of gaining a form of political power that was difficult to oppose.

One dilemma for feminists has been, in Kate Soper's words, how to base theory

> on the uniqueness of feminine experience without reifying a particular definition of femaleness as paradigmatic and thus succumbing to essentialist discourse.[14]

Another use of "difference" has been to argue that women's entry points differ and that theories and strategies devised by one group provide overall perspectives that eclipse the lives and ideas of others. This has created important openings for considering how race or ethnicity defines gender. It challenges hidden forms of privilege and power among feminists. It argues not merely for inclusion but shifts the whole axis of assumptions. As Claudette Earle says, "It is not always true that all invention takes place in the white industrial North."[15]

Some feminist theorists of "difference," however, have elaborated the metaphor of marginality into a fixed stance and argued that the very project of attempting any totalizing political perspectives is inherently oppressive. This has had an emotional appeal as authoritarian forms of state socialism in Eastern Europe and the Soviet Union have crumbled. It also presents a critique of theories that are based on Western women's perspectives alone. But it does not indicate how to put Humpty Dumpty together again.

Himani Bannerji argues that "diversity, particularity, multiple and changing subject positions and self-representation"[16] have been useful as a means for "non-white women"[17] to challenge textual invisibility, or a segregation that is confining and always "peripheral to the everyday workings of society."[18]

But she shows that the expression of different experience is not sufficient for the recreation of the self and social transformation. She writes in "But Who Speaks for Us?"

> The political sphere is modelled on the market place and freedom amounts to the liberty of all political vendors to display their goods equally in competition. But this view of society as an aggregate of competing individuals or at best as fragmented groups or communities, makes the notion of an over all social organization theoretically inconceivable and thus unnamable.[19]

To simply present "difference" actually disguises inequalities among the vendors. Thus a miner's wife interested in the history of women's action in mining communities, an aboriginal woman struggling to challenge concepts of law, enter not only at different points than the American woman banker or the British university teacher, they have less access to resources and less clout within the prevailing culture. Some vendors get onto the cosmopolitan High Street. Others are shunted off to poor suburbs or even back to shanty towns, and pit villages where the collieries are closing. It also removes a vital weapon, that radical impetus that was within the original claim for rights, "the grounding for any moral demand that they be treated equally."[20] As Kate Soper observes, "Why should they be, if they are not comparable in any respect at all."[21] This particular theoretical tack in feminism has thus "pulled the rug from under feminism as politics."[22]

Not only does this make it difficult to question the "social topogra-phy"[23] as a whole as Himani Bannerji points out, it pessimistically insinuates a generalized impossibility of any concerted action. Because some women, in some historical contexts, have conflicting interests, it does not follow that other women, in other situations, must be without any common interests. The possibility of groups of women combining with one another across differing circumstances and also forming coalitions with men is a matter of vital significance in the actual world. The consequences of recession and the obeisance to the market are devastating the lives of poor and working-class people.

Kumari Jayawardena and Govind Kelkar[24] have recently argued that in the Third World, workers and peasants movements for social change, human rights issues, peace, ecology, struggles against commu-nal violence, and antifundamentalist agitation are all important areas for feminist action. Similarly, engagement with the economic and social problems in the First World has brought women to campaign for many causes from public transport to peace that do not affect only women. From the late 1980s in the United States a series of coalitions have been formed to link various groups and connect labor and com-munity needs. Bell Hooks remarked in 1991 that the isolation of gender makes it impossible to look outward at what has actually been happen-ing. She stresses that women need to confront men and also to form alliances with them. "I do not feel the luxury of choice . . . Black communities are in crisis."[25] She adds,

> Black women, women of colour, feminist activists have brought to femi-nist theory and practice some of the most integrated ways to think about questions of inclusion and exclusion.[26]

Alma M. Garcia describes how, from the 1980s, Chicana feminists "stressed the interrelationship of race, class and gender in explaining the conditions in American society."[27] These new urgencies will un-doubtedly begin to undermine theories that deny the possibility of connection, simply by making them in practice.

However, the theoretical knots raise confusions and disagreements not only about how to proceed but what future is envisaged. Protest is greatly weakened when it lacks any compelling vision of an alternative. For some privileged women this is not too much of a problem as feminism (or indeed postfeminism) is taken to mean a bit more of the same for an elite. But many feminists are concerned about a wider possibility of social change, consequently questions about how consciousness is formed, whether women's interests overlap with men, whether the aim is to protect women from male sexual desire, or enable women to define and express sexuality, how to link autonomy and mutuality, and how to value what women have traditionally done without confining them in "difference" are all vital issues not only for now but for envisaging a better future.

All those wrenching tussles around the boundaries of personal and public transformation are in fact processes through which new social desires take shape. Kate Soper enquires,

> are we wanting an upgrading of the derided "private" aims, values, and activities or an obliteration of the distinction: a "utopia" without a "public" realm of emulation, competition, fame and recognition, or a "utopia" which held traditional "male" activities of little account but esteemed everything "womanly."[28]

She argues that instead what is needed is a redefinition of both public and private spheres and of the values they carry in existing society. Indeed many of the practical struggles of feminism as a movement suggest that the original assumption that the personal and political would *merge* was mistaken; what many feminists have tended to do amid much labor and pain is to seek greater control over how the boundaries are socially defined. Power to shift the boundary stones has characterized the mapping of both inner and outer subjugation.

These themes are imaginatively pursued in science fantasy, which is a way of staking out new territory through playing with the fantastic. But the power of imagination is needed also in the mundane. Speculation about how a better society can be shaped and how less exploitative economies can develop are not remote impossibilities; they concern our daily lives, women as well as men.

27

THE PROTESTS WITHOUT A NAME: WOMEN IN COLLECTIVE ACTION

Running counterpoint with the emergence of women's liberation and its struggles to define one set of problems that had no name has been a whole range of other social protests in which women have participated.[1] They include women's militancy at work, organization in support of men on strike, action around consumption in communities, both in terms of prices and of the quality of goods and social welfare, defense of the environment, and peace and human rights.

These collective actions seek access to social resources; they aim to safeguard natural resources or other people in the family or society. Like women's liberation they have involved negotiation around the boundaries of personal and public life. Women can move into a public sphere through resisting the invasion of daily life by exploitative or oppressive economic or political policies. They have started, however, not from women's search for autonomy, but from relations to others: class, race, community, and family. They are not based predominantly on the desire to create a different destiny for women, but often rebel against the impossibility of being women in accustomed ways.

They have been ambiguous in their political orientation, for example, community grass roots organizing can contribute to both left wing revolutionary upsurges and racist or communalist violence. They are also socially and culturally complex. For example, defense of a personal sphere can take the form of support for human rights or for fundamentalist religion.[2] They are sometimes antifeminist; however, they can also be seen interacting with the women's movement in many countries.

There is no single definition that adequately covers all these movements. They are sometimes called "new social movements," but, as we have seen, certain of these forms of social protest are not absolutely new, they simply lack recorded histories. They are sometimes analyzed as being completely distinct from feminism, arising only from class or poverty or from violations of human rights, yet there are cases when interaction has been apparent. Collective action around consumption has been described as "female consciousness." But not all consumption struggles are exclusively female.

On the other hand they are sometimes designated as "working class feminism," "third world feminism," "popular feminism," "unconscious feminism," and partly included in some definitions of "black feminism" or "non-white feminism," regardless of whether the participants themselves would use such terms. While ascribing people with a consciousness they do not claim themselves is problematic and can be arrogant and misleading, the issue is complicated because women in some social protests identify with feminism and others do not. So no term encapsulates all the forms of women's social protest in which thousands and thousands of women have participated in the past two decades. They appear simply as innumerable instances; protests that have no name.

Lack of a category does not prevent us from seeing how they derive from changing forms of social and economic life and organization. The more continuous involvement of women in paid employment and the growth of public services have contributed to women developing a more assertive presence in trade unions in many Western capitalist countries. Restructuring of employment has also created new forms of production that have affected many Third World women. Global economic pressures have been transforming rural and urban communities. For example, during the 1980s recession and export-oriented policies produced a wave of rebelliousness among desperate consumers in the urban slums and shanty towns of Latin America. Women demonstrated and organized alternatives, not because there was a feminist movement, but because they could not feed their families. In Lourdes Arizpe's words "the repressive state apparatus and the market encroach increasingly on private life."[3] Similarly in Britain, during the miner's strike in 1984–1985, women formed groups, initially in response to their need to claim welfare, which government policy had severely restricted.

However, the existence of a women's movement has been extremely important, because it presents women with the means of contesting a culture that denies the significance of women's experience and gender subordination in the widest sense. Feminism demonstrates the possibility of redefining the scope of politics. There has also been considerable direct interaction between feminists and women's protests at work and in the communities. So although not *caused* by feminism, certain similarities emerge. Women in social protest have partially found a language through feminism, though their action and demands raise many questions about existing theoretical paradigms.

All over the world feminists have taken themselves off to factory gates, to pickets, to mothers and toddlers groups, to women's church groups. They have talked to women at work, in the shops and in the trade union branches, leafleted in markets, and provided health and welfare services. Ideas have been disseminated in journals, magazines, films, television, and radio. Women's centers have been set up in many countries, not only the United States, Australia, New Zealand, and Europe but in the Third World, for example, India, Sri Lanka, Mexico,

Peru, and the Philippines. Women's publishing groups have started in for instance India and Morocco.

Feminists have publicized conditions at work and in working class and peasant communities. In Mexico, they have campaigned about the sweated garment industry; in Mauritius they have challenged multinational capital in the free trade zones.

Joint conferences and meetings have occurred. In India, for instance, broad based women's liberation conferences were held in Bombay in 1980 and 1985 when feminists, along with working-class and peasant women, discussed rape, health, religion, and communalism. Similar conferences occurred in Calcutta in 1986 and Bihar with rural women in 1988.

Feminists have helped to create service groups and community projects in many countries. Korea, where rapid and harsh industrialization has exacerbated social problems, is a notable example. Hong Min, a member of the Korean feminist group "Women for Equality and Peace," formed in the mid-1980s, is from a wealthy family and studied sociology at the university.

> I was doing educational work for middle-class housewives, and I felt a kind of emptiness. This is why I decided that my role is to work at consciousness raising for women at the bottom of society.[4]

Women for Equality and Peace supported her decision and formed a fundraising committee. She began a center for school children that provided care and cultural education after school because many mothers were working. Then she opened a literacy class for mothers and set up counselling on health and child-care. This was followed by advice services on workers' accident compensation for those injured in factories and organization around slum eviction. The aim was to develop "close relationships"[5] so that the women will gain confidence. "Women in the slums have been oppressed for so long that they can't speak up."[6]

However, women's social protest action has not appeared simply because ideas have been taken from outside. Arising from situations different than those that provoked the emergence of women's liberation "consciousness raising" groups in the 1970s, they have their own histories, often unwritten, and their own agendas.

The mobilization of women to claim access to resources in communities or at work does not necessarily involve a demand to be equal to men, which has been one important strand in feminism. This is partly because they arise out of a defense of what is done customarily by women. Also class as well as race inequality, as we have seen, makes the notion of equality less clearly an advantage than it would be for a middle-class professional woman without children.

However, when women's situation is comparable to men's at work inequality is more likely to rankle. Heather Jon Maroney quotes a Canadian woman trade unionist as saying,

> Of course jobs are a feminist issue; and equal pay and training. Getting women into non-traditional jobs is important right now because of what will happen with tech[sic] change.[7]

Although contesting the power of men to set union priorities, she had no doubts about the need for alliance.

> unions give you power, and they educate you. It's the only way to unite the working class through unions and working together.[8]

Though there have been some autonomous women's groups, like the American office workers organization 9 to 5, organization within the mainstream has been the more general approach.

In some cases women trade unionists have raised the whole sexual division of labor. In Britain, as more women went out to work, men doing housework has found its way onto the agenda at the Trade Union Congress. In 1978 the First Congress of Women Metal Workers was held in Brazil and one woman observed,

> Woman works in the factory and in the house, she gets more worn out, she ages. And he sits around like a doll, . . . Men only do housework when they don't have a woman to do it for them, . . . I think housework should be divided between husband and wife if the woman works outside the home.[9]

The demand for equality, extended into domestic life by working-class women, would involve fundamental changes in the organization of caring activities and labor, both production and paid services. A socially egalitarian gender perspective has arisen both among women manual workers and the new strata of educated women who have been most affected by feminism.

It is conceivable, however, not only in an industrial or a professional context. Exceptional circumstances of militancy that disrupt daily life can evoke a similar response among other groups of women. For example, in Bihar in the course of a militant peasant movement in which some men were involved full time in the late 1980s, peasant women, who had contact with feminists, argued that these men should do their share, not only of paid work but unpaid domestic work.

The *idea* of equality is vital in such protests. However, it is not always a matter of equal economic and social rights with men but of an egalitarian concept of social need. Gita Sen and Caren Grown argue in *Development Crises and Alternative Visions* for this concept of equality:

> Our vision of feminism has at its very core a process of economic and social development geared to human needs through wider control over and access to economic and political power.[10]

The protests of Latin American women over prices, the creation of alternative communal forms of eating together, the democratic organization of basic social provision for children, like the milk program in Peru, which is funded partly by left-wing municipalities and by aid organizations, are all collective forms through which women connect the needs of their family to society and demand the redistribution of resources. These are often based on customary concepts of what is due to a mother. They thus seek not a *change* in gender relations but better circumstances *from* a gendered class experience.

Action based on a sense of maternal difference can be both conservative and radical. The circumstances of the women involved, the overall political context, the ideas that are available, and currents within specific cultures affect how the relationship is socially expressed. Moreover, peoples' attitudes can be contradictory and they change. Women differ in how they are mothers and one's experience of mothering changes over time. Nor is there a single cultural definition of motherhood.

Aspirations for "difference" and "equality" express the conflicting realities in which women are situated in society. Thus in some circumstances equality with men seems desirable; in others it does not meet the needs of poor women. Linda Gordon has suggested that instead of using these "trends in feminist thinking"[11] in "adversarial ways"[12] it should be possible to see them as both part of the feminist legacy. What we need to do is find ways of "transcending this tension and creating a new synthesis."[13]

By understanding better how women are actually experiencing their needs and desires in many differing contexts and places, the interconnections between the social experiences that arise from gender can be seen in relation to other forms of subordination. Then it becomes clearer why women do not all want the same kind of changes or present their aspirations in any uniform manner. Collective action around claims for social and economic resources can sometimes be expressed as a *gendered* consciousness, a sense of being a woman in different ways, or it can be articulated as entering a universal humanity.

For example, the Self Employed Women's Association (SEWA) in India organizes thousands of paper pickers, home workers, contract cleaners, and small vendors as well as poor rural women. In summer 1987, five thousand women vendors marched through the streets of Ahmedabad demanding "Dignity and Daily Bread." They wanted licenses to prevent police harassment and the right to space to sell in the city, thus playing a part in planning decisions.

Empowerment, which has been important in the feminist movement, also characterizes many grass roots movements. Creativity and celebration, songs and dancing, confidence, and power arise out of action. As a Brazilian working-class woman said "a woman who participates is the owner of her own nose."[14] This new awareness of self in relation to collectivity can be found in working-class and poor women's organizing in many countries. An active tenant organizer in South Wales in the late 1970s said her husband used to tell her she "was like a mouse and ask me why I didn't stand up for myself. Now he tells me I'm dictatorial and bossy so you can't win."[15] In 1983 a member of the Brooklyn borough wide welfare rights union BWA (1966–1970) reflected on her involvement: "I learned I am somebody. . . . I am a person you can't push aside, I have the right to be."[16]

How do these exceptional periods of mobilization affect people in the long term? This is hard to answer because "history" loses track of grass roots activists; ordinary life takes over. But the Brooklyn campaigner said they are still struggling in

> "PTAs", school boards, even political classes. An organization for and by poor people, a women's movement that addresses real survival issues. Its concepts and promises live in us and our children.[17]

Memory is exceedingly powerful and is passed on resiliently through families and communities in resistance to prevailing hegemonies of class, race, or ethnicity; in defiance of slavery, colonization and multinational capital.

A persistent dilemma the rebellions among subordinate people face is their need to close ranks against the culture and values of dominant groups and a desire to reach beyond themselves, which can emerge in the process of collective movement.

The struggles of daily life at work and in communities can open what Sylvia E. Alvarez describes as "an ideological space."[18] These can open to assimilate other peoples' memories, stories, experience, and concepts. They can include a responsiveness to personal and sexual issues that would probably have been dismissed otherwise. Heather Jon Maroney describes an incident in the late 1970s when socialist feminist support for a strike contract at Fleck Ontario brought two workers on to the International Women's Day march in 1978. One was disturbed by the banner "Lesbian Organisation of Toronto." Her friend told her, "well that's the women's movement and you'll just have to put up with it."[19] Similarly, during the 1984–1985 miner's strike in Britain men and women's attitudes to gays and lesbians, black and Asian people, the disabled, feminists, the Irish, or peace campaigners shifted because support came from these groups.

New syntheses thus come out of rebellions in one set of circum-

stances encountering others. Consciousness is not just externally transferred but mutually developed. It does not evolve mechanically from
one aspect of life without affecting others. An active awareness on one
issue can mean that others take on new perspectives.

Maria O'Reilly, a tenants' organizer in Liverpool, who campaigned for safety on her council estate after a child died, told the
feminist magazine *Spare Rib* in 1977,

> I have faced male-chauvinism I failed to see existed before . . . we came
> to understand politics, usually thought of as a man's world, and expected
> more of ourselves. People now call us women's libbers.[20]

In Britain black women in the late 1970s, organizing around their
children's education and tenants issues in London, formed a women's
group. Race and class protest resulted in an awareness of gender. There
are several ways of becoming a feminist, and differing entry points to
politics. All consciousness is not cut and dried, it moves through
various aspects of life.

Lourdes Arizpe says of the social movements among women in
Latin America that they have been "insisting that their demands enter
the arena of debate and political negotiation."[21] The shift from the
personally experienced problem into the terrain defined as "politics"
resembles aspects of the feminist movement. But the area of concern
tends to differ because the circumstances of the women becoming
active in social protests are not the same.

Similar processes can be seen in auxiliary organizing. In Sudbury,
Ontario during a strike in 1978 at the International Nickel Company
a "wives supporting the strike" committee was formed partly on the
initiative of the local women's center. In 1958 the women had opposed
a strike, but in 1978 they began to make private domestic activities
communal—eating, sharing children's clothes, and parties. As they
got more involved in defending the strike they demanded, in Heather
Jon Maroney's words, "a greater voice in the direction of the whole
strike."[22]

In 1987 "Women Against Pit Closures" in Britain broke through
the demarcation in much modern working class organizing between

work and home, when the National Union of Mineworkers included them as associate members.

Auxiliary organizing, along with other ways in which women in communities have exerted collective pressure over resources, has a history internationally. That this is a fragmented record is part of the lack of visibility. The right to be part of humanity and politics involves the right to remember, otherwise the wheel is being constantly reinvented and scattered protests never fuse into a more general social critique. There is a power in memory too. By relating to others akin to oneself in the past an unrealized potential is touched.

In 1989 during the long miners' strike at Pittston, in the United States, a group of 40 women, meeting to support the strike, decided to call themselves "Daughters of Mother Jones." This preserved their anonymity, but it also paid tribute to the miners' organizer Mother Jones who had been involved in militant battles in the early twentieth century. A union organizer Marad Moore said that naming themselves seemed "to spark a kind of fire—the traditional word 'auxiliary' just doesn't have the same kind of effect."[23]

Auxiliary movements span not only work and home, production and reproduction, they can question how decisions are made about the use of resources, as happened in the British mining community in 1984–1985.

Environmental devastation has also caused action. In 1980, in the Peruvian mining town of Cerro de Pasco, when a child died, women mobilized against the mining company that was polluting the main street with toxic and radioactive waste.

Women in India have taken part in movements to safeguard trees, which for forest people are vital aspects of livelihood. In Kenya in 1983 the Mombamba Women's Self-Help Group got involved in an energy program that set about redesigning stoves, learning agroforestry techniques, and growing firewood. Similarly the Association of Women's Clubs in Zimbabwe in the mid-1980s embarked on tree planting after a drought. In Senegal the Féderation des Associations Féminine du Sénégal organizes groups on deforestation and afforestation.

Access to water, its transportation, storage, and purification are all aspects of everyday management that take effort and skill in the Third World. Thus women have been involved in dam projects and in hand pump installation. Women's groups internationally and women working in aid organizations have brought these social needs and women's skills on to planning agendas. These self-help survival endeavors thus raise important questions about democracy and demonstrate the possibility of technological and economic alternatives.

Devastating environmental and economic forces have been bringing new threats. For example, women in Bhopal, India organized after the disaster at Union Carbide brought illness and death to their families and the argument arose with the company how to compensate loss of human life and livelihood.

Women in the United States have also mobilized against environmental hazards. Nell Grantham from Tennessee became frightened about water near a chemical dump, not only for herself, but for her children and grandchildren. "What kind of life are they gonna have?"[24] In Harlem, New York, Helene Brathwaite noticed white powder flaking off the ceilings in her child's school in 1978. She and other parents agitated to develop thorough and safe methods of doing the repairs. They not only protested but presented alternative solutions. American Indian women in South Dakota revealed a range of environmental hazards resulting in birth defects on the Pine Ridge reservation in 1979. Poor Mexican and black "Mothers of Los Angeles" blocked construction of a toxic waste incinerator in 1989.

These networks for survival and resistance are vital not only for the lives of women whose action brings them into politics but also for any project of social transformation serious about fundamentally changing women's lives. They are crucial indicators of economic and social problems that require urgent solutions.

At present they remain external to the main theoretical debates in women's studies writing. They raise fundamental questions that cannot be comprehended within existing feminist paradigms. For social protest action frequently relates also to men and is about issues that affect men. Nor are the participants all women.

Some strands of the women's movement in both the North and

South in the last two decades have been concerned about social change in general, but if "feminism" is taken to be about gender relations alone, then there are distinctions that make the feminist label inappropriate.

For example, Yayori Matsui describes a young Korean worker Chun Tae-il who was distressed by the conditions of girls aged 12 to 15 who were assistants in the "Peace Market," a garment factory where they were brutally abused and likely to get tuberculosis. The right to unionize was denied and he was sacked. When five hundred of the women demonstrated in 1970 with placards saying "We are not machines" the police stopped them. Chun Tae-il set himself alight crying "Protect young women workers."[25] As he died in the hospital he said to his mother "Don't waste my death. Please be mother of the workers."[26]

Lee So-Sun's own life had been hard. She had worked as a pedlar, a domestic servant, and begged for her children. Her son's action brought her into a new public sphere, organizing the Chonggye Garment Labour Union in the Peace Market, opening a school for workers to learn about their rights with help from students.

Her daughter has been drawn into what became a wider movement for human rights not only labor issues. During 1986 a number of students burned themselves in protests for democracy. Their mothers formed an "Association of Families of the Democratic Movement" and Lee So-Sun was elected its president while she was in prison.

There are, moreover, many examples of women entering a public political sphere for humanitarian reform as "mothers." Actions based on this gendered relationship have been both apart from and connected with feminism.

The involvement of mothers through their children in public defiance of tyranny has been an important influence on politics in Latin America. In Argentina women whose children had "disappeared" and were not known to be alive or dead began walking in small groups in the Plaza de Mayo in 1977. The "Madres" action inspired others to brave Galtieri's dictatorship. Tragically, it has been compelled to continue.

Personal grief combined with a sense among women, regardless of their class, that the responsibilities of mothering, so often invoked by rulers to remind women of their duties, involved the right to protest against inhuman acts of dominion. The demand for human rights became an ethical movement for democracy that challenged the public power of the state.

Motherhood has been invoked both for war and for peace in the past. The modern women's movement itself has been both committed to armed struggle (in support of Vietnam or South Africa, for example, and to some extent Palestine or Ireland). It has also been *against* war and colonization. Feminists camped outside the U.S. military base at Greenham Common from the early 1980s in Britain; Some saying that men are the ones who make wars; others simply declaring that they are women against nuclear weapons. In Israel in the early 1980s a women's group formed against the Lebanon war. From the mid-1980s the "Women in Black" have protested against Israel's treatment of the Palestinians. These vigils have spread not only in Israel but to many other countries. "Women in Black" combines groups who act as "mothers" and as "women against war."

Modern feminists differ (as in the past) about whether women are either inherently or socially less militaristic than men. Women demand peace sometimes as "mothers," sometimes as political "human beings." For an ambivalence still exists about whether to value one's difference or challenge male colonization of universal concepts.

Not surprisingly, human rights and peace movements contain similarly both assertions of women's difference from men socially or culturally and a claim of universal rights as part of a common humanity.

Movements such as the "Madres" in Latin America express a social power based on the intensity of the personal bond between child and mother. For this they are prepared to risk death and torture, shifting values of love and nurture into public opposition to the state. A movement of black mothers that crystallized during the 1980s in South African townships outside Capetown possessed a comparable vision of community.

However, a persistent problem has proved to be how to make the move from being a social force, into the political arena, in the context of the transition to democracy. Mothers can be at once revered and marginalized.

The difficult process of making such a transition has been evident in the mobilization of women in nationalist and socialist movements as well. The questions posed by recent national liberation struggles in the Third World, by attempts to establish socialism amid wars and trade embargoes in poor countries such as Cuba or Mozambique or Nicaragua, have been debated in innumerable feminist meetings, articles, and books.[27] There has been disagreement about the extent to which women's specific relations with men should be the emphasis or whether women's concerns are bound up with the collective enterprise of transition to a different society.

But there has also been an awareness coming from the women's movement internationally that the formulations of both Western feminism and the old Marxist "Woman Question" have to be reworked. Recognition of the need to acknowledge women's autonomy and gender relations has combined with the realization that these cannot be abstracted from material circumstances and social relations as a whole. As Sonia Kruks, Rayna Rapp, and Marilyn Young observe in *Promissory Notes,* a collection of studies about the transition to socialism,

> macro-planning issues (such as production goals for light over heavy industry) and even micro issues (such as providing running water or designing public housing), are all vital to women and have gender implications.[28]

In the context of South Africa's future, Jo Beall, Shireen Harrison, and Alison Todes[29] point out that simply involving women in production neglects the social wage and redistribution of economic assets that are significant factors in how women's domestic work is done. So power to determine how social and economic policy is conceived and priorities determined along with participation in a democratic process committed to a more egalitarian society is part of "the woman question."[30]

A Nicaraguan campesina in campaigning for an autonomous organization of women during the mid-1980s told an FSLN commander he was "up the spout on women"[31]—a defiance of male authority that would have been inconceivable under the former regime led by Somosa. The Sandinistas were overwhelmed, but they struggled in adverse conditions to break with the authoritarian legacy of socialism that was set by the pattern of the Soviet Union. Commenting on women's struggle within the Nicaraguan revolution, Hermione Harris observes that "women's participation . . . made women agents of their own emancipation, not just objects of reform."[32]

Varied forms of women's action for emancipation carry differing aspects of women's experience and various understandings about change. Those problems without names that Betty Friedan uncovered among American women in the 1960s were only part of a much wider predicament in which the diverse circumstances of women's lives lead to a new awareness of self. It is important that these are all sources for critical thinking about what kind of society promises a better life for those vast populations of women who are still excluded from political power and from that partial, and often socially prejudiced, terrain called 'theory.' Then the protests which at present have no name will come into their own and the tocsin of reason change its tune. Olympe de Gouges' "moment" has not been squandered, even though emancipation is yet to be realized.

CONCLUSION

In the mid-1980s Maxine Molyneux put forward a "dual challenge,"[1] in examining and understanding the contemporary collective action of women. She said it was necessary to take account of both feminism and

> the widespread and growing involvement of women in the realm of politics on a global scale, as participants in popular movements together with men, as actors with specific women's demands, and in their own autonomous movements.[2]

All these forms of political involvement have a long and entangled history. Understanding the debates and demands which have appeared in the past provides a means of placing women's claim for emancipation in a wider context than simply the story of feminism- or even feminisms. The choices and priorities of politics have gender implications which affect women's responses. Women both now and in the past have been involved in struggles which have not only been about women's needs as women.

Broader definitions of women's engagement in politics are not just historically illuminating they have practical implications for the kind of future we can envisage. In a period of material and theoretical crisis the question of what kind of emancipatory vision has become a matter of urgency.

From a few small groups meeting in the United States from the mid-1960s, internationally women's movements have grown to redefine the initial assumptions and aims in many parts of the globe. Their influence has ranged from the Indian countryside to the townships of South Africa. However, in the same period the lives of poor women in particular have been badly affected by economic and social changes that they have lacked the power to determine. Increasing poverty and violence have been borne by women with the least access to resources. Of course not all women are poor; indeed, demands for equal opportunities in the richer countries have enabled a minority of women to enter better jobs. Nonetheless, although women are not the only people who are poor, women constitute a significant element among the have nots.

So an incongruity exists; awareness of the disparity in gender relations and a recognition that social inequality as a whole has a gendered aspect have come into being as feminist ideas have spread and developed, but the lives of the mass of women have not improved.

Practical change has been difficult not only because of opposition from powerful interests, but because of disagreement and uncertainty about how to create a society that would improve women's lives.

Feminism, always, as we have seen a movement with several political meanings, has retained its ambiguities in our time. Is its aim for a few women to rise, for an elect to retire to a citadel of purity, or for a wider social transformation? Is it to be a movement of liberated women or a movement for the liberation of all women?

Women's participation with men in combined popular movements has involved historically a struggle on two fronts. Not only have women sacrificed their lives to the dream of a better future—that good society without poverty and fear, where no one would be subordinate, but they have had to confront the attitudes of some men in radical movements. A male vision of greater democracy has frequently denied the specific needs of women and not acknowledged women as equals within the public political realm.

Socialist and national liberation movements are now in considerable disarray. This is partly because they have met with ruthless opposition from conservative forces, concerned to safeguard privilege amidst economic and social upheaval, but also because the political forms, created in the name of socialism, have been so clearly oppressive and undemocratic that their claim to be bearers of freedom has been muddied. Although the social and economic structures of state-led socialist societies did provide more security for women than capitalism, they also were bureaucratic, corrupt, and clumsy in responding to both material and cultural needs. In developing countries concern about economic scarcity has frequently overwhelmed the struggle to create more equal relationships.

The outcome of all egalitarian and democratic dreams is uncertain for we are in the midst of a profound reassessment of many notions that provided the framework for assumptions about how human beings could act to improve their lives and societies. Certainly there is abundant historical evidence to show that reason, progress, control, and modernization cannot be taken as somehow unqualified good things, but as concepts that have brought harm as well as benefits. The enlightenment heritage thus has turned sour, leading many people to reject it in its entirety, including the optimistic vision that by applying human reason and planning to institutions it would be possible to increase human well-being. Indeed the view that the kindest course is to do nothing at all but to live our own personal lives as quietly and unpretentiously as we can has gained an influential following. From the point of view of those who are poor or subordinated, however, such quietism is hardly satisfactory. Past efforts might have not succeeded; this does not remove the problems that previous movements for human emancipation sought to address. Nor does it necessarily imply that the endeavor to bring thought and action to the project of creating a better society should be abandoned.

Feminism itself has not evaded the turbulence, for it too is partly a daughter of the enlightenment, albeit an unruly and argumentative offspring, carrying, like other radical strands, its ambivalent heritage. However, the proposal of rational social change was, from the start, problematized by the loaded meanings given to biological difference. Women thus were never in the same relationship as men to the project of the enlightenment because biological difference was posited by many radical men as sufficient cause to exclude women from what was in reality always a male-defined notion of humanity. The female gender was the point where the radical notion of universal rights was inclined to start making exceptions. Women were presented as part of nature, to be controlled, the symbols of continuity in a world of flux.

A protracted argument of feminism from its origins then has been for the right to both enter and redefine the public space of male democratic politics. Historically the emphasis has varied depending on circumstance and there is a long history of women disagreeing about whether it was more important to get included or to put specific needs forward. Broadly the attempt to combine both the struggle for access and the effort of transformation has been more evident when an impact on society as a whole has appeared to be feasible. In reactionary periods, in response to the failure of efforts to change all aspects of relationships, withdrawal has appeared to be a more realistic approach.

Implicit within the debates among contemporary feminists have been fundamental theoretical questions about the relationship of the material to the spiritual or cultural and the interconnection between human beings and the natural world. A challenge is emerging to the assumption that control over nature is the goal, along with a rejection of the complacency that progress is carried inherently within history.

A persistent confusion however is whether these are essentially women's visions or whether feminist theoretical questioning is part of a broader redefinition of human social emancipation.

CONCLUSION

Some feminist theories, now and in the past, have maintained that women have not only been excluded from politics historically, but that women are necessarily apart from politics because this is an inherently male sphere. Although this opens up the possibility of imagining how the purpose of politics might change by taking on women's needs and desires, it suppresses the important creative record of what women have done and thought and it presents a misleading impression of women's actual circumstances. For being not seen within a culture and not being there are not at all the same—though this has been a persistent source of confusion, for to be denied and scorned is humiliating and weakening.

If we look a little closer, it is possible, however, to find that it is not only women who are marginalized through the perceptions and views of more powerful groups. Also as we observe feminism over time, we will note that feminism has always interacted with other political ideas. Moreover, it has been worked out historically by particular social groups, embodying meanings from partial vantage points and containing its own exclusions.

So although "women" have been invoked politically by feminists and others, it is important to be clear about who is being labeled and for what purposes. Real women are a complicated and argumentative lot. Instead of presenting "women" as an abstract category, it is better to see "women" as people, who within particular historical situations are continually making choices about how they see and align themselves.

So by placing feminism alongside other forms of women's social protest and viewing both within an historical context, it becomes possible to show how various groups of women have tried to change their circumstances and how they have fared. This can indicate what kind of blocks are likely to occur again and help to reveal how a new political paradigm might emerge. History does not repeat itself; it can, nonetheless, provide some hints and clues.

Though books are valuable forms of communication, it would be a mistake to assume that the only individuals endowed with ideas about change have been those with access to publishers. The women of the French revolution who complained about prices and Chartist women resisting unemployment and the upheaval caused by the factory system had views about the economy and the state. Resistance against slavery, the conditions of workers, tenants' movements, and communal insurrections of the poor have contained convictions about political and social rights and wrongs as have the rebellions of peasant women.

The reconstruction of a vision of society among poor women historically and in the present day requires interpreting not only words but actions. The range of protest has involved many aspects of social existence and included notions of justice that are not based on concepts of abstract rights but on rights established by custom. Very often a past is invoked by popular movements. Thus an idealized Golden Age and a mythological version of tradition can be a powerful element in popular mobilization. These can be incorporated either into movements for democracy or those that seek to impose hierarchical and authoritarian regimes.

Human desires are frequently contradictory and consciousness shifts and moves elusively. Moreover, when people act on their assumptions and beliefs, there are always many variables affecting the consequences that can be far from what they intended. So it is never an easy matter to determine how and why people take the courses they choose. This is one of the great quests in history, as relevant and problematic for women as for men.

How individuals position themselves in relation to their situation in society is another big debate that has had an important impact upon arguments that women should have the power to decide how they should live. One way of thinking places individuals within the structures of society; gender, race, and class, for instance. Others focus on the individual, telling people how to become more assertive, healthy, less emotionally dependent, in harmony with nature, how to enjoy sex more, or whatever. In the first the individual is in danger of vanishing within theoretical structures of domination and becomes quite powerless, whereas the other is often overly optimistic about what can be done without taking account of the real barriers that constrain liberating oneself while every one else is in a mess. The missing link is a perspective that can include the needs of individuals, while placing these within a network of relationships formed within particular societies.

Although it is important to recognize that neither self-emancipation nor social transformation are as straightforward as their earlier advocates sometimes imagined for women, or for men, and that the obstacles to be encountered include both inner and outer fears and resistances, there are compelling reasons for reworking proposals that can show how human beings can make a better society. Thus those aspects of the enlightenment that presented a critique of inequality, injustice, and human subordination, along with the view of the individual as responsible for change and improvement in society are as vital as ever. Accompanying the gleaning of insights from the enlightenment, there are the sources of lived experience.

Movements of women, now and in the past, provide more than criticism, they can be a basis for valuable knowledge about needs and well-being that have been theoretically disregarded. They also enable us to think about society and the economy in new ways and discover a great deal about the processes of politics and culture. Not only feminism, but environmental and ecological protests, the efforts to reorganize consumption, daily life and work, and the stand on human rights and peace all contain a wealth of understanding about how the aspirations of women can tackle the powerful economic and political institutions that control vast resources. Within these practical struggles, there are many theoretical questions about how to resist; what should be the proper relation between the grassroots and leaders, the implications of the means used for the end that is desired, the connection between the personal and the political, nature and culture, or the material and the spiritual.

An understanding of such movements now and in the past as well as of feminism can thus help us envisage how we might conceive a better way of life, by enabling questions to crystallize that do not take what exists for granted: Is the aim to be equality or difference? To assert or deny the body? To map the interior world or lay claim to a public terrain? To reshape society or restructure political power?

Where do opposing values come from and how do we imagine this new world? Will the emphasis be placed on freedom or security?

Do we conceive of all women becoming manly and men womanly? Or do we assume a new woman and a new man? Or do we simply want to find a new human being? Would such beings be recognizable to us? If so, what aspects of our present selves might we trace in the future we would wish to make?

Imagination can enlighten the body politic, reason and strategic action can reconstruct its contours, but our understanding and memory of past efforts at reform and transformation can also help shape a future; one that is mindful of recurring tensions and sensitive to the complex ramifications of human desire. The fabric of experience, long claimed by conservatives, can also serve the project of emancipation.

NOTES

CHAPTER 1
WHAT DO WOMEN WANT?

1. Edith Hoshino Altbach, *From Feminism to Liberation*. Schenkman, Cambridge, Massachusetts, 1971.

2. Amanda Sebestyen, Introduction. In ed. Amanda Sebestyen, '68, '78, '88, *From Women's Liberation to Feminism*. Prism Press, London, 1988, p. x (U.S. distribution, Avery).

3. Judith Astellara, *Feminism and Democratic Transition in Spain,* Canadian Woman Studies, les cahiers de la femme, Vol. 16, No. 1. York University, Ontario, p. 71.

4. Rebecca West, In ed. Jane Marcus, *The Young Rebecca, Writings of Rebecca West, 1911–1917*. Macmillan in association with Virago, London, 1982, p. 119.

5. Mari Jo Buhle, *Women and American Socialism 1870–1920*. University of Illinois Press, Urbana, 1983, p. 290.

6. Arabella Kenealy, *Feminism and Sex Extinction*. T. Fisher Unwin, London, 1920, p. v.

7. Olive Schreiner, *Woman and Labour*. T. Fisher Unwin, London, 1911, p. 125.

8. Louise A. Tilly, Women and Collective Action in Europe. In ed. Dorothy G. McGuigan, *The Role of Women in Conflict and Peace*. The University of Michigan, Center for Continuing Education of Women, Ann Arbor, Michigan, 1977, p. 41.

9. Lucille Mathurin, *The Rebel Woman in the British West Indies during Slavery*. African-Caribbean Publications, no date. (Distributed in Britain by Third World Publications, 151, Stratford Road, Birmingham BII 1RD.) See also Hilary McD Beckles, *Natural Rebels, A Social History of Enslaved Black Women in Barbados*. Zed Books, London, 1989.

10. Charlotte Woodward, quoted in Gerda Lerner, *The Woman in American History*. Addison Wesley, Menlo Park, California, 1971, p. 84.

CHAPTER 2
WOMEN, POWER, AND POLITICS

1. Maxine Molyneux, Prologue to Gail Omvedt, *Women in Popular Movements: India and Thailand during the Decade of Women*. United Nations Research Institute for Social Development (UNRISD), Geneva, Report No. 86.9, 1986, p. x.

2. Trieu Thi Trinh, quoted in Sheila Rowbotham, *Women, Resistance and Revolution*. Allen Lane, London, 1972, p. 20.

3. Christine de Pisan, quoted in Joan Kelly, Early Feminist Theory and the Querelle des Femmes. In ed. Joan Kelly, *Women, History and Theory*. University of Chicago Press, Chicago, 1984, p. 71.

4. Fatima Mernissi, *Beyond the Veil, Male-Female Dynamics in Muslim Society*. Al Saqi Books, London, 1985 (first edition Schenkman, Cambridge, Massachusetts, 1975), p. 71, and Fatima Mernissi, Women in Muslim History: Traditional Perspectives and New Strategies. In ed. S. Jay Kleinberg, *Retrieving Women's History*. Berg/UNESCO Comparative Studies, 1987.

5. Ursula King, *Women and Spirituality, Voices of Protest and Promise*. Macmillan Education, London, 1989, p. 103.

6. Quoted in Sheila Rowbotham, *Women, Resistance and Revolution*, p. 17.

7. Catherine Macauley, quoted in Sylvana Tomaselli, The Enlightenment Debate on Women. *History Workshop,* a journal of socialist and feminist historians, Issue 20, Autumn 1985, p. 107.

8. Mary Wollstonecraft, quoted in Jean Grimshaw, Mary Wollstonecraft and the Tensions in Feminist Philosophy. In ed. Sean Sayers and Peter Osborne. *Socialism, Feminism and Philosophy, A Radical Philosophy Reader.* Routledge, London, 1990, p. 19.

9. Ibid.

10. William Godwin, Memoirs of the Author of the Rights of Woman (1st ed. 1798) in ed. Richard Holmes, Mary Wollstonecraft and William Godwin, Penguin, London, 1987, p. 231.

CHAPTER 3
THE TOCSIN OF REASON: WOMEN IN THE FRENCH REVOLUTION

1. Olympe de Gouges, Declaration of the Rights of Woman. In eds. Darline Gay Levy, Harriet Branson Applewhite, and Mary Durham Johnson, *Women in Revolutionary Paris 1789–1795.* University of Illinois Press, Urbana, 1979, p. 92.

2. Pétition des femmes du Tiers-Etat au Roi (January 1789), quoted in Elizabeth Racz, The Women's Rights Movement in the French Revolution. In ed. Ann Forfreedom, *Women out of History, a Herstory Anthology.* Ann Forfreedom, Los Angeles, 1972, p. 143.

3. The Women of Paris Respond to the Delaying Tactics of the National Convention, February 25 1793. In eds. Darline Gay Levy et al., *Women in Revolutionary Paris, 1789–1795,* p. 132.

4. Olympe de Gouges, Declaration of the Rights of Woman in ibid, p. 93.

5. Ibid.

6. Ibid.

7. Ibid.

8. Citoyenne Lacombe's Report to the Society of Revolutionary Republican Women Concerning What Took Place, September 16 at the Jacobin Society, in ibid, p. 190.

9. The Women of the People Revolt Against the Jacobin Regime, in ibid, p. 268.

10. Ibid.

CHAPTER 4
A NEW MORAL WORLD: EARLY RADICALS, COOPERATORS, AND SOCIALISTS

1. Female Reformers of Blackburn, quoted in Ruth and Edmund Frow, *Political Women, 1800–1850*. Pluto Press, London, 1989, p. 22.

2. William Thompson, *Appeal of One-Half the Human Race, Women against the Pretentions of the Other Half, Men to Retain Them in Civil and Domestic Slavery*. London, 1825, p. 165.

3. Ibid, p. 189.

4. Frances Wright, Explanatory Notes Respecting the Nature and Objects of the Institution of Nashoba, quoted in Raymond Lee Muncy, *Sex and Marriage in Utopian Communities*. Penguin, Baltimore, 1974, p. 201.

5. A Page for the Ladies, *Pioneer*, 5 April 1834, quoted in Ruth and Edmund Frow, *Political Women*, 1800–1850, p. 158.

6. Straw Bonnet Makers Organize, *Pioneer*, 24 May 1834, quoted in ibid, p. 178.

7. Women's Page, *Pioneer*, 26 April 1834, quoted in ibid, p. 169.

8. Ibid, p. 168.

9. Ibid, p. 169.

CHAPTER 5
THE ABOLITION OF SLAVERY AND WOMEN'S EMANCIPATION

1. Maria Stewart, quoted in Jane Rendall, *Origins of Modern Feminism, Women in Britain, France and the United States, 1780–1860*. Macmillan, London, 1985, p. 248.

2. Angelina Grimké, quoted in ibid, p. 251.

3. Elizabeth Cady Stanton and Lucretia Mott, quoted in Gerda Lerner, *The Woman in American History*. Addison Wesley, Menco Park, California, 1971, pp. 82–83.

4. "An Operative" Voice of Industry, January 22 1847, quoted in Philip S. Foner, *Women and the American Labour Movement, From the First Trade Unions to the Present*. The Free Press, Macmillan, New York, 1974, p. 33.

5. "An Operative," quoted in ibid, pp. 33–34.

6. Sojourner Truth, quoted in Gerda Lerner, *The Woman in American History*, pp. 67–68.

7. Quoted in Paula Giddings, *When and Where I Enter, The Impact of Black Women on Race and Sex in America.* Bantam Books, New York, 1984, p. 54.

8. Ibid.

9. Ibid.

10. Ed. Jean Fagan Yellin, *Harriet A. Jacobs, Incidents in the Life of a Slave Girl, 1861.* Harvard University Press, Cambridge, Massachusetts, 1987, p. xix.

11. Sojourner Truth, quoted in Paula Giddings, *When and Where I Enter,* p. 65.

12. Charles Reymond, quoted in ibid, fn. p. 68.

13. Lottie Rollins, quoted in ibid, p. 71.

14. Quoted in ibid, p. 69.

CHAPTER 6
CLASS AND COMMUNITY: WOMEN AND THE CHARTIST MOVEMENT

1. Female Public Meeting 1838. In eds. Ruth and Edmund Frow, *Political Women, 1800–1850.* Pluto Press, London, 1989, p. 191.

2. Ibid, p. 192.

3. Ibid.

4. Address of the Female Political Union of Newcastle-upon-Tyne to their Fellow Countrywomen, *The Northern Star,* 2 February 1839. In ed. Dorothy Thompson, *The Early Chartists.* Macmillan, London, 1971, p. 128.

5. Ibid, p. 129.

6. Ibid, p. 128.

7. *The Northern Star,* 2 February 1839, quoted in Dorothy Thompson, *The Chartists.* Temple Smith, London, 1984, p. 126.

8. *The Northern Star,* 13 March 1841, quoted in ibid, p. 146.

9. Ibid.

10. Ibid.

11. Women's Rights Association, 19 December 1851. In eds. Ruth and Edmund Frow, *Political Women, 1800–1850,* p. 201.

12. Ibid.

13. Ibid.

14. Dorothy Thompson, Women and Nineteenth-Century Radical Politics: A Lost Dimension. In ed. Juliet Mitchell and Ann Oakley, *The Rights and Wrongs of Women.* Penguin, London, 1976, p. 136.

15. Ibid.
16. Ibid.
17. Ibid.
18. Ibid.

CHAPTER 7
WOMEN IN REVOLUTION: NINETEENTH-CENTURY FRANCE

1. Laura S. Strumingher, *Women and the Making of the Working Class: Lyon 1830–1870*. Eden Press Women's Publications, St. Alban's, Vermont, 1979, p. 38.

2. *La Politique des Femmes,* 5 August 1848, in Maria Mies, Utopian Socialism and Women's Emancipation. In ed. Maria Mies and Kumari Jayawardena, *Feminism in Europe, Liberal and Socialist Strategies, 1789–1919*. Institute of Social Studies, The Hague, Netherlands, 1981, p. 76.

3. Ibid, p. 77.

4. Jeanne Deroin, quoted in Evelyne Sullerot, Journaux Féminin et Lutte Ouvière, 1848–1849. In ed. Jacques Godechot, *La Presse Ouvrière*. Presses Universitaries, Paris, 1968, p. 97.

5. Jeanne Deroin and Pauline Roland, quoted in June Hannam, *Isabella Ford*. Basil Blackwell, Oxford, 1989, p. 121.

6. Karl Marx, quoted in Philip S. Foner, *Women and the American Labor Movement, From the First Trade Unions to the Present*. The Free Press, Macmillan, New York, 1979, p. 62.

7. André Léo, quoted in Lawrence Klejman and Florence Rochefort, *L'Égalité En Marche, Le Féminisme sous la Troisième République*. Presses de la Foundation des Sciences Politiques, des Femmes, Antoinette Fouque, Paris, 1989, p. 313.

CHAPTER 8
EQUALITY AND INDIVIDUALISM: HARRIET TAYLOR AND JOHN STUART MILL

1. Harriet Taylor and John Stuart Mill, 1851, quoted in Dorothy Thompson, Women, Work and Politics in Nineteenth-Century England, The Problem of Authority. In Jane Rendall, *Equal or Different, Women's Politics 1800–1914*. Basil Blackwell, Oxford, 1987, p. 74.

2. John Stuart Mill, *The Subjection of Women*, 1869. Virago, London, 1983, p. 38.

3. John Stuart Mill, *The Globe*, April 18 1832, quoted in Richard Pankhurst, *The Saint Simonians, Mill and Carlyle, A Preface to Modern Thought, Lalibela Books*. Sidgwick Jackson, London, no date, p. 74.

4. Ibid.

5. Anna Jameson, Sisters of Charity and the Communion of Labour, London 1859, quoted in Jane Rendall, *The Origins of Modern Feminism, Women in Britain, France and the United States 1780–1860*. Macmillan, London, 1985, p. 316.

6. Milicent Garrett Fawcett, *What I Remember*. T. Fisher Unwin, London, 1924, p. 64.

7. Mary Hume-Rothery, Letter to Gladstone, quoted in Judith R. Walkowitz, *Prostitution and Victorian Society, Women, Class, and the State*. Cambridge University Press, Cambridge, 1980, p. 130.

8. Lucinda Chandler, Motherhood. *Woodhull and Claflin's Weekly*, May 13 1871, quoted in William Leach, *True Love and Perfect Union, The Feminist Reform of Sex and Society*. Routledge and Kegan Paul, London, 1981, p. 81.

9. Matilda Joslyn Gage, National Woman's Suffrage Society, July 4 1874, in ibid.

10. Harriet Taylor, Enfranchisement of Women, quoted in Anne Phillips, *Divided Loyalties, Dilemmas of Sex and Class*. Virago, London, 1987, p. 77.

11. Lydia Becker, 1877, quoted in Philippa Levine, *Victorian Feminism, 1850–1900*. Hutchinson, London, 1987, p. 74.

CHAPTER 9
SENSUOUS SPIRITS: VICTORIA WOODHULL AND TENNESSEE CLAFLIN

1. Emanie Sachs, *The Terrible Siren, Victoria Woodhull 1838–1927*. Harper and Brothers, New York, 1928, p. 60.

2. Elizabeth Cady Stanton, quoted in ibid, p. 79.

3. Friedrich Albert Sorge, quoted in David Herreshoft, *The Origins of American Marxism, From the Transcendentalists to De Leon*. Monad Press distributed by Pathfinder Press, New York, 1967, p. 82.

4. Ibid.

5. Ibid, p. 93.

6. Victoria Woodhull, quoted in Arlene Kisner, *The Lives and Writings of Notorious Victoria Woodhull and Her Sister Tennessee Claflin*. Times Change Press, Washington, 1972, p. 28.

7. Ibid.

8. Elizabeth Cady Stanton, quoted in Linda Gordon, *Woman's Body Woman's Right, A Social History of Birth Control in America*. Grossman, Viking Press, New York, 1976, p. 109.

9. Victoria Woodhull quoted in Emanie Sachs, The Terrible Siren, Victoria Woodhull 1838–1927, p. 74.

CHAPTER 10
TRANSFORMING DOMESTIC LIFE:
COOPERATIVES AND THE STATE

1. Stephen Pearl Andrews, quoted in Dolores Hayden, *The Grand Domestic Revolution,* The MIT Press, Cambridge Massachusetts, 1981, p. 102.

2. Edward Bellamy, *Looking Backward,* quoted in ibid, p. 135.

CHAPTER 11
MORAL UPLIFT, SOCIAL PURITY, AND
TEMPERANCE

1. Anna Haslam, quoted in Rosemary Cullen Owens, *Smashing Times, A History of the Irish Women's Suffrage Movement, 1889–1922*. Attic Press, Dublin, 1984, p. 27.

2. Mari Jo Buhle, *Women and American Socialism, 1870–1920*. University of Illinois Press, Urbana, 1983, p. 64.

3. Ibid, p. 65.

4. Ibid.

5. Nellie Letitia Mooney McClung, quoted in Alison Prentice, Paula Bourne, Gail Cuthbert Brandt, Beth Light, Wendy Mitchinson, and Naomi Black, *Canadian Women, A History*. Harcourt Brace, Toronto, 1988, p. 198.

6. Frances Willard, quoted in Dorothy Sterling, *Black Foremothers, Three Lives*. The Feminist Press, New York, 1988, p. 91.

7. Ibid.

8. Ibid.

9. Ibid.

10. Paula Giddings, *When and Where I Enter, The Impact of Black Women on Race and Sex in America*. Bantam Books, Toronto, 1985, p. 100.

CHAPTER 12
NATIONALIST MOVEMENTS AND
WOMEN'S PLACE

1. Deniz Kandiyoti, End of Empire: Islam, Nationalism and Women in Turkey. In ed. Deniz Kandiyoti, *Women, Islam and the State*. Macmillan, London, 1991.

2. Qasim Amin, quoted in Fatima Mernissi, *Beyond the Veil, Male-Female Dynamics in Muslim Society*. Al Saqi Books, London, 1985, p. 14.

3. Raden Adjeng Kartini, quoted in Kumari Jayawardena, *Feminism and Nationalism in the Third World*. Zed Books, London, 1986, p. 143.

4. Bolivar, quoted in Bell Gale Chevigny and Gari Laguardia, *Reinventing the Americas, Comparative Studies of Literature of the United States and Spanish America*. Cambridge University Press, Cambridge, 1986, p. 140.

5. Ibid, p. 141.

6. Michael Davitt, quoted in Margaret Ward, *Unmanageable Revolutionaries, Women and Irish Nationalism*. Pluto Press, London, 1983, p. 13.

7. *The Times,* ibid, p. 22.

8. Michael Davitt, quoted in ibid, p. 33.

9. Ibid.

10. Tim Harrington, quoted in ibid, p. 44.

11. Ibid, p. 49.

12. Honor Ford Smith, Introduction. In ed. Sistren with Honor Ford Smith, *Lionheart Gal*. Women's Press, London, 1986, p. xxiv.

13. Ibid, p. xxxi.

CHAPTER 13
SOCIAL REFORM: PROTECTION BY THE STATE

1. Emma Paterson, quoted in Sheila Lewenhak, *Women and Trade Unions. An Outline History of Women in the British Trade Union Movement*. Ernest Benn, London, 1977, p. 69.

2. Mrs. Mason, quoted in Barbara Drake, *Women in Trade Unions*. Virago, London, 1984 (first edition, 1920), p. 16.

3. Henry Broadhurst, quoted in ibid.

4. Clementina Black, London County Council Special Committee on Contracts, Inquiry into the Condition of the Clothing Trade, 12 December 1890. In ed. Rodney

Mace, *Taking Stock, A Documentary History of the Greater London Council's Supplies Department, Celebrating Seventy Five Years of Working for London*. The Greater London Council, London, 1984, pp. 27–29.

5. Ada Nield Chew, Life in a Crewe Factory, *Crewe Chronicle*, 14 July 1894. In ed. Doris Chew, *Ada Nield Chew, The Life and Writings of a Working Woman*. Virago, London, 1982, p. 104.

CHAPTER 14
WELFARE AND SOCIAL ACTION

1. John Ruskin to Octavia Hill, August 30 1870. In ed. Emily S. Maurice, *Octavia Hill, Early Ideals*. George Allen and Unwin, London, 1928, p. 180.

2. Quoted in Meredith Tax, *The Rising of the Women*. Monthly Review Press, New York, 1980, p. 60.

3. Jane Addams, quoted in Dolores Hayden, *The Grand Domestic Revolution*. MIT Press, Cambridge, Massachusetts, 1981, p. 167.

4. Paula Giddings, *When and Where I Enter, The Impact of Black Women on Race and Sex in America*. Bantam Books, Toronto, 1985, p. 102.

CHAPTER 15
SOCIALISM, WOMEN, AND THE NEW LIFE

1. Tom Maguire, quoted in eds. A. Mattison and E. Carpenter, *Tom Maguire: A Remembrance*. Manchester Labour Press Society, Manchester, 1895, pp. v–vi.

2. Kathleen St John Conway, quoted in Laurence Thompson, *The Enthusiasts, A Biography of John and Bruce Glasier*. Gollancz, London, 1971, p. 85.

3. Isabella Ford, quoted in June Hannam, *Isabella Ford*. Basil Blackwell, Oxford, 1989, p. 54.

4. Edith Lees, quoted in Sheila Rowbotham, Edward Carpenter, Prophet of the New Life. In Sheila Rowbotham and Jeffrey Weeks, *Socialism and the New Life*. Pluto, London, 1977, p. 86.

5. Helena Born, *The Last Stand Against Democracy in Sex, Helen Tufts, Whitman's Ideal Democracy*. Boston, Massachusetts, 1902, p. 74.

6. Kathleen St John Conway, quoted in Sheila Rowbotham, Edward Carpenter, Prophet of the New Life. In Sheila Rowbotham and Jeffrey Weeks, *Socialism and the New Life,* p. 68.

7. Hannah Mitchell, *The Hard Way Up*. Faber, London, 1968, p. 88.

8. Ibid.

9. Isabella Ford, quoted in June Hannam, *Isabella Ford*, p. 51.

10. Averil Sanderson Furniss, quoted in Christine Collette, *For Labour and for Women, The Women's Labour League, 1906–18*. Manchester University Press, Manchester, 1989, p. 162.

11. Enid Stacey, quoted in Jill Liddington and Jill Norris, *One Hand Tied Behind Us, The Rise of the Women's Suffrage Movement*. Virago, London, 1978, p. 130.

12. Ibid.

13. Ibid.

14. Ibid.

15. Margaret McMillan, quoted in ibid, p. 131.

CHAPTER 16
MARXISTS AND THE WOMAN QUESTION

1. Annie Sleet, *Justice*, 2 November 1895. (I am grateful to Beverley Thiele for this reference.)

2. Ibid.

3. Ibid.

4. E. Marx and E. Aveling, 'The Woman Question', A Socialist Point of view. *Westminster Review*, 1885, volume VI, no. 25, p. 211.

5. Frederick Engels, ed. Eleanor Burke Leacock, *The Origin of the Family, Private Property and the State*, Preface to the first edition. Lawrence and Wishart, London, 1972, p. 71.

6. Ibid.

7. Jenny to Laura, 22 April 1881, Letter 42. *The Daughters of Karl Marx, Family Correspondence 1866–1898*. Andre Deutsch, London, 1982, p. 131.

8. Jenny to Laura, end March 1882, Letter 51, in ibid, p. 152.

9. Jules Guesde, quoted in Patricia Hilden, *Working Women and Socialist Politics in France 1880–1914. A Regional Study*. Oxford University Press, Oxford, 1986, p. 177.

10. Ibid, p. 185.

11. Clara Zetkin, quoted in Richard J. Evans, *Comrades and Sisters, Feminism, Socialism and Pacifism in Europe 1870–1945*. Wheatsheaf Books, Brighton, 1987, p. 21.

12. Ibid, p. 22.

13. Hal Draper and Anne G. Lipow, Marxist Women versus Bourgeois Feminism. In

eds. Ralph Miliband and John Saville, *The Socialist Register*. Merlin, London, 1976, p. 217.

14. Ibid.

15. Ibid, p. 218.

16. Richard J. Evans, *Comrades and Sisters, Feminism, Socialism and Pacifism in Europe 1870–1945*, p. 27.

17. Hopeful, *Justice*, 23 September 1893. (I am grateful to Beverley Thiele for this reference.)

18. Eduard Bernstein, quoted in John Lauristen and David Thorstad, *The Early Homosexual Rights Movement, 1865–1935*. Times Change Press, Washington, New Jersey, 1974, p. 58.

CHAPTER 17
ANARCHISM AND REBEL WOMEN

1. Emma Goldman, quoted in June Sochen, *Movers and Shakers, American Women Thinkers and Activists 1900–1970*. Quadrangle, The New York Times Book Co., New York, 1973, p. 63.

2. Louise Michel, quoted in Edith Thomas, *Louise Michel*. Black Rose Books, Montreal, 1981, p. 294.

3. Vera Figner, in eds. Barbara Alpern Engel and Clifford N. Rosenthal, *Five Sisters: Women Against the Tsar*. Alfred A. Knopf, New York, 1975, p. 35.

4. Emma Goldman, quoted in June Sochen, *Movers and Shakers, American Women Thinkers and Activists 1900–1970*, p. 62.

5. Emma Goldman, *Living My Life*. Pluto, London, 1987, p. 253.

6. Lou Andreas—Salomé, quoted in Walter Sorell, *Three Women, Alma Mahler—Werfel, Gertrude Stein, Lou Andreas—Salomé, Lives of Sex and Genius*. Oswald Wolff, London, 1975, p. 166.

7. Ibid.

8. Ibid.

9. Ibid.

10. Madeleine Pelletier, quoted in Felicia Gordon, *The Integral Feminist, Madeleine Pelletier, 1874–1939*. Polity Press, Oxford, 1990, p. 91.

11. Ibid.

12. Frances Swiney, quoted in Sheila Jeffreys, *The Spinster and Her Enemies, Feminism and Sexuality 1880–1930*. Pandora Press, London, 1985, p. 36.

13. Ibid, p. 38.

14. Madeleine Pelletier, quoted in Felicia Gordon, *The Integral Feminist, Madeleine Pelletier, 1874–1939*, p. 134.

15. Margaret Anderson, quoted in Richard Drinnon, *Rebel in Paradise: A Biography of Emma Goldman*. Chicago University Press, Chicago, 1961, p. 56.

16. Linda Gordon, *Woman's Body, Woman's Right, A Social History of Birth Control in America*. Grossman, New York, 1976, p. 223.

17. Elizabeth Gurley Flynn, quoted in Rosalyn Fraad Baxandall, *Words on Fire. The Life and Writings of Elizabeth Gurley Flynn*. Rutgers' University Press, New Brunswick, 1987, p. 103.

18. Ibid, p. 137.

19. Lily Gair Wilkinson, *Women's Freedom*. Freedom Press, London, c1914, p. 15.

20. Ibid.

21. Ibid.

22. Hélène Brion, *La Voie Féministe. Collection Memoire des Femmes*, dirigée par Huguette Bouchardeau. Editions Synos, Paris, 1978, p. 63.

23. Philip S. Foner, *Women and the American Labor Movement. From the First Trade Unions to the Present*. The Free Press, Macmillan, New York, 1979, p. 197.

CHAPTER 18
THE SUFFRAGE: PATRIOTS AND INTERNATIONALISTS

1. Rebecca West, A Reed of Steel. In ed. Jane Marcus, *The Young Rebecca, Writings of Rebecca West, 1911–1917*. Macmillan in association with Virago Press, London, 1982, p. 255.

2. Rebecca West, The Labour Party's Treachery. *The Clarion*, 25 October 1912, in ibid, p. 109.

3. Christabel Pankhurst, quoted in Sheila Jeffreys, *The Spinster and Her Enemies, Feminism and Sexuality 1886–1930*. Pandora, London, 1985, p. 47.

4. Christabel Pankhurst quoted in ibid., p. 46.

5. Ibid.

6. Ibid.

7. Rebecca West, The Nature of Woman. *The Clarion*, 7 March 1913, in ed. Jane Marcus, *The Young Rebecca*, p. 162.

8. Rebecca West, Time and Tide, 1920, in ibid, p. 5.

9. Ibid, p. 6.

10. See ed. Tierl Thompson, *Dear Girl, The Diaries and Letters of Two Working Women 1897–1917*. The Women's Press, London, 1987.

11. Kate Richards O'Hare, quoted in June Sochen, *Movers and Shakers, American Women Thinkers and Activists, 1900–1970*. Quadrangle/The New York Times Book Co., New York, 1973, p. 55.

12. Ibid.

13. Charlotte Perkins Gilman, quoted in Jill Liddington, *The Long Road to Greenham, Feminism and Anti-Militarism in Britain since 1820*. Virago, London, 1989, p. 67.

14. Rebecca West, So Simple, *The Freewoman*, 12 October 1912, in ed. Jane Marcus, *The Young Rebecca*, pp. 70–74.

15. Ichikawa Fusae, quoted in Kumari Jayawardena, *Feminism and Nationalism in the Third World*. Zed Books, London, 1987, p. 249.

CHAPTER 19
WOMEN AND REVOLUTION IN RUSSIA

1. Moscow Union for Women's Equality, quoted in Richard Stites, *The Women's Liberation Movement in Russia, Feminism, Nihilism and Bolshevism, 1860–1930*. Princeton University Press, Princeton, 1978, p. 207.

2. Vera Zasulich, in eds. Barbara Alpern Engel and Clifford N. Rosenthal, *Five Sisters: Women Against the Tsar*. Alfred A. Knopf, New York, 1975, p. 69.

3. Nadezhda Stasova, quoted in Richard Stites, *The Women's Liberation Movement in Russia*, p. 67.

4. Elisaveta Garshina, quoted in Cathy Porter, *Fathers and Daughters, Russian Women in Revolution*. Virago in association with Quartet Books, London, 1976, pp. 88–89.

5. Olga Lyubatovich, quoted in eds. Barbara Alpern Engel and Clifford N. Rosenthal, *Five Sisters, Women Against the Tsar*, p. 195.

6. Inessa Armand, quoted in Richard Stites, *The Women's Liberation Movement in Russia*, p. 255.

7. Ibid.

8. Alexandra Kollontai, The Social Basis of the Woman Question. In ed. Alix Holt, *Selected Writings of Alexandra Kollontai*. Allison and Busby, London, 1977, p. 69.

9. Quoted in Temma Kaplan, Woman and Communal Strikes in the Crisis of 1917–1922. In eds. Renate Bridenthal, Claudia Koonz, and Susan Stuard, *Becoming Visible, Women in European History*. Houghton Mifflin, Boston 1987, p. 440.

10. Ibid.

11. Angelica Balabanova, quoted in Richard Stites, *The Women's Liberation Movement in Russia*, p. 324.

12. Ibid.

13. Alexandra Kollontai, quoted in Ibid, p. 332.

14. Alexandra Kollontai, quoted in Ibid, p. 249.

15. Cathy Porter, *Alexandra Kollontai, a Biography*. Virago, London, 1980, p. 176.

16. Alexandra Kollontai, Love and the New Morality. In ed. Alix Holt, *Alexandra Kollontai, Sexual Relations and the Class Struggle, Love and the New Morality* (Pamphlet). Falling Wall Press, Bristol, 1972, p. 17.

17. Lenin, Speech at First All-Russian Congress of Women Workers, November 19, 1918. In *Women and Communism, Selections from the Writings of Marx, Engels, Lenin, Stalin*. Lawrence and Wishart, London, 1950, p. 43.

18. Ilin, quoted in Richard Stites, The Women's Liberation Movement in Russia, p. 409.

19. Quoted in Elizabeth Waters, In The Shadow of the Comintern. The Communist Women's Movement, 1920–43. In eds Sonia Kruks, Rayna Rapp, and Marilyn B. Young, *Promissory Notes, Women in the Transition to Socialism*. Monthly Review Press, New York, 1989, p. 32.

CHAPTER 20
INDIAN WOMEN AND SELF-RULE

1. See Margaret Ward, *Unmanageable Revolutionaries, Women and Irish Nationalism*. Pluto Press, London, 1983; Sheila Rowbotham, *Women Resistance and Revolution*. Allen Lane, The Penguin Press, 1972; Rhoda Reddock, Elma Françoise, *the NWCSA and the Workers' Struggle for Change in the Caribbean in the 1930's*. New Beacon Books, 1988; ed. Christine Quinta, *Women in Southern Africa*. Allison and Busby, London, 1987; ed. Miranda Davis, *Third World, Second Sex*. Zed Books, London, 1983.

2. Rassundari Devi, Amar Jiban, quoted in eds. Susie Tharu and K. Lalita, *Women Writing in India 600 B.C. to the Present. Volume 1: 600 B.C. to the Early 20th Century*. The Feminist Press, City University, New York, 1991, p. 194.

3. Ibid, p. 201.

4. Ibid, p. 202.

5. Ibid.

6. Sakhawat Hussain, quoted in ibid, p. 340.

7. Hukma Devi, quoted in Vir Bharat Talwar, Feminist Consciousness in Women's

Journals in Hindi, 1910–20. In eds. Kumkum Sungari and Sudesh Vaid, *Recasting Women. Essays in Colonial History*. Kali for Women, New Delhi, 1989, p. 215.

8. Hridayamohini, quoted in ibid, p. 221.

9. Ibid.

10. Ibid.

11. Ibid.

12. Uma Nehru, quoted in ibid, p. 227.

13. Stri Dharma, quoted in Kumari Jayawardena, *Feminism and Nationalism in the Third World*. Zed Books, London, 1986, p. 97.

14. Ibid.

15. Amiya Devi, quoted in Radha Kumar, *A History of Doing, An Illustrated History of the Women's Movement in India*. Kali for Women, New Delhi, 1991, p. 58.

16. Radha Kumar, ibid, p.

17. Dayani Priyamvada, quoted in Stree Shakti Sanghatana (K. Lalita, Vasantha Kannabiran, Rama Melkote, Uma Maheshwari, Susie Tharu, Veena Shatugna), *'We Were Making History . . .' Life Stories of Women in the Telengana People's Struggle*. Zed, London, 1989, p. 71.

18. Ashapurna Debi, Ja Noy Tai, quoted in eds. Susie Tharu and K. Lalita, *Women Writing in India 600 B.C. to the Present. Volume I: 60 B.C. to the Early Twentieth Century*, p. 487.

19. Ibid.

CHAPTER 21
THE LONG MARCH OF CHINESE WOMEN

1. Bobby Siu, *Women of China, Imperialism and Women's Resistance, 1900–1949*. Zed, London, 1982, p. 21.

2. Elizabeth Croll, *Feminism and Socialism in China*. Routledge and Kegan Paul, London, 1978, p. 66.

3. Jiu Jin, quoted in ibid, p. 67.

4. Ibid, p. 67.

5. Ibid, p. 68.

6. Ibid, p. 69.

7. Japanese journalist, quoted in ibid, p. 63.

8. Ibid.

9. Quoted in ibid, p. 124.

10. Ibid, p. 130.

11. Wang Shih-wei, Wild Lily, 1942. In Gregor Benton, The Yenan 'Literary Opposition'. *New Left Review* no. 92, July –August 1975, p. 96.

12. Ibid.

13. Ibid.

14. Ibid.

15. Elizabeth Croll, *Feminism and Socialism in China,* p. 162.

16. Mao Zedong (Tse-Tung), quoted in Kumari Jayawardena, *Feminism and Nationalism in the Third World.* Zed Books, London, 1986, p. 192.

17. Chi-hsi Hu, The Sexual Revolution in the Kiangsi Soviet. *The China Quarterly* no. 59, July–September 1974, p. 489.

18. He Zizhen, quoted in Janice R. Mackinnon and Stephen R. Mackinnon, *Agnes Smedley, The Life and Times of an American Radical.* Virago, London, 1988, p. 190,

19. Ding Ling (Ting Ling), Thoughts on 8 March (Women's Day). In Gregor Benton, *The Yenan "Literary Opposition,"* p. 103.

20. Ibid.

21. Ibid.

22. Ibid, pp. 103–104.

23. Quoted in Elizabeth Croll, *Feminism and Socialism in China,* p. 316.

CHAPTER 22
SEXUAL POLITICS

1. Ross S., quoted in Mark Finnane, Asylums, Families and the State. *History Workshop* Issue 20, Autumn 1985, p. 138.

2. Eli Zaretsky, Female Sexuality and the Catholic Confessional. In eds. Catherine R. Stimpson and Ethel Spector Person, *Women, Sex and Sexuality.* The University of Chicago Press, Chicago, 1980, p. 326.

3. Martin Bauml Duberman, "I Am Not Contented', Female Masochism and Lesbianism in Early Twentieth Century New England, in ibid, p. 323.

4. Mary Hunter Austin, quoted in ed. Elaine Showalter, *These Modern Women, Autobiographical Essays from the Twenties.* The Feminist Press, New York, 1978, p. 15.

5. Ibid.

6. Ibid.

7. Ibid.

8. Crystal Eastman, Mother-Worship. In ed. Blanche Wiesen Cook, *Crystal Eastman on Women and Revolution*. Oxford University Press, London, 1978, p. 45.

9. Ed. Franklin Rosemont, *Isadora Speaks, Isadora Duncan*. City Lights Books, San Francisco, 1981, p. 48.

10. Ibid.

11. Ibid.

12. Mrs. Bertrand Russell (Dora Russell), *The Right to be Happy*. Garden City Publishing Company, New York, 1927, p. viii.

13. Ibid, p. vii.

14. Crystal Eastman, Birth Control in the Feminist Program. In ed. Blanche Wiesen Cook, *Crystal Eastman, on Women and Revolution*, p. 47.

15. Nelly Roussel, quoted in Lawrence Klejman and Florence Rochefort, *L'Égalité en Marche, Le Féminisme sous La Troisiéme République*. Presses de la Foundation Nationale des Sciences Politique, des femmes Antoinette Fouque, Paris, 1989, p. 331.

16. Stella Browne letter to *The Communist*, 19 August 1922, quoted in Sheila Rowbotham, *A New World for Women: Stella Browne Socialist Feminist*. Pluto Press, London, 1977, p. 62.

17. Stella Browne, *The New Generation*, November 1922, quoted in ibid.

18. Ibid, p. 63.

19. Dora Russell, *The New Generation*, August 1926, quoted in Barbara Brookes, *Abortion in England, 1900–1967*. Croom Helm, London, 1988, pp. 86–87.

20. Ibid, p. 87.

21. Stella Browne, Women and Birth Control. In eds. Eden and Cedar Paul, Population and Birth Control, a Symposium New York 1917, quoted in Sheila Rowbotham, *A New World for Women: Stella Browne Socialist Feminist*.

22. W.E.B. Du Bois, quoted in Jessie M. Rodrique, The Black Community and the Birth Control Movement. In eds. Kathy Reiss and Christina Simmons with Robert A. Padgug, *Passion and Power, Sexuality in History*. Temple University Press, Philadelphia, 1989, p. 142.

23. The Women's Political Association of Harlem, quoted in ibid, p. 145.

24. Delmar, "Bad Girl," *Courier*, 3 January 1931, quoted in ibid, p. 143.

25. Helene Johnson, quoted in Paula Giddings, *When and Where I Enter, the Impact of Black Women on Race and Sex in America*. Bantam Books, Toronto, 1985, p. 185.

26. The Abortion Law Reform Association Conference 15 May 1936, quoted in Barbara Brookes, *Abortion in England 1900–1967*, p. 95.

27. Stella Browne, *The Right to Abortion*, 1935, in Sheila Rowbotham, *A New World for Women: Stella Browne Socialist Feminist*, p. 114.

28. Alec Craig 1936, quoted in Barbara Brookes, *Abortion in England, 1900–1967*, p. 96.

29. Atina Grossman, Abortion and Economic Crisis: The 1931 Campaign Against §218 in Germany. *New German Critique,* no. 14, Spring 1978, p. 129.

30. Else Kienle, quoted in ibid, p. 130.

31. Ibid.

32. Thea vonn Harbou, quoted in ibid, p. 131.

33. Ibid, p. 133.

34. Richard J. Evans, *Comrades and Sisters, Feminism, Socialism and Pacifism in Europe 1870–1945.* Wheatsheaf Books, Sussex, 1987, p. 172.

35. Claudia Koonz, *Mothers in the Fatherland, Women, the Family and Nazi Politics.* Jonathan Cape, London, 1987, p. 123.

36. Ibid.

37. F. W. Stella Browne, The Sexual Variety and Variability among Women and Their Bearing upon Social Reconstruction. In Stella Rowbotham, *A New World for Women: Stella Browne Socialist Feminist,* p. 94.

38. Ibid, p. 103.

39. Ibid, p. 102.

40. Ibid, p. 103.

41. F. W. Stella Browne, Studies in Feminine Inversion. *Journal of Sexology and Psychology,* New York. In ed. Jonathan Katz, *Gay American History, Lesbians and Gay Men in the USA.* Thomas Y. Crowell, New York, 1976, p. 385.

42. Ibid.

43. Ibid.

44. Ibid, p. 384.

45. Ibid.

46. Ibid.

47. Ibid.

48. Mary Austin, in ed. Elaine Showalter, *These Modern Women,* p. 15.

49. Stella Browne, Studies in Feminine Inversion. In ed. Jonathen Katz, *Gay American History, Lesbians and Gay Men in the USA,* p. 384.

50. Ibid, p. 385.

51. Gertrude Stein, quoted in Walter Sorell, *Three Women, Alma Mahler-Werfel, Gertrude Stein, Lou Andreas-Salomé.* Oswald Wolff, London, 1975, p. 107.

52. Mary Casal, quoted in Lillian Faderman, *Surpassing the Love of Men, Romantic Friendship and Love Between Women from the Renaissance to the Present.* The Women's Press, London, 1985, p. 358.

53. Natalie Barney, quoted in ibid, p. 371.

54. Vera Brittain, *Halcyon or the Future of Monogamy.* Kegan Paul, Trench, Trubner, London, 1929, p. 23.

55. Ibid.

56. Gertrude Stein, quoted in Walter Sorell, *Three Women*, p. 126.

57. Ibid, p. 87.

58. Lorraine Hansberry, in *The Ladder*, 1957. In ed. Jonathan Katz, *Gay American History, Lesbians and Gay Men in the USA*, p. 425.

59. Ibid.

60. Gertrude Stein, quoted in Walter Sorell, *Three Women*, p. 126.

CHAPTER 23
BATTLES AROUND BOUNDARIES: CONFLICTING STRATEGIES AFTER WORLD WAR I

1. Crystal Eastman, Now We Can Begin, *The Liberator,* December 1920. In ed. Blanche Wiesen Cook, *Crystal Eastman on Women and Revolution*. Oxford University Press, London, 1978, p. 52.

2. Virginia Woolf introduction to ed. Margaret Llewellyn Davis, *Life as We Have Known It by Co-operative Working Women*. Hogarth Press, London, 1931, p. xxxv.

3. Elise Johnson McDougald, quoted in Paula Giddings, *When and Where I Enter, The Impact of Black Women on Race and Sex in America*. Bantam Book with William Morrow, New York, 1984, p. 183.

4. Crystal Eastman, Now We Can Begin, *The Liberator,* December 1920. In ed. Blanche Wiesen Cook, *Crystal Eastman on Women and Revolution,* p. 54.

5. Ibid.

6. Ibid.

7. Ibid.

8. Ibid.

9. Ibid, p. 55.

10. Ibid, p. 55.

11. Ibid, p. 56.

12. Ibid, p. 57.

13. Ibid.

14. Ibid.

15. Ibid, p. 53.

16. Ibid.

17. Ibid.

18. Ibid.

19. Eleanor F. Rathbone, Changes in Public Life. In ed. Ray Strachey, *Our Freedom and Its Results*. Hogarth Press, London, 1936, p. 57.

20. Eleanor Rathbone, quoted in Suzie Fleming, Introduction, Eleanor Rathbone: Spokeswoman for a Movement. In Eleanor Rathbone, *The Disinherited Family*. Falling Wall Press, Bristol, 1986 (first edition 1924), p. 52.

21. Dora Russell, *The Tamarisk Tree, My Quest for Liberty and Love*. Elek/Pemberton, London, 1975, p. 175.

22. Ellen Wilkinson, quoted in Betty D. Vernon, *Ellen Wilkinson*. Croom Helm, London, 1982, p. 98.

23. Mary McLeod Bethune, quoted in Paula Giddings, *When and Where I Enter, The Impact of Black Women on Race and Sex in America*, p. 214.

24. Linda Gordon, Black and White Visions of Welfare: Women's Welfare Activism 1890–1945. *Journal of American History*, September 1991, pp. 559–590.

25. Anne Summers, *Damned Whores and God's Police, The Colonisation of Women in Australia*. Penguin Books, London, 1975, p. 393.

26. Judith van Allen, 'Aba Riots' or Igbo 'Women's War'? Ideology, Stratification and the Invisibility of Women. In eds. Nancy J. Hafkin and Edna G. Bay, *Women in Africa*. Stanford University Press, Stanford, 1976, p. 72.

27. Ibid.

28. Vera Leff, quoted in Jill Liddington, *The Long Road to Greenham, Feminism and Anti-Militarism in Britain Since 1920*. Virago, London, 1989, p. 165.

29. Virginia Woolf, *A Room of One's Own and Three Guineas*. Chatto and Windus, The Hogarth Press, London, 1984, p. 267.

30. Simone de Beauvoir, quoted in Mary Evans, *Simone de Beauvoir, a Feminist Mandarin*. Tavistock, London, 1985, p. 60.

31. Simone de Beauvoir, quoted in Judith Okely, *Simone de Beauvoir*. Virago, London, 1986, p. 90.

32. Ibid, p. 115.

CHAPTER 24
"BORNINGS" AND BEGINNINGS: ORIGINS OF WOMEN'S LIBERATION IN MANY COUNTRIES

1. Betty Friedan, *The Feminine Mystique*. Penguin, London, 1968, p. 17.

2. The Borning Struggle: The Civil Rights Movement (interview with Bernice Reagon). In ed. Dick Cluster, *They Should Have Served That Cup of Coffee*. Southend Press, Boston, 1979, p. 38.

3. Casey Hayden and Mary King, quoted in Sara Evans, *Personal Politics, The Roots of Women's Liberation in the Civil Rights Movement and the New Left*. Alfred A. Knopf, New York, 1979, p. 86.

4. Alice Echols, *Daring to Be Bad, Radical Feminism in America, 1967–1975*. University of Minnesota Press, Minneapolis, 1989, p. 83.

5. Rosalyn Fraad Baxendall, Feminizing the Sixties. *Socialist Review*, no. 1, 1991, p. 192x.

6. Ibid.

7. Revolutionary Peoples Constitutional Convention, September 1970, Philadelphia. Appendix in George Katsiaficas, *The Imagination of the New Left: A Global Analysis of 1968*. South End Press, Boston, 1987, p. 269.

8. Ellen Willis, Radical Feminism and Feminist Radicalism. In eds. Sohnya Sayers, Anders Stephanson, Stanley Aronowitz, and Fredric Jameson, *The '60s without Apology*. University of Minnesota Press, Minneapolis, 1984, p. 94.

9. Ibid.

10. Françoise Picq, The MLF: Run for your life. In ed. La Revue d'en Face no. II. 1981. *Claire Duchen, French Connections, Voices from the Women's Movement in France*. Hutchinson, London, 1987, p. 24.

11. Ibid.

12. Monique Wittig, Gille Wittig, Marcia Rothenburg, and Margaret Stephenson, Combat Pour la Liberation de la Femme. *Idiot International*, Paris, no. 6, May 1970.

13. Ibid.

14. Ibid.

15. Helke Sander, Action Committee for the Liberation of Women, quoted in Sheila Rowbotham, *Dreams and Dilemmas*. Virago, London, 1983, p. 96.

16. Ibid.

17. Ibid.

18. Lynn Walter, The Embodiment of Ugliness and the Logic of Love: The Danish Red Stocking Movement. *Feminist Review*, no. 36, Autumn 1990, p. 118.

19. Anon. *Why Miss World* Pamphlet, no. date, no page numbers.

20. Ireland, in *Women's Newspaper*, no. 3, June 5, 1971.

21. The New Feminists, quoted in Alison Prentice, Paula Bourne, Gail Cuthbert Brandt, Beth Light, Wendy Michison, and Naomi Black, *Canadian Women, a History*. Harcourt Brace, Toronto, 1988, p. 287.

22. Judith Adler Hellman, *Journeys among Women, Feminism in Five Italian Cities*. Oxford University Press, New York, 1987, p. 67.

23. Anne Summers, Where's the Women's Movement Moving To? In ed. Jan Mercer, *The Other Half, Women in Australian Society*. Penguin, London, 1975, p. 412.

24. Hema Goonatilake, quoted in Yayori Matsui, *Women's Asia*. Zed Books London, 1987, p. 151.

25. Yayori Matsui, *Women's Asia,* p. 2.

26. Ibid.

27. Ibid, pp. 3–4.

28. Ibid, p. 4.

29. Ibid, p. 152.

30. Domitila Barrios dela Chungara, Women and Organisation. In ed. Miranda Davies, *Third World—Second Sex, Women's Struggles and National Liberation, Third World Women Speak Out*. Zed Books, London, 1983, p. 41.

31. Ibid.

32. Women for Equality and Peace, quoted in Yayori Matsui, *Women's Asia,* p. 151.

33. Kamla Bhasin and Nighat Said Khan, "Some Questions on Feminism and Its Relevance in South Asia," Kali for Women, New Delhi, no date, p 4

34. Ibid.

35. Helga Rapusi, oral statement at meeting of the North South Round Table, Rome, Autumn 1990. (I owe this reference to Swasti Mitter.)

36. Anastasia Posadskeya, The Role and the Task of National Machinery for the Advancement of Women in the Period of Social and Economic Reform in the Countries of Eastern Europe and the USSR, Regional Seminar on the Impact of Economic and Political Reform on the Status of Women in Eastern Europe and the USSR, Vienna, 8–12 April 1991 (unpublished paper). Division for the Advancement of Women, United Nations Office at Vienna, 1991, p. 4.

37. Ibid.

38. Ibid.

39. Ibid, p. 11.

40. Ibid.

CHAPTER 25
PERSONAL POLITICS: CHANGING DEFINITIONS THROUGH ACTION

1. Mary Wollstonecroft, quoted in Jean Grimshaw, Mary Wollstonecroft and the Tensions in Feminist Philosophy. eds. Sean Sayers and Peter Osborne, *Socialism, Feminism and Philosophy, a Radical Philosophy Reader*. Routledge, London, 1990, p. 19.

2. Alice Echols, *Daring to Be Bad, Radical Feminism in America 1967–1975*. University of Minnesota Press, Minneapolis, 1989, p. 10.

3. Paula Giddings, *When and Where I Enter, The Impact of Black Women on Race and Sex in America*. Bantam Books, Toronto, 1985, p. 345.

4. Rosalind Delmar, What is Feminism? In eds. Juliet Mitchell and Ann Oakley, *What Is Feminism?* Basil Blackwell, London, 1986, p. 23.

5. Ibid.

6. Radha Kumar, Contemporary Indian Feminism. *Feminist Review* no. 33, Autumn 1989, p. 22.

7. See Awa Thiam, *Black Sisters Speak Out, Feminism and Oppression in Black Africa*. Pluto Press, London, 1986.

8. Lynne Segal, *Is the Future Female? Troubled Thoughts on Contemporary Feminism*. Virago, London, 1987, p. 126.

9. Janet Sayers, *Sexual Contradictions, Psychology, Psychoanalysis, and Feminism*. Tavistock Publications, London, 1986, p. x.

10. Ursula King, *Women and Spirituality, Voices of Protest and Promise*. Macmillan Education, London, 1989, p. 116.

11. Ibid.

12. Mira Savara (India), Report of a Workshop on "Women, Health and Reproduction:" In ed. Miranda Davies, *Third World—Second Sex*. Zed Books, London, 1983, p. 221.

13. Carol Scmid, Women in the West German Green Party: The Uneasy Alliance of Ecology and Feminism. In eds. Guida West and Rhoda Lois Blumberg, *Women and Social Protest*. Oxford University Press, New York, 1990, p. 237.

14. Sr Maria, quoted in Jenny Beale, *Women in Ireland, Voices of Change*. Macmillan Education, London, 1986, p. 164.

15. Judith Adler Hellman, *Journeys among Women, Feminism in Five Italian Cities*. Oxford University Press, New York, 1987, p. 6.

16. Heather Jon Maroney, Feminism at Work. In eds. Juliet Mitchell and Ann Oakley, *What Is Feminism?* Basil Blackwell, London, 1986, p. 107. See also ibid. In eds. Heather Jon Maroney and Meg Luxton, *Feminism and Political Economy, Women's Work, Women's Struggles*. Methuen, Toronto, p. 87.

17. Ibid.

18. Sue Findley, Facing the State. In eds. Heather Jon Maroney and Mex Luxton, *Feminism and Political Economy, Women's Work, Women's Struggles*, p. 48.

CHAPTER 26
KNOTS: THEORETICAL DEBATES

1. Lourdes Benería and Martha Roldán, *The Crossroads of Class and Gender, Industrial Homework, Subcontracting, and Household Dynamics in Mexico City*. The University of Chicago Press, Chicago, 1987, p. 10.

2. Ibid.

3. Himani Bannerji, But Who Speaks for Us? Experience and Agency in Conventional Feminist Paradigms. In eds. Himani Bannerji, Kari Dehli, Kate McKenna; Linda Carty, and Susan Heald, *Unsettling Relations*. Canadian Women's Educational Press, Toronto, 1991, p. 81.

4. Ibid, pp. 93–94.

5. Anne Leclerc, Woman's Word (extracts from Femme, Editions Grasset, Paris, 1974), In ed. Claire Duchen, *French Connections, Voices from the Women's Movement in France*. Hutchinson, London, 1987, p. 58.

6. Ibid.

7. Ibid.

8. Ibid.

9. Ursula King, *Women and Spirituality, Voices of Protest and Promise*. Macmillan Education, London, 1989, p. 170.

10. Ibid.

11. Ibid.

12. Bernice Johnson Reagon, quoted in Carol Anne Douglas, *Love and Politics, Radical Feminist and Lesbian Theories*. ism press, San Francisco, 1990, pp. 260–261.

13. Interview by A. Gottlieb with Joan Nestle, *Cayenne: A Socialist Feminist Bulletin*, Toronto, 2. 1., March 1986, quoted in Sheila Rowbotham, *The Past Is Before Us, Feminism in Action since the 1960s*. Pandora, 1989, p. 255.

14. Kate Soper, Feminism as Critique. In ed. Kate Soper, *Troubled Pleasures, Writings on Politics, Gender and Hedonism*. Verso, London, 1990, p. 198.

15. Claudette Earle, Media Concepts for Human Development in the Caribbean with Special Reference to Women. In ed. Pat Ellis, *Women of the Caribbean*. Zed Books, London, 1988, p. 116.

16. Himani Bannerji, But Who Speaks For Us? Experience and Agency in Conventional Feminist Paradigms, p. 76.

17. Ibid.

18. Ibid, p. 72.

19. Ibid, pp. 78–79.

20. Kate Soper, Feminism as Critique, in *Troubled Pleasures*, p. 208.

21. Ibid.

22. Kate Soper, Feminism, Humanism, Post-Modernism, in Ibid, p. 234.

23. Himani Bannerji, But Who Speaks For Us?, p. 80.

24. Kumari Jayawardena and Govind Kelkar, The Left and Feminism, Economic and Political Weekly, September 23, 1989, p. 2126.

25. Bell Hooks, Challenging Patriarchy Means Challenging Men To Change, *Z Magazine,* February 1991, p. 35.
26. Ibid.
27. Alma M. Garcia, The Development of Chicana Feminist Discourse 1970–1980. In eds. Ellen Carol DuBois and Vicki L. Ruiz, *Unequal Sisters, a Multi-Cultural Reader in U.S. Women's History.* Routledge, New York, 1990, p. 427.
28. Kate Soper, Feminism as Critique, in *Troubled Pleasures,* p. 205.

CHAPTER 27
THE PROTESTS WITHOUT A NAME: WOMEN IN COLLECTIVE ACTION

1. For accounts of these women's social protests see Heather Jon Maroney, Feminism at Work. In eds. Juliet Mitchell and Ann Oakley, *What Is Feminism?* Basil Blackwell, Oxford, 1986; Anne Phillips, *Divided Loyalties, Dilemmas of Sex and Class.* Virago, London, 1987; Carol Andreas, *When Women Rebel, The Rise of Popular Feminism in Peru.* Lawrence Hill, Westport, Connecticut, 1985; Paula Giddings, *When and Where I Enter: The Impact of Black Women on Race and Sex in America.* William Morrow, New York, 1984; Linda Carty, Black Women in Academia. In eds. Himani Bannerji, Kari Dehli, Kate McKenna, Linda Carty, and Susan Heald, *Unsettling Relations.* Canadian Women's Educational Press, Toronto, 1991. Vinay Bahl, Women in the Third World: Problems in Proletarianization and Class-Consciousness. *Race Relations Abstracts* Vol. 14, no. 2, May 1989; Kumarti Jayawardena and Govind Kelkar, The Left and Feminism. *Economic and Political weekly,* September 23 1989; Temma Kaplan, Community and Resistance in Women's Political Cultures. *Dialectical Anthropology* no. 15, 1990; Maxine Molyneux, Mobilization without Emancipation? Women's Interests, the State and Revolution in Nicaragua. *Feminist Studies II,* Summer 1985; Jennifer Schirmer, Those Who Die for Life Cannot Be Called Dead. *Feminist Review* Autumn 1989; ed. Jane S. Jacquette, *The Women's Movement in Latin America, Feminism and the Transition to Democracy.* Unwin Hyman, Boston, 1989; ed. Elizabeth Jelin, *Women and Social Change in Latin America.* Zed Books, London, 1990; eds. Guida West and Rhoda Blumberg, *Women and Social Protest.* Oxford University Press, New York, 1990; Sheila Rowbotham, *The Past Is Before Us, Feminism in Action since the 1960s.* Pandora, London, 1989.
2. See Linda Gordon, The Peaceful Sex? on Feminism and the Peace Movement. *National Women's Studies Association Journal,* Vol. 2, no. 4, Autumn 1990; ed. Deniz Kandiyoti, *Women, Islam and the State.* Macmillan, London, 1991; Ximena Buster, The Mobilization and Demobilization of Women in Militarized Chile. In ed. Eva Isaksson, *Women and the Military System.* Proceedings of a Symposium arranged by

the International Peace Bureau and Peace Union of Finland, Harvester, Wheatsheaf, New York, 1988; Nira Yuval-Davis and Gita Sahgal, *Refusing Holy Orders, Women and Fundamentalism in Contemporary Britain.* Virago, London, 1992; Radha Kumar, *A History of Doing, An Illustrated History of the Indian Women's Movement*, Kali for Women, New Delhi, 1992.

3. Lourdes Arizpe, Foreword. In ed. Elizabeth Jelin, *Women and Social Change in Latin America,* p. xvii.

4. Hong Min, quoted in Yayori Matsui, *Women's Asia.* Zed Books, London, 1987, p. 133.

5. Ibid.

6. Ibid.

7. Heather Jon Maroney, in eds. Juliet Mitchell and Ann Oakley, *What Is Feminism?,* p. 104.

8. Ibid.

9. Quoted in Sonia E. Alvarez, Women's Movements and Gender Politics in the Brazilian Transition. In ed. Jane S. Jacquette, *The Women's Movement in Latin America,* p. 32.

10. Gita Sen and Caren Grown, *Development Crises and Alternative Visions.* Earthscan, London, 1987, p. 20.

11. Linda Gordon, *The Peaceful Sex?, On Feminism and the Peace Movement,* p. 631.

12. Ibid.

13. Ibid.

14. Quoted in Sonia E. Alvarez, Women's Movements and Gender Politics in the Brazilian Transition. In ed. Jane S. Jacquette, *The Women's Movement in Latin America,* p. 32.

15. Quoted in Sheila Rowbotham, The Past Is Before Us, p. 271.

16. Quoted in Jackie Pope, Women in the Welfare Rights Struggle: The Brooklyn Welfare Action Council. In eds. Guida West and Rhoda Lois Blumberg, *Women and Social Protest,* p. 73.

17. Ibid.

18. Sonia E. Alvarez, Women's Movements and Gender Politics in the Brazilian Transition. In ed. Jane S. Jacquette, *The Women's Movement in Latin America,* p. 32.

19. Quoted in Heather Jon Maroney, Feminism at Work. In eds. Juliet Mitchell and Ann Oakley, *What Is Feminism?,* p. 115.

20. Maria O'Reilly, quoted in Sheila Rowbotham, *The Past Is Before Us,* p. 271.

21. Lourdes Arizpe, Foreword. In ed. Elizabeth Jelin, *Women and Social Change in Latin America,* p. xvii.

22. Heather Jon Maroney, Feminism at Work. In eds. Juliet Mitchell and Ann Oakley, *What Is Feminism?,* p. 112.

23. Marat Moore, quoted in Jenny Burnam, Daughters of Mother Jones. *Z Magazine* November 1989, p. 44.

24. Nicholas Freudenberg and Ellen Zaltzburg, From Grassroots Activism to Political Power: Women Organizing Against Environmental Hazards. In ed. Wendy Chavkin, *Double Exposure, Women's Health Hazards on the Job and at Home*. Monthly Review Press, New York, 1981, p. 247.

25. Chun Tae-il, quoted in Yayori Matsui, *Women's Asia*, p. 135.

26. Ibid.

27. There is a vast literature but see Sonia Kruks, Rayna Rapp, and Marilyn B. Young, *Promissory Notes, Women in the Transition to Socialism*. Monthly Review Press, New York, 1989. Stephanie Urdang, *Fighting Two Colonisations, Women in Guinea-Bissau*. Monthly Review Press, New York, 1974; Stephanie Urdang, *And Still They Dance, Women, War and the Struggle for Change in Mozambique*. Earthscan, London, 1989; Amrit Wilson, *The Challenge Road, Women and the Eritrean Revolution*. Earthscan, London, 1991; Adriana Angel and Fiona Macintosh, *The Tiger's Milk, Women of Nicaragua*. Virago, London, 1987; Valentine M. Moghadam, *Gender, Development, and Policy: Towards Equity and Empowerment*. WIDER UNU Research for Action, (pamphlet), Helsinki, 1990.

28. Sonia Kruks, Rayna Rapp, and Marilyn Young, Introduction, *Promissory Notes*, p. 10.

29. Jo Beall, Shiream Hassim, and Alison Todes, 'A Bit on the Side?', Gender Struggles in the Politics of Transformation. *Feminist Review* no. 33, Autumn 1989.

30. On Eastern Europe, see articles collected in *Feminist Review*, Autumn 1991, and Maxine Molyneux, "The Woman Question" in the Age of Perestroika. *New Left Review*, no. 183, 1991.

31. Flor Raminez, quoted in Hermione Harris, Women and War: The Case of Nicaragua. In ed. Eva Isaksson, *Women and the Military System*, p. 200.

32. Ibid, p. 198.

CONCLUSION

1. Maxine Molyneux, Prologue to Gail Omvedt, *Women in Popular Movements: India and Thailand during the Decade of Women*. United Nations Research Institute for Social Development (UNRISD), Geneva, Report No. 86.9, 1986, p. x.

2. ibid.

FURTHER READING

These books and articles can be used along with those in the notes to go into the topics covered more deeply.

★   Indicates that the book or articles could be read without much knowledge of the historical context or other ideas. Some of these are works by contemporaries or collections of documents. Personal letters and diaries are included. Where possible fiction is also introduced as an imaginative rather than factual means of approaching topics and ideas.

★★   Indicates texts that provide summaries. These are good starting points for students who are not familiar with either the history or the theoretical debates.

The references without asterisks indicate works that assume some background in either history or political concepts of women's position. They deal with historical themes or respond to theories and provide students with sources for reflection.

You will find that there is considerable overlap. Some of the books cited can be used in several of the sections. You will spot some of these connections if you browse through as many as you can find in a library or shop. You will see too how these accumulate as you read through the sections over time. If you want to go further follow up the notes in the bibliographies.

The main basis for selection in these short bibliographies is history and political theory. In Chapters 24 to 27, however, the sources span contemporary feminist writing that covers not only political theory, but sociology, cultural studies, philosophy, psychology, anthropology, and women in development.

The assumption behind the varied source material is that people's interests vary and that individuals can learn in more than one dimension at a time.

CHAPTER 1
WHAT DO WOMEN WANT?

** Diana H. Coole, *Women in Political Theory, From Ancient Misogyny to Contemporary Feminism*. Wheatsheaf Books, Sussex, Brighton, and Lynne Riene Publishers, Boulder, 1988.

** Nancy A. Hewitt, Beyond the Search for Sisterhood: American Women's History in the 1980's, in ed. Ellen Carol DuBois and Vicki L. Ruiz *Unequal Sisters, A Multi-Cultural Reader in U.S. Women's History*. Routledge New York and London, 1990.

** Eds. Juliet Mitchell and Ann Oakley, *What Is Feminism?* Basil Blackwell, Oxford, 1986.

Eds. Patricia Mohammed and Catherine Shepherd, Gender in Caribbean Development. Papers Presented at the Inaugural Seminar at the University of the West Indies, Women and Development Studies project, the University of the West Indies, Mona, Jamaica, 1988.

** Ed. Anne Phillips, Introduction, *Feminism and Equality*, Basil Blackwell, Oxford, 1987.

** Alice S. Rossi, The Feminist Papers. From Adams to de Beauvoir (1st edition Columbia Press 1973), Northeastern University Press 1988, Introductions to Part 1, 2 and 3.

** Guida West and Rhoda Lois Blumberg, Reconstructing Social Protest from a Feminist Perspective. In ed. Guida West, *Women and Social Protest*. Oxford University Press, New York, 1990.

CHAPTER 2
WOMEN, POWER, AND POLITICS

* Marion Zimmer Bradley, *Firebrand*. Simon & Shuster, New York, 1987 (fiction).

** Jean Grimshaw, Mary Wollstonecraft and the Tensions in Feminist Philosophy, and Val Plumstead, Women, Humanity and Nature. In ed. Sean Sayers and Peter Osborne, *Socialism, Feminism and Philosophy, A Radical Philosophy Reader*. Routledge, London, 1990.

** Temma Kaplan, Women and Communal Strikes in the Crisis of 1917–1922 in ed. Renate Bridenthal, Claudia Koonz, Susan Stuard, Becoming Visible, Women in European History, Second Edition, Houghton Mifflin Company, Boston, 1987.

Joan Kelley, *Women, History and Theory, The Essays of Joan Kelly*. The University of Chicago Press, Chicago, 1984.

* Susie Tharu and K. Lalita, Introduction to Literature of the Reform and Nationalist Movements. In eds. Susie Tharu and K. Lalita, *Women Writing in India 600 B.C. to the Present. Volume I: 600 B.C. to the Early 20th Century*. The Feminist Press, City University of New York, New York, 1991.

* Mary Wollstonecraft, *A Vindication of the Rights of Woman* (1792). Everyman's Library, Dent, London, 1970.

CHAPTER 3
THE TOCSIN OF REASON: WOMEN IN THE
FRENCH REVOLUTION

** ed. Carol R. Berkin and Clara M. Lovett, *Women, War and Revolution*. Holmes and Meier, New York, 1980, Chapters 1, 5, and 9.

** Elizabeth Fox-Genovese, Women and the Enlightenment, and Darline Gay Levy and Harriet Branson, Women and Political Revolution in Paris. In eds. Renate Bridenthal, Claudia Koonz, and Susan Stuard, *Becoming Visible, Women in European History*, 2nd ed. Houghton Mifflin, Boston, 1987.

* Darline Gay Levy, Harriet Branson Applewhite, and Mary Durham Johnson, *Women in Revolutionary Paris, 1789–1795*. University of Illinois Press, Chicago, 1979.

** Linda Kelly, *Women of the French Revolution*. A Hamish Hamilton Paperback. London, 1987; Penguin, London, 1989.

Jane Rendall, *The Origins of Modern Feminism: Women in Britain, France and the United States 1780–1860*. Macmillan, London, 1985, Chapters 1 and 2.

Joan Wallach Scott, French Feminists and the Rights of 'Man', Olympe de Gouges' Declaration. In *History Workshop, a journal of socialist and feminist historians*, issue 28, Autumn 1989.

CHAPTER 4
A NEW MORAL WORLD: EARLY RADICALS, COOPERATORS, AND SOCIALISTS

* Celia Morris Eckhardt, *Fanny Wright, Rebel in America*. Harvard University Press, Cambridge, Massachusetts, 1984.

** eds. Ruth and Edmund Frow, *Political Women, 1800–1850*. Pluto Press, London, 1989.

* Richard Pankhurst, *William Thompson, Britain's Pioneer Socialist, Feminist and Co-operator*. Watts, London, 1954; Pluto Press, London, 1990.

Jane Rendall, *The Origins of Modern Feminism, Women in Britain, France and the United States 1780–1860*. Macmillan, London, 1985, Chapters 5, 6, 7, and 8.

** Barbara Taylor, *Eve and the New Jerusalem, Socialism and Feminism in the Nineteenth Century*. Virago, London, 1983.

* William Thompson, *Appeal on Behalf of One Half of the Human Race, Women* (1825). Virago, London, 1983.

CHAPTER 5
THE ABOLITION OF SLAVERY AND WOMEN'S EMANCIPATION

** Louis Billington and Rosamund Billington, 'A Burning Zeal for Righteousness', Women in the British Anti-Slavery Movement, 1820–1860. In ed. Jane Rendall, *Equal or Different, Women's Politics 1800–1914*. Basil Blackwell, Oxford, 1987.

Ellen Carol Du Bois, *Feminism and Suffrage: The Emergence of an Independent Women's Movement in America, 1848–1869*. Cornell University Press, Ithaca, New York and London, 1978.

** Philip S. Foner, *Women and the American Labour Movement: From the First Trade Unions* *to the Present.* The Free Press, a Division of Macmillan Publishing Co., New York, Collier Macmillan Publishers, 1979. Chapters 1, 2, and 3.

★★ Paula Giddings, *When and Where I Enter, The Impact of Black Women on Race and Sex in America.* William Morrow, New York, 1984; Bantam, Toronto, New York, 1985. Chapters 2 and 3.

★ Toni Morrison, *Beloved.* Chatto and Windus, 1987; Picador, London, 1987 (fiction).

★ ed. Jean Fagan Yellin, *Harriet A. Jacobs, Incidents in the Life of a Slave Girl, Written by Herself.* Harvard University Press, Cambridge, Massachusetts, 1987.

CHAPTER 6
CLASS AND COMMUNITY: WOMEN AND THE CHARTIST MOVEMENT

★★ eds. Ruth and Edmund Frow, *Political Women, 1800–1850.* Pluto Press, London, 1989.

★ Elizabeth Gaskell, *Mary Barton* (1848). Panther, London, 1966 (fiction).

★★ Anne Phillips, *Divided Loyalties, Dilemmas of Sex and Class.* Virago, London, 1987.

Jane Rendall, *The Origins of Modern Feminism Women in Britain, France and the United States, 1780–1860.* Macmillan, London, 1985, Chapters 5, 6, 7 and 8.

★★ Dorothy Thompson, *The Chartists.* Temple Smith, London, 1984; Women and Nineteenth Century Radical Politics: A Lost Dimension. In eds. Ann Oakley and Juliet Mitchell, *The Rights and Wrongs of Women.* Penguin, London, 1976.

CHAPTER 7
WOMEN IN REVOLUTION: NINETEENTH-CENTURY FRANCE

Claire G. Moses, *French Feminism in the Nineteenth Century.* State University of New York Press, Albany, 1984.

★★ Karen Offen, Liberty, Equality and Justice for Women, The Theory and Practice of Feminism in Nineteenth Century Europe. In eds. Renate Bridenthal, Claudia Koonz, and Susan Stuard, *Becoming Visible, Women in European History,* 2nd ed. Houghton Mifflin, Boston, 1987.

★★ Eugene Schulkind, Socialist Women in the 1871 Commune. *Past and Present* no. 106, February 1985.

Joan Wallach Scott, *Gender and the Politics of History.* Colombia University Press, New York, 1988, Chapters 5, 6, and 7.

Laura S. Strumingher, *Women and the Making of the Working Class, Lyon, 1830–1870*. Eden Press Women's Publication, St. Albans, Vermont, 1979.

★★ Edith Thomas, *The Women Incendiaries*. Secker and Warburg, London, 1967.

CHAPTER 8
EQUALITY AND INDIVIDUALISM: HARRIET TAYLOR AND JOHN STUART MILL

★★ Richard J. Evans, *The Feminists, Women's Emancipation Movements in Europe, America and Australasia, 1840–1920*. Croom Helm, London; Baron and Noble, A division of Harper & Row, New York, 1979, Chapters 1 and 2.

★★ Patricia Hollis, *Women in Public, The Women's Movement, 1850–1900*. Allen & Unwin, London, 1979.

★★ Susan Moller Okin, *Women in Western Political Thought*. Virago, London, 1980, Chapter 9.

 ★ John Stuart Mill, *The Subjection of Women,* and Harriet Taylor Mill, *Enfranchisement of Women,* Introduction by Kate Soper. Virago, London, 1983.

ed. Anne Phillips, *Feminism and Equality*. Basil Blackwell, Oxford, 1987.

Judith R. Walkowitz, *Prostitution and Victorian Society, Women, Class and the State*. Cambridge University Press, Cambridge, 1980.

CHAPTER 9
SENSUOUS SPIRITS: VICTORIA WOODHULL AND TENNESSEE CLAFLIN

★★ Lucy Bland, The Married Woman, the 'New Woman' and the Feminist: Sexual Politics of the 1890's. In ed. Jane Rendall, *Equal or Different*. Basil Blackwell, Oxford, 1987.

★★ Linda Gordon, *Woman's Body, Woman's Right, A Social History of Birth Control in America*. Grossman Viking, New York, 1976, Chapters 5, 6, and 7.

Linda Gordon and Ellen Du Bois, Seeking Ecstasy on the Battlefield: Danger and Pleasure in Nineteenth Century Feminist Sexual Thought. *Feminist Studies* 9, Spring 1983.

★★ Ed. Arlene Kisner, *The Lives and Writings of Notorious Victoria Woodhull and Her Sister Tennessee Claflin*. Times Change Press, Washington, 1972.

William Leach, *True Love and Perfect Union, The Feminist Reform of Sex and Society*. Routledge and Kegan Paul, London, 1981, Chapters 1, 2, 3, 4, and 5.

** Raymond Lee Muncy, *Sex and Marriage in Utopian Communities, Nineteenth Century America*. Indiana University Press, Bloomington, 1973; Penguin Books, Baltimore, 1974.

CHAPTER 10
TRANSFORMING DOMESTIC LIFE:
COOPERATIVES AND THE STATE

* Ed. Margaret Llewelyn Davies, *Life as We Have Known It, by Co-operative Working Women* (first edition, Hogarth Press, 1931). Virago, London, 1977.

* Charlotte Perkins Gilman, *Herland,* with an introduction by Ann J. Lane. Pantheon Books, New York, 1979 (fiction).

** Dolores Hayden, *The Grand Domestic Revolution.* The MIT Press, Cambridge, Massachusetts, 1981.

   Mary A. Hill, *Charlotte Perkins Gilman, The Making of a Radical Feminist, 1860–1896*. Temple University Press, Philadelphia, 1980.

** ed. Jane Lewis, *Labour and Love, Women's Experience of Home and Family 1850–1940*. Basil Blackwell, Oxford, 1986, Chapters 3, 4, 5, and 6.

** Temma Kaplan, Female Consciousness and Collective Action: The Case of Barcelona, 1910–1918. *Signs Journal of Women in Culture and Society* no. 17, no. 3, 1982.

CHAPTER 11
MORAL UPLIFT, SOCIAL PURITY, AND
TEMPERANCE

** Olive Banks, *Faces of Feminism, A Study of Feminism as a Social Movement*. Marlin Robertson, Oxford, 1981; Basil Blackwell, Oxford, 1986, Chapter 5.

   Mari Jo Buhle, *Women and American Socialism 1870–1920*. University of Illinois Press, Urbana, 1983, Chapters 2 and 7.

* Linda Gordon, Feminism and Social Control: The Case of Child Abuse and Neglect. In eds. Juliet Mitchell and Ann Oakley, *What Is Feminism?* Basil Blackwell, Oxford, 1986.

* Gerda Lerner, Community Work of Black Club Women. In ed. Gerda Lerner, *The Majority Finds Its Past, Placing Women in History*. Oxford University Press, New York, 1979.

** Betty Searle, *Silk and Calico, Class, and Gender and the Vote* (Australia). Hale and Ire-
monger, Sydney, 1988.

** Dorothy Sterling, *Black Foremothers, Three Lives*. The Feminist Press, New York, 1988.

CHAPTER 12
NATIONALIST MOVEMENTS AND WOMEN'S PLACE

** Kumari Jayawardena, *Feminism and Nationalism in the Third World*. Zed Books, London,
1986.

ed. Deniz Kandiyoti, *Women, Islam and the State*. Macmillan, London, 1991.

** Radha Kumar, *A History of Doing, An Illustrated History of the Indian Women's Movement*.
Kali for Women, New Delhi, 1991.

* Huda Shaarawi, *Harem Years, The Memoirs of an Egyptian Feminist*, translated and introduced by Margot Badran. Virago, London, 1986.

* eds. Susie Tharu and K. Lalita, *Women Writing in India 600 B.C. to the Present, Volume
I: 600 B.C. to the Early Twentieth Century*. The Feminist Press and the City University
of New York, New York, 1991.

** Margaret Ward, *Unmanageable Revolutionaries, Women and Irish Nationalism*. Pluto Press,
London, 1983, Chapters 1 and 2.

CHAPTER 13
SOCIAL REFORM: PROTECTION BY THE STATE

** Olive Banks, Faces of Feminism, *A Study of Feminism as a Social Movement*. Martin
Robertson, Oxford, 1981; Basil Blackwell, Oxford, 1986, Chapter 7.

** Rosalyn Baxandall, Linda Gordon, and Susan Reverby, *America's Working Women*.
Random House, New York, 1976.

** Alice Kessler Harris, Protection for Women, Trade Unions and Labour Laws. In ed.
Wendy Charkin, *Double Exposure, Women's Health Hazards on the Job and at Home*.
Monthly Review Press, New York, 1984.

* Sheila Lewenhak, *Women and Trades Unions, An Outline History of Women in the British
Trade Union Movement*. Ernest Benn, London, 1977, Chapters 4, 5, 6, 7, 8, and 9.

* Meredith Tax, *The Rising of the Women*. Monthly Review Press, New York, 1980.

* Meredith Tax, *Rivington St*. William Heinnemann, London, 1983 (fiction).

CHAPTER 14
WELFARE AND SOCIAL ACTION

★★ Paula Giddings, *When and Where I Enter, the Impact of Black Women on Race and Sex in America*. William Morrow, New York, 1984; Bantam Books, Toronto, 1985, Chapters 3, 4, 5, 6, 7, 8, and 9.

Linda Gordon, Black and White Visions of Welfare: Women's Welfare Activism 1890–1945. *Journal of American History* (forthcoming).

★★ Dolores Hayden, *The Grand Domestic Revolution*. The MIT Press, Cambridge, Massachusetts, 1981.

★★ Patricia Hollis, Women in Council: Separate Spheres, Public Space. In ed. Jane Rendall, *Equal or Different, Women's Politics 1800–1914*. Basil Blackwell, Oxford, 1987.

 ★ Meredith Tax, *The Rising of the Women*. Monthly Review Press, New York, 1980.

Martha Vicinus, *Independent Women, Work and Community for Single Women 1850–1920*. Virago, London, 1985.

CHAPTER 15
SOCIALISM: WOMEN AND THE NEW LIFE

Mari Jo Buhle, *Women and American Socialism, 1870–1920*. University of Illinois Press, Urbana, 1983, Chapter 7.

★★ Angela Davis, *Women, Race and Class*, Random House, New York, 1981.

 ★ June Hannam, In the Comradeship of the Sexes Lies the Hope of Progress and Social Regeneration, Women in the West Riding ILP, c. 1890–1914. In ed. Jane Rendall, *Equal or Different*. Basil Blackwell, Oxford, 1987.

 ★ Jill Liddington, *The Life and Times of a Respectable Rebel, Selina Cooper (1864–1946)*. Virago, London, 1984.

 ★ *The Daughters of Karl Marx, Family Correspondence 1866–1898*. Commentary and notes by Olga Meir, translated and adapted by Faith Evans, introduction by Sheila Rowbotham, André Deutsch, London, 1982.

★★ Sheila Rowbotham, *Hidden from History*. Pluto Press, London, 1973.

CHAPTER 16
MARXISTS AND THE WOMAN QUESTION

★★ Diana H. Coole, *Women in Political Theory: From Ancient Misogyny to Contemporary Feminism*. Wheatsheaf Books, Sussex, 1988, Chapters 8 and 9.

** Richard J. Evans, *Comrades and Sisters, Feminism, Socialism and Pacifism, 1870–1915*. Wheatsheaf Books, Sussex, 1987.

 * Yvonne Kapp, *Eleanor Marx*, Volume 1 and 2. Lawrence and Wishart, London, 1972 and 1976.

   Joan B. Landes, Marxism and the "Woman Question." In eds. Sonia Kruks, Rayna Rapp, and Marilyn B. Young, *Promissory Notes, Women in the Transition to Socialism*. Monthly Review Press, New York, 1989.

 * ed Eleanor Burke Leacock, *Frederick Engels, The Origin of the Family, Private Property and the State*. Lawrence and Wishart, London, 1972.

** Charles Sowerwine, The Socialist Women's Movement from 1850–1940. In eds. Renate Bridenthal, Claudia Koonz, and Susan Stuard, *Becoming Visible, Women in European History*, 2nd ed. Houghton Mifflin, Boston, 1987.

CHAPTER 17
ANARCHISM AND REBEL WOMEN

** Rosalyn Fraad Baxandall, *Words on Fire, The Life and Writings of Elizabeth Gurley Flynn*. Rutgers University Press, New Brunswick, 1987.

   Candace Falk, *Love, Anarchy and Emma Goldman*. Holt, Rinehart & Winston, New York, 1984.

 * Emma Goldman, *Living My Life*, Vols. 1 and 2; introduction Daughter of the Dream by Sheila Rowbotham. Pluto Press, 1987 (first edition 1931 Alfred Knopf).

   Felicia Gordon, *The Integral Feminist, Madeleine Pelletier, 1874–1939, Feminism, Socialism and Medicine*. Polity Press, London, 1990.

** Temma Kaplan, Other Scenarios: Women and Spanish Anarchism. In eds. Renate Bridenthal and Claudia Koonz, Becoming Visible, Women in European History. Houghton Mifflin Company, Boston, 1977 (first edition).

 * Ed. Alix Kates Shulman, *Red Emma Speaks, Selected Writings and Speeches by Emma Goldman*. Vintage Books, Random House, New York, 1972.

CHAPTER 18
THE SUFFRAGE: PATRIOTS AND
INTERNATIONALISTS

** Richard J. Evans, *The Feminists, Women's Emancipation Movements in Europe, America and Australasia, 1840–1920*. Croom Helm, London; Baron and Noble, New York, A division of Harper & Row Publishers, 1979.

Sandra Stanley Holton, *Feminism and Democracy, Women's Suffrage and Reform Politics in Britain 1900–1918*. Cambridge University Press, Cambridge, 1986.

** Kumari Jayawardena, *Feminism and Nationalism in the Third World*. Zed Press, London, 1986.

** Aileen S. Kraditor, *The Ideas of the Woman Suffrage Movement, 1890–1920*. W. W. Norton, New York, 1981 (first edition, Columbia University Press, 1965).

** Jill Liddington, *The Long Road to Greenham, Feminism and Anti-Militarism in Britain since 1820*. Virago, London, 1989.

* Ed. Tierl Thompson, Dear Girl. *The Diaries and Letters of Two Working Women, 1897–1917*. The Women's Press, London, 1987.

CHAPTER 19
WOMEN AND REVOLUTION IN RUSSIA

** Eds. Barbara Alpern Engel and Clifford N. Rosenthal, *Five Sisters, Women Against the Tsar*. Alfred A. Knopf, New York, 1975.

* Alexandra Kollontai, *Love of Worker Bees*. Virago, London, 1971 (reissued 1991) (fiction).

** Cathy Porter, *Women in Revolutionary Russia, Women in History*. Cambridge University Press, Cambridge, 1987.

* Cathy Porter, *Alexandra Kollontai, A Biography*. Virago, London, 1980.

** Maxine Molyneux, The Woman Question in the Age of Perestroika. *New Left Review* no. 183, 1991.

Richard Stites, *The Women's Liberation Movement in Russia, Feminism, Nihilism and Bolshevism, 1860–1930*. Princeton University Press, Princeton, 1978.

CHAPTER 20
INDIAN WOMEN AND SELF-RULE

** Kumari Jayawardena, *Feminism and Nationalism in the Third World*. Zed Books, London, 1986.

** Radha Kumar, *A History of Doing, An Illustrated History of the Indian Women's Movement*. Kali for Women, New Delhi, 1992.

Eds. Kumkum Sangari and Sudesh Vaid, *Recasting Women, Essays in Colonial History*. Kali for Women, New Delhi, 1989.

* Agnes Smedley, *Daughter of Earth*. Feminist Press, New York, 1986 (first edition Coward McCann, New York, 1929).

* Stree Shakti Sanghatana, *We Were Making History, Women and the Telengama Uprising*. Zed Books, London, 1989.

* eds. Susie Tharu and K. Lalita, *Women Writing in India 600 B.C. to the Present: Volume 1: 600 B.C. to the Early Twentieth Century*. The Feminist Press, City University of New York, New York, 1991.

CHAPTER 21
THE LONG MARCH OF CHINESE WOMEN

* Elisabeth Croll, *Feminism and Socialism in China,* Routledge and Kegan Paul, London, 1978.

Christina Gilmartin, Gender, Politics and Patriarchy in China: The Experiences of Early Women Communists, 1920–27; Marilyn B. Young, Chicken Little in China: Women After the Cultural Revolution; Delia Davin, Of Dogmas Dicta and Washing Machines, Women in the People's Republic of China. In eds. Sonia Kruks, Rayna Rapp, and Marilyn B. Young, *Promissory Notes, Women in the Transition to Socialism.* Monthly Review Press, New York, 1989.

** Kumari Jayawardena, *Feminism and Nationalism in the Third World.* Zed Books, London, 1986.

* Zhang Jie, *Leaden Wings.* Virago, London, 1987 (fiction).

* Maxine Hong Kingston, *The Woman Warrior, Memoirs of a Girlhood Among Ghosts.* Alfred A. Knopf, New York, 1976 (fiction).

** Sheila Rowbotham, *Women, Resistance and Revolution.* Allen Lane, The Penguin Press, London, 1972, Chapter 7.

CHAPTER 22
SEXUAL POLITICS

** Lillian Faderman, *Surpassing the Love of Men, Romantic Friendship and Love between Women from the Renaissance to the Present.* The Women's Press, London, 1985.

Ed. Jonathan Katz, *Gay American History, Lesbians and Gay Men in the U.S.A.* Thomas Y. Crowell, New York, 1976.

** Claudia Koonz, The Fascist Solution to the Woman Question in Italy and Germany. In eds. Renate Bridenthal, Claudia Koonz, and Susan Stuard, *Becoming Visible, Women in European History,* 2nd ed. Houghton Mifflin, Boston, 1987.

Eds. Kathy Peiss and Christina Simmons with Robert A. Padgug, *Passion and Power, Sexuality in History*. Temple University Press, Philadelphia, 1989.

** Dora Russell, *The Tamarisk Tree, My Quest for Liberty and Love*. Elex/Pemberton, London, 1975.

Ed. Elaine Showalter, *The New Feminist Criticism, Essays on Women, Literature and Theory*. Pantheon Books, New York, 1985, Part 2, Feminist Criticisms and Women's Cultures.

CHAPTER 23
BATTLES AROUND BOUNDARIES: CONFLICTING STRATEGIES AFTER WORLD WAR I

** Olive Banks, *Faces of Feminism, A Study of Feminism as a Social Movement*. Martin Robertson, Oxford, 1981; Basil Blackwell, Oxford, 1986.

* Simone de Beauvoir, *The Second Sex* (1949). A Four Square Book, London, 1960.

** Nancy F. Cott, Feminist Theory and Feminist Movements, The Past Before Us, and Jane Lewis, Feminism and Welfare. In eds. Juliet Mitchell and Ann Oakley, *What Is Feminism?* Basil Blackwell, Oxford, 1986.

* ed. Ruth Milkman, *Women, Work and Protest, A Century of US Women's Labor History*. Routledge and Kegan Paul, Boston, 1985.

* Meredith Tax, *Union Square*. William Morrow, New York, 1988 (fiction).

* Virginia Woolf, *A Room of One's Own* (1929) and *Three Guineas* (1938), with an introduction by Hermione Lee. Chatto and Windus, The Hogarth Press, London, 1984.

CHAPTER 24
"BORNINGS" AND BEGINNINGS: ORIGINS OF WOMEN'S LIBERATION IN MANY COUNTRIES

* Nancy Adamson, Linda Briskin, and Margaret McPhail, *Feminist Organising for Change*. Oxford University Press, Toronto, 1988.

Alice Echols, *Daring to Be Bad, Radical Feminism in America, 1967–1975*. University of Minnesota Press, Minneapolis, 1989.

** Sara Evans, Personal Politics, *The Roots of Women's Liberation in the Civil Rights Movement and the New Left*. Alfred A. Knopf, New York, 1979.

* Judith Adler Hellman, *Journeys among Women, Feminism in Five Italian Cities*. Oxford University Press, New York, 1987.

★★ Radha Kumar, Contemporary Indian Feminism. *Feminist Review* no. 33, Autumn 1989.

★★ Yayori Matsui, *Women's Asia*. Zed Books, London, 1987.

CHAPTER 25
PERSONAL POLITICS: CHANGING DEFINITIONS THROUGH ACTION

★★ Carol Anne Douglas, *Love and Politics, Radical Feminist and Lesbian Theories*. ism press, San Francisco, 1990.

 ★ Rohini, *To Do Something Beautiful*. Sheba Feminist Press, London, 1990 (fiction).

★★ Bell Hooks, *Ain't I a Woman*. South End Press, Boston, 1981.

★★ Ursula King, *Women and Spirituality, Voices of Protest and Promise*. Macmillan Education, London, 1989.

Eds. Heather Jon Maroney and Meg Luxton, *Feminism and Political Economy, Women's Work, Women's Struggles*. Methuen, Toronto, 1987.

★★ Sheila Rowbotham, *The Past Is Before Us, Feminism in Action Since the 1960's*. Pandora, London, 1989.

CHAPTER 26
KNOTS: THEORETICAL DEBATES

eds. Himani Bannerji, Kari Dehli, Kate McKenna, Linda Corty, and Susan Heald, *Unsettling Relations*. Canadian Women's Educational Press, Toronto, 1991.

★★ Hester Eisenstein, *Contemporary Feminist Thought*. Unwin Paperbacks, London, 1984.

eds. Patricia Mohammed and Catherine Shepherd, Gender in Caribbean Development. Papers Presented at the Inaugural Seminar of the University of the West Indies, Women and Development Studies Project, The University of the West Indies, Women and Development Studies Project, Mona, Jamaica, 1988.

★★ Sheila Rowbotham, The Trouble with Patriarchy. In ed. Sheila Rowbotham, *Dreams and Dilemmas, Collected Writings*. Virago, London, 1983.

Janet Sayers, *Sexual Contradictions, Psychology, Psychoanalysis, and Feminism*. Tavistock Publications, London, 1986.

★★ Lynne Segal, *Is The Future Female? Troubled Thoughts on Contemporary Feminism*. Virago, London, 1987.

CHAPTER 27
THE PROTESTS WITHOUT A NAME: WOMEN IN COLLECTIVE ACTION

* Carol Andreas, *When Women Rebel, The Rise of Popular Feminism in Peru*. Lawrence Hill, Westport Connecticut, 1985.

* Adrianna Angel and Fiona Macintosh, *The Tiger's Milk, Women of Nicaragua*. Virago, London, 1987.

** Temma Kaplan, Community and Resistance in Women's Political Cultures. *Dialectical Anthropology* no. 15, 1990. Kluwer Academic Publishers. The Netherlands.

** Radha Kumar, *A History of Doing, An Illustrated History of Women's Movement*. Kali for Women, New Delhi, 1992.

** Jennifer Schirmer, Those Who Die for Love Cannot Be Called Dead. *Feminist Review* Autumn 1989.

** eds. Guida West and Rhoda Lois Blumberg, *Women and Social Protest*. Oxford University Press, New York, 1990.

CONCLUSION

** ed. Elizabeth Jelin, *Women and Social Change in Latin America*. Zed Books, London, 1990.

** Anne Phillips, So what's wrong with the individual. In ed Peter Osborne, Socialism and the Limits of liberalism. Verso, London, 1991.

** Janet Sayers, *Biological Politics, Feminist and Anti-feminist Perspectives*. Tavistock Publications, London, 1982.

** Lynne Segal, *Slow Motion, Changing Masculinities, Changing Men*. Virago, London, 1990.

Kate Soper, *Troubled Pleasures, Writing on Politics, Gender and Hedonism*. Verso, London, 1990.

* Alice Walker, *In Search of Our Mothers Gardens*. The Women's Press, London, 1984.

INDEX

INDEX

De Gouges, Olympe, 27–28, 30, 38, 42, 307
De la Chungara, Domitila Barrios, 268
De Pisan, Christine, 18
De Silva, Agnes, 175
Demuth, Freddy, 149
Deroin, Jeanne, 60, 63–65, 67, 92, 162
Despard, Charlotte, 125, 166–167
Development of Capitalism in Russia, 182
Development Crises and Alternative Visions, 298
Dewey, John, 209
Die Neue Zeit, 150
Dilke, Lady, 118
Ding Ling (Ting Ling), 215–216
Dollan, Agnes, 169, 174
Dolle Minas, 262
Douglass, Frederick, 46
Douglass, Sarah, 45
Drucker, Wilhelmina, 262
Du Bois, WEB, 228
Duncan, Isadora, 223

Earle, Claudette, 289
East London Federation of the Suffragettes, 168
Eastman Crystal, 172–173, 223–224, 235, 239, 241–243, 247
Echols, Alice, 274
Ellis Havelock, 158, 233, 235
Emerson, Ralph Waldo, 51–52
Engels, Frederick, 141–147, 149–150, 156, 159, 183
Enlightenment, 22, 27–28, 311–312
English Woman's Journal, 70
Equality League of Self-Supporting Women, 171
Equal Rights Amendment, 243, 274
England's Ideal, 130
Eroticism, 155
Evrard, Constance, 31
Explanatory Notes Respecting the Nature and Objects of the Institution of Nashoba, 40

Fabians, 91, 132, 136–137
Factory Girls' Voice, 47
Faithfull, Emily, 115
Family Limitation, 159
Fauset, Jessie, 228

Fawcett, Henry, 70
Fawcett Milicent, 70, 147, 173–174
Féderations des Associations Féminine du Senegal, 302
Felix, Concepción, 175
Female Political Union, 55
Female Reform Association, 47
Female Reform Society, 36–37
The Feminine Mystique, 258
Feminism and Sex Extinction, 10
Findley, Sue, 282
La Femme Libre, 59
Figner, Vera, 153, 181
First International, 65, 73, 79
Flynn, Elizabeth Gurley, 159, 235, 264
Ford, Isabella, 132, 135–136, 167–168, 173
Forten, Margaretta, 45
Forten, Sarah, 45
Fourier, Charles, 8, 38, 57, 68, 88, 142
Fourierists, 64, 90
Françoise, Elma, 194
Frankel, Leo, 65
French Revolution, 22, 27–35, 59, 108
Freud, Sigmund, 155, 235, 262
Friedan, Betty, 258
Fuller, Margaret, 51–52
Fusae, Ichikawa, 175

GABRIELA, 267
Gandhi, Mahatma, 201–202
Garcia, Alma M., 291
Garrett circle, 74
Garrett, Elizabeth (See Anderson)
Garrett, Milicent (See Fawcett)
Garrison, William Lloyd, 46, 78
Garshina, Elisaveta, 180
Garvey, Marcus, 228
Gay, Desirée, 60–62, 64
Gay, Jules, 60, 61
Gilman, Charlotte Perkins, 91, 113, 137, 160, 173–174
Glasier, Bruce, 131, 134
Godwin, EW., 89
Godwin, William, 23–24
Goldman, Emma, 151–156, 159, 162, 186
Gonne, Maud, 110
Goonatilake, Hema, 266
Gordon, Linda, 299

INDEX

INDEX